EXIT

FROM

BREXIT

TIME TO EMIGRATE?

GEORGE WALDEN

GIBSON SQUARE

For Oliver, Francis and Celia.

Also by George Walden

The Oligarch (Joseph Clyde)
A State of Fear (Joseph Clyde)
China: A Wolf in the World?
God Won't Save America
Who's a Dandy?
New Elites

This edition first published in 2016 by Gibson Square

UK Tel: +44 (0)20 7096 1100
US Tel: +1 646 216 9813

rights@gibsonsquare.com
www.gibsonsquare.com

ISBN 9781783341221

Printed by CPI Books Ltd

Contents

Author's Note

This book is about the future of life in Britain. It focuses on the prospects for families on average earnings in a dramatically changing country, and asks whether some are right to consider emigration.

The new edition takes the discussion forward, post-Brexit. It takes the form of a father's letters to his children – first Guy, then Emma, both of them young parents. Emigration is an emotive business, involving personal preferences and feelings, and it seemed best to convey these in imaginary letters to imaginary children, rather than in a dry factual study.

In real life I have three grown-up children, one or two of whom may end up working at least some time abroad. Some of their friends think about emigration, especially after the referendum. So we have often discussed the subject, as well as the state of Britain, and I learn from them.

For obvious reasons both Guy and Emma are entirely fictional, as are their spouses. The voice of the father is of course my own. Although not all incidents in the book happened, either to me or my children, and the locations are not specific, others are based on fact.

Dear Emma,

'Families torn apart by Brexit.' Everywhere you hear it, yet in our case it seems to have had the opposite effect. You being a human rights lawyer with politics to match, and me a lapsed Conservative MP, father and daughter have had their battles over the years, but Brexit has brought us together.

During the campaign we had a stand-off. You suspected that I was a clandestine Brexiteer, because some years back I'd warned about the consequences of mass immigration. It was a time when you were beginning to take on asylum cases, and were probably embarrassed at the idea your MP dad putting his head above the parapet when everyone except right-wingers were keeping theirs firmly down.

The ice broke, you remember, when I rang to console you the day after the referendum result. After I unleashed a string of curses, you said:

'So you didn't vote Brexit?'

At first I thought you were joking, and I can't remember my reply. Something along the lines of 'Vote for a Pantaloon? Of course I was a Remainer! That was the whole point of what I was saying about immigration! To warn that if we didn't listen to decent Brits on the rough side of it, then God help us. Well, we didn't, and He hasn't.'

You had the grace to say you must have got the wrong idea of what I was saying. Not surprising, since such discussions as we had at the time on the subject had a parliamentary flavour, with more sound than significance and more heat than light.

Never mind, we've both come out on the losing side, and our defeat has brought us closer. It isn't often that politics are a healing agent. I can't tell you how relieved I am that our spat is over, and how nice it is to be absolved by your lawyer daughter from a racism charge.

I came round to your office after work to take you for a drink. Champagne for you, an Old Fashioned for me. A couple, in fact, to celebrate a father/daughter reconciliation and drown our Brexit sorrows. But I took you to the wrong place: a poncy hotel bar full of loud, well-heeled old parties, who turned out to be a bunch of cavorting Brexiteers, while we sat in our corner echoing each other's sighs and lamentations.

In fact it was troubling how much we agreed. We'd independently decided that the defeat was a turning point for the country, in the wrong direction, and that life was not going to be like it was before. Not in the short term, maybe never.

Over-dramatic? Not when your daughter casually informs you that she and her husband were thinking about emigration. For us it was a double shock. It's beginning to look as though we lose a child to foreign parts with every setback the country faces: first the recession, when your brother went, now Brexit, and you contemplating going as well. It was before we came to France on holiday that you told us, and with anyone else we might have suspected that it was an over-hasty reaction, but not you, with your lawyer's cool.

When you came round and we discussed it over dinner we could see you were serious. By then you knew there could be less work coming your way (cutbacks in legal aid), and if things turned sour Robert's work could also be affected. When Guy was thinking about going, I wrote to him about 'the flimsiness and precariousness' of the economy, and it's even less predictable now.

We know you both well enough to understand that with you it's a 'state of the nation' issue, as well as jobs and cash. Which worried us all the more. We took your news with us to the South of France, and it's pointless to pretend it hasn't troubled our holiday. It's eerie to find myself writing to you about it from our French friend's house – the same place I wrote my letters to Guy. I wasn't so much trying to dissuade him – parental pressure tends to backfire – as to set out the pros and cons, because ultimately it's a personal thing.

He went anyway, to Canada, and has never regretted it. As well as skipping the worst of the recession (less severe there than here) he missed the referendum's nationalistic hogwash, and the Brexit backwash that's got us clinging to our canoes while we shoot the financial rapids, grinning with inane optimism as we go. Your brother was a big loss to us, but at least it's a comfort that, as you know from your visits, he's secure and happy.

After the vote he sent an email quoting back at me a remark I'd made in one of my letters about Arthur Koestler saying that Britain was a cross between a lion and an ostrich: a country with its head deeply buried, though capable of rising to a challenge. 'If ever you hear the sound of an ostrich wrenching its head from the sand and of a lion roaring,' I wrote, 'you could always come back.'

Post-referendum, his response was, 'The ostrich's head has just gone deeper, and your blond-maned lion roaring away about Brexit making Britain greater than ever has a mangy look about him.'

*

Obviously I'm bound to say it, but what I wrote to your brother stands up pretty well today, notably about immigration. I warned him that 'over-abrupt changes could provoke an extreme response,' and together with austerity, by Jesus it has.

I also promised that I would never again write or speak about it, and till now I haven't. Given the level of public discussion, with its evasions, taboos and hypocrisies, simply to be involved gives you a shoddy feeling. But your thoughts of leaving the country have forced my hand. It's an ignoble sentiment, I admit, but an irresistible one, so if you detect a whiff of 'I told you so' in some of what follows, so be it.

You may not agree, but I suspect that our heads are still in the sand about why people voted the way they did, particularly in the North and Midlands. Partly it was economic: blind, anti-austerity rage, which after the tour your mother and I made of the region I can understand. And socially? We are asked to believe that the vote was a backlash against Polish plumbers, Bulgarian fruit-pickers and the like, because ethnic etiquette means that no-one can admit that a lot of it was about fear and resentment of minorities from outside Europe, and far more difficult to assimilate.

Neither of us can prove our point: who knows what's in the mind of the average voter when they're alone in the booth, and the politically correct factor is left at the polling station door? Analysts are not going to enlighten us. Nobody's going to tell a pollster that they voted 'leave' because Muslims give them the heebie-jeebies, and make them feel insecure. But the increased hate attacks against them after Brexit, of which you've seen examples in your work, point that way, don't they?

A lot of voters must have bought the UKIP line about the EU being behind Muslim immigration, and our less clued-up fellow citizens probably believed that a 'leave' vote would force them out. A slur on the working classes? Remember that Google recorded large numbers of Brits googling 'What is the EU?' in the hours after the referendum. How dumb is that? Answer – as dumb as their social betters for holding the bloody thing in the first place.

It was you who said that, in a sense, it was never a referendum on Europe, but one about the British themselves: a test of their sobriety, their sense of proportion, their intelligence and their once-famed good sense. And collectively, we failed, because there is no common ground between the social classes – no collective – except in the form of manipulation from above. When rightwing elites combine with the masses to do their own country down, you told me over our drink, the nation is in trouble. It's that, I sense, that's behind your growing disillusionment about the future.

*

While you ponder whether to go or stay, I thought you might like some top-up impressions of where things stand today, to help with your decision. I apologise if some of them seem light-minded or over-the-top, but I'm on holiday, don't forget, so a little self-indulgence is in order. And if you think I was a bit too satirical about our dear country a decade ago, things are beyond satire now.

Let's get two things out of the way before we start. I do not believe you should make your decision on the basis of the referendum alone, and have no solid advice to give on whether Brexit will pan out for good or ill. In the uncertainty it has created nobody can know, there are no precedents, so don't listen to anyone who assures you it's going to be a triumph or disaster.

Obviously I want it to succeed, because it's all we've got – if it doesn't we're in deep trouble. But patriotic posturing is not my style, and I wouldn't be doing my parental duty if I disguised my doubts and fears. If it all comes good I'll be happy to write an abject *mea culpa* for voting Remain.

The second thing to say is that in Britain everyone is consigned a role, like stock characters in a play, so as a former diplomat I still get cast as a foreigner-loving FCO type. In fact, I was never an unconditional Remainer, or unequivocally pro-Brussels. How could I be? I've worked there, negotiated there, fumed there, sat in on EU summits with my boss Peter Carrington and Margaret Thatcher, who did a bit of fuming herself. I also watched it extend from a sensible nine members to an unmanageable twenty-eight, and make the catastrophic blunder of inventing the Euro.

I need no persuading about the tragic mediocrity of the leaders Brussels throws up – over-promoted time-servers like the wretched duo Juncker and Schulz (both with a drink problem, but then the bureaucracy must drive you to it). And yet confronted with the In/Out question Thatcher would have been cautious. 'What is the alternative?' I can hear her say. 'If we leave, where do we go?' As a realist, she wouldn't have banged on about how we're the fifth biggest economy in the world and could go it alone.

Fifth in the world? Looking at the living conditions of the people you deal with, it doesn't feel like that, I remember you saying. London has more billionaires than any other city – about 80 – though the fact that our nearest rival – Moscow, with around 50 – is capital of one of most corrupt countries on earth doesn't say much for the nature of the competition.

What matters is income per head, and on that we're way down the league. (We're about $40,000 annually, the US is $50,000, Norway $75,000). So chest-beating about the size of the economy is just more pap our Oxbridge union debaters toss down to the don't-wanna-know brigade. The thing about Oxbridge debaters is that they're playing at politics, and not all of them grow up.

Behind it all lies something a lugubrious old hand I worked under in the Foreign Office explained to me years ago, when I was a novice diplomat specializing in Russia and China. A right-wing minister, Sir Julian Amery, kept calling me in to ventilate his opinions on grand strategy in East-West relations over a whisky and soda at eleven in the morning. His solution to the division of Europe by the Iron Curtain was of the club-chunter variety: 'why don't we just roll them back?'

When I told my boss about my difficulty in responding to half-arsed questions, he sighed and said: 'Ah yes, you'll get plenty of that from ministers. Left or Right, whether it's an 'ethical foreign policy' they're after, or instant intervention in some distant corner of the globe, the illusion is that we can throw ourselves around the world like we did in the nineteenth century.' He was right, and I was to hear a lot more nostalgia about how we should sort things out, single-handedly. 'The illusion of options', was my name for it.

Sure enough, now we are told we must return to the Victorian spirit that made us the greatest trading nation on earth, and assert ourselves as Commonwealth leaders, as if the twentieth century never happened. Whether quitting the EU was a serious option, or a *Boys' Own* fantasy, ('with one bound Jack was free'), and whether the world is once again our oyster, is something we are about to discover.

*

In our post-referendum talk we agreed on the Guilty Men. How the Brexit boys loved all that jolly campaigning, those precious moments of concord between the upper and lower orders! The problem being, as we now discover, that the upper-crust Brexiteers had little idea what they were doing, and the lower lot didn't either. To Guy I suggested that mass immigration had been a leap in the dark, and the referendum result has proved it. The irony is that we've now taken a second blind leap to escape the consequences of the first. Blair and Cameron, take a bow.

I hate to say, you being a one-time Blair supporter, but it is Blair, who today rages against the stupidity of Brexit, who bears the greatest responsibility for it. It was he who set the whole mass immigration machine in motion. And yet as Ed Balls has just confirmed in his autobiography, astonishingly, neither he nor Gordon Brown bothered to discuss it as the problems mounted.

For the moment, of course, there's no problem. It's all still up in the air. Like the guy who jumps from a hundred storey building against strenuous advice, we're still counting the floors down – ninety, eighty, seventy – it feels fine so far! What were all those naysayers on about?

The sense of freedom, the rush of air – it's exhilarating!

For the record, I had a hunch that it would happen. I told people I occasionally advise in the City that although the case for staying seemed persuasive, my gut told me that we could get a 51% Brexit vote. I wasn't just covering my back: before the vote I went out and bought a stash of Euros for our holiday. Pity I didn't have the courage to stake the lot on Brexit. And now that the country's entire future is a lottery, subject to populist mood swings whipped up by irresponsible charlatans, you might just as well say goodbye to rational argument and give your money to the bookies.

How did it happen? Don't worry, I'm not going to re-live the debate, but if people your age have lost faith in the future of their country it's as well to understand how we got here. Your own view – and I agree – is that we are where we are because of three men: a suavely over-confident Prime Minister for calling the vote, an old school pal for playing careerist games with it, and on the Labour side an antediluvian bonehead for doing his best not to win it.

Personal foibles aside, whatever you think of him (and in your case it was never much), Cameron played the part of Prime Minister with competence and occasional brio, and for all my carping I suspect we may come to look back at him with grudging admiration. Except for this mammoth miscalculation. How could he have taken such a colossal risk? Because for him, there wasn't one. Things had always gone his way in the past, so why not now?

The whole thing was a kind of schoolboy dare. Johnson took the bet without expecting to win, as if it were a bit of a jape, the Eton wall game played out on the back of a prostrate nation. Does that make the Tories guilty of putting party before country? No, because in the Cameron/Johnson world the Tory party *is* the country, just as Eton had become the Tory Party, complete with school clowns.

Remember those American Indian tribal leaders, who used to

demonstrate their superiority over one another by publicly trashing their possessions at a grand ceremony? A potlatch it was called. One chieftain would burn his most treasured goods and chattels, and the other would build an even bigger bonfire of his. The pair who set up the referendum and headed the Brexit campaign are the same, except they pretended they weren't chieftains. And it wasn't their own possessions they were trashing, it was the country's.

We've had a surfeit of Johnson, so let me get him out of the way by quoting a few sentences from the smartest thing I've seen on him, by Robert Armstrong in *The Financial Times*. It explains why the shambolic, adolescent clothes are very much the man, and why he may smarten up as Foreign Secretary – 'though whether he can carry off adulthood remains to be seen':

> 'Casual disorder is one of the few stylistic habits of the aristocratic British male that reliably succeeds (whether the aristocrat is the genuine article or an arriviste wannabe is beside the point). Devil-may-care style is usually an expression of privilege… When decisions have real consequences for people, when the game is for keeps, messages of privileges, which suggest that the man is bigger than the job, are horrific. Casualness of dress can, at crucial times, send a message of power and entitlement.'

The bit about him smartening up may have been premature. I've just seen a picture of him ambling along late, hands in pockets, for a group photo of an EU foreign ministers' meeting. An example of deliberately casual disorder that will be perceived as pseudo-aristocratic arrogance by his twenty-seven waiting colleagues. Two of them, the French and the German, on whose goodwill you and I will depend when the EU Brexit negotiations finally begin, have criticized him sharply in the past. Displays of discourtesy, suggesting that 'the man is bigger than the job', are unlikely to help.

Why did the celebrity-soused Brits buy the product in the first place? The answer is in the question, but when you have time I recommend reading the nineteenth century classic by Charles Mackay, *Extraordinary Popular Delusions and the Madness of Crowds*. Celebrity and other mass idiocies, it turns out, are older than we think, including in socially advanced Britain.

As for Corbyn – and again I quote you – there is something fundamentally amiss with a country where someone of his non-calibre can become leader of the opposition, and as such exercise the power over events that he did in the referendum.

My own view is that you can be intelligent and uneducated, and educated but not too bright, but you can't be unintelligent, under-educated and a wannabe Prime Minister. At best he is a pious moralist aspiring to the condition of a holy fool. The poor man is not of this world and would do better to enter the church – any church – where he can chant its eternal verities to his heart's content. As it is, intellectually he is rag doll manipulated by a couple of Winchester-educated neo-Marxist puppeteers. Note how, in Britain, even on the far left the upper-caste top-down ethos prevails.

But here's the point for you, and your future. Corbyn was content to lose because he and his coven of Lilliput Lenins stand to benefit from any economic mayhem that could ensue. Lenin's most characteristic utterance, you may recall, was 'the worse, the better', and Corbyn and his playpen revolutionaries hope and believe that for all the post-Brexit calm, if confidence fades we could still be heading for industrial upheaval and trouble on the streets. As I write trade union leaders are flexing their muscles, speaking openly of politically coordinated strikes in public services, in defiance of the law.

*

Enough about our Three Great Men of destiny. To understand how

they got us into this historic hole you have to look at the performance of Labour MPs on the ground. Remain would almost certainly have
won if they'd got their troops out, and one of those who failed spec-
tacularly was the former telly don, Tristram Hunt. Personally I was
unsurprised, because I'd met him.

I once debated immigration with him on the *Today* programme.
The contribution of this entitlement-breathing, velvet-jacketed,
tousle-haired left-wing Fauntleroy (daddy is a Lord), was to insist that
there was no problem, none whatsoever. By raising it at all, he suggested, I was behaving like the eugenicists at the turn of the twentieth century: in other words, like the forerunners of the Nazis.

In the green room later I suggested it would be a good idea for him
to apologise. In declining he said something you don't expect to hear
from adult folk: 'The trouble with people like you,' he spat out, like a
petulant child, 'is that you have no idea of the depth and breadth of
my knowledge.' Not the kind of talk that makes friends in the House
of Commons.

Because the fun part is that the Honourable Tristram is today an
MP for Stoke on Trent, a desolate, down-at-heel, high-immigration
backwater with a council house waiting list of 1,600. Had I lived there
I would have voted Brexit myself, and by God they did. Un-persuaded
by the depth and breadth of their MP's knowledge, and ignoring his
advice to remain, 70% of them voted out, one of the highest tallies in
the country.

Naturally he's changed his tune. Labour must show it cares, the
post-referendum Hunt explained earnestly to the cameras: review free
movement, restrict access to benefits, tighten frontier checks. If I'd
suggested anything like that he wouldn't have bothered with snide academic innuendo, he'd have called me an out-and-out racist. Little Lord
Fauntleroy has grown up a bit, but too late.

Note that Tristram the left-wing liberal patrician was behaving very much like the right-wing financial fraternity, who denied any immigration problem too. To hell with the impact on society, low wages and a flooded labour market were good for business. I've heard many a cheery City gent explaining the benefits to us all of letting in a couple more million. They're not in the Stoke on Trent council house list, and for the denizens of Kensington or Notting Hill it was a matter of supreme indifference how many Poles or Pakistanis pitched up in our dowdier towns and cities.

Now that the public have struck back, a little Schadenfreude is in order. A top American banker handling Europe recently told a friend of mine that he'd spent his entire career working on the assumption that Britain was a rock solid country that would never do anything stupid under either Party. After blinking in our gyrations in the last few months he said he would never make the same mistake again.

As a result of this single mogul's change of mind a number of our bankers are likely to lose their jobs. Though unless he gets himself deselected, Tristram won't suffer, any more than leftist media folk like the former *Guardian* editor Alan Rusbridger, who enjoyed his £500,000 a year salary while many in his paper dismissed the concerns of millions on less sumptuous incomes, adversely affected by a swelling population and the cultural tensions it brought.

Never mind. Once we're out of the EU there'll be no more coming from Europe, they assure us, and the Scots could go for independence. So we'll be estranged from our cultural cousins, and can settle down cosily in what remains of the country with our biggest, most rapidly growing and most difficult to integrate non-European minority, some of whose beliefs and activities inspire fear and dread.

I know, just teasing, and I'm sorry if that upsets you – I can see you grimacing. But your dad's not as young and prudent as he was, he just comes out with stuff, and you mustn't hold it against him if from time to time he inadvertently stumbles on the truth.

Our actors, writers, artists and singers, you will have noted, voted Remain to a man and a woman, and weep tragic tears about Brexit. Fine, except that as with Hunt a little self-flagellation is needed. If a single one of them had the grace to apologize for not taking the grievances of ordinary folk about migration seriously, it would make me feel better about the entire luvvie class.

I fear my wait for Emma Thompson to reflect on the social, health or educational pressures that drove normal folk to vote leave will be a long one. Like Tristram, our arts folk, comedians and pop stars included, are increasingly creatures of privilege. And though they assure us that empathy with the less fortunate is what the arts are all about (they're not, but leave that aside), our artistic toffocracy have written off 52% of the country as an alien tribe of Ukippers.

But wait – I've discovered an exception: a long piece in *The New York Review of Books* by Zadie Smith, a favourite novelist of yours. Maybe it's because her youth was spent as a black girl on a council estate in Willesden that she talks some good sense. A passionate Remainer who at first cursed the outers as imbeciles, she now shows empathy with simple Brexit folk. Better than that, she shows remorse for failing to appreciate the problems endured by the white working class who live cheek by jowl with recent immigrants and struggle for resources. Best of all she has a go at the smug London left, who lecture the rest of the country on race but rarely meet 'them' in their schools or social circles.

'The middle-class left so delights in being right!' Smith concludes. Tell it to Tristram, or Emma.

*

The reason I go on about the insouciant, gamblers' mentality of those behind Brexit is because they're forcing people like you to take risks yourself. The referendum was a big-ticket game played by high rollers, but the outcome means that we're all gamblers now. Your decision whether to go or stay will be a bet on what the market might call 'British futures,' if there were such a stock, namely how long it could take to sort things out. Two years, three, a decade? Nobody knows.

How on earth are you to make a judgement? As I write the air is shrill with the sound of people whistling to keep their spirits up. The front pages of much of the non-leftwing press tend to be bathed in an increasingly lurid optimism, while the financials pages discreetly point up the downsides, muttering about it being early days. I hope the optimists are right, though talk about the Brexit bounce or bonanza unnerves me, not to speak of the 'Brexit spirit.' If things go wrong, it'll be the Blitz spirit next.

Will the non-EU world throw open its doors to us eagerly – the image we get of China, India, the Commonwealth beating a path to our door. Out of what, one wonders? Post-colonial nostalgia? What we know is that India became independent more than 60 years ago, and that China is keen on the EU, with its orderly, half-a-billion strong market.

So beware the official line – 'talks on a trade deal are under way.' We're in a hurry for new agreements, they're not, each one could take years, and as a supplicant on bended knee the price we pay might turn out to be the unrestricted inflow of (for example) Chinese or Indian goods, undercutting our own. But then Brexiteers can't be choosers.

We live in strange times, with a growing gap between triumphant British talk about our future as a world leader in free trade, and the stony facts. The US, China and the EU itself – quite a chunk of that world – frowned on Brexit. The EU and America continue to warn about the consequences, while relations with China are shaky for other reasons. True, Putin is making eyes at us, because he sees us as weak and isolated and a handy tool to break EU solidarity over sanctions. So we've got one suitor, if we want to play his game, which Corbyn would but May commendably doesn't. Instead she's taken to making sobering reminders, which I'm sure you've noticed, that there will be few savings from Brexit and that hard times could lie ahead.

I'm not trying to frighten you into leaving – I couldn't if I wanted, you're too well-grounded (can we claim any credit for that?). I'm just saying that in your position I wouldn't base my decision about my own and my family's future on 'chin up!' headlines, or cocky talk by hardline Brexit ministers.

In this phoney war, this summer and autumn limbo, all you can do is wait and see. What does the future hold, one wonders, for the people who voted out in the North and Midlands, and got what they wanted? The poor devils have already fallen victim to many a southern scam. Heseltine promised Liverpool a rose garden, literally. Under Blair they were to enjoy a cultural blooming, every town a hotbed of creativity, Gateshead, Bolton or Wigan the equivalent of 16th century Italian city states.

Then it was Osborne's Northern powerhouse. Of powerhouses I'm in favour, though I distrust the means and the motivation behind the one proposed, which smells of yet more southern condescension. One moment there's no such thing as a North/South divide, our condescenders insist, and life begins north of Enfield. Next thing we're going to spend £50 billion on HS2 to get anyone to go there. Or endow them with directly elected mayors, in a nod back to the grand nineteenth-century Joseph Chamberlain era.

And yet May, a Chamberlain fan, has scotched this policy, it seems, ostensibly to prevent Labour re-grouping in major cities. Could it be that there was something else? In the North and Midlands, with their tight, self-sealing immigrant communities, there could be dangers. Look at Lafur Rahman, mayor of Tower Hamlets, elected on a high ethnic vote in a low turnout, with hundreds of millions of Whitehall grants at his disposal. No Chamberlain he, though a master of corrupt and illegal practices to get himself elected. You don't re-invent defunct civic institutions overnight, and I fear we could see many an aspirant Rahman of the Midlands and the North.

The next pig-in-a-poke our Northerners may be offered, I suspect, will be promises of a glorious industrial revival on the back of a cheap post-Brexit pound. Already the manufacturing sector is buoyant, and the instant economics I understand. I just don't see the longer term. Keep the UK's international outlook down or uncertain, the logic seems to be, and the pound with it, and you're laughing.

*

'Britain is different from Europe, and has thrived as such,' the historian Andrew Roberts informs us. Very true. One reason being that we don't do plebiscites, like Napoleon and Hitler, who of course fixed theirs. We're big on parliamentary democracy, and two thirds of Parliament was pro-Remain. So why was Roberts such a fan of a simple majority referendum?

Being different is also why we came out of recession earlier than others (though shouldering a vastly bigger debt), and why Roberts and his chums boast *ad nauseam* about London being the greatest city in the world. Which raises a question. If we've thrived in the EU for decades, while being agreeably different, to the point of becoming the world's greatest city, why should we up and leave?

Not that we should expect too much political wisdom from Roberts, a strutting Brexiteer and an excitable fellow. In the war with Serbia Roberts wrote that NATO should use, or threaten to use, nuclear weapons. A humane act, he said, because it would prevent further slaughter of Albanians. I seem to recall something equally loopy about us going to extreme lengths to defy the Chinese and keep Hong Kong British.

Nowadays you get more sense out of London cabbies. Have you noticed how silent they've become? They don't launch into anti-Brussels tirades any more, and you get monosyllabic answers if you strike up a conversation. Always a bit torn between Brexit-preaching and allergies to the then London mayor, victory has struck them dumb.

'Well, at least you won't have to drive all those overpaid City bankers around any more,' I remarked to one cheerily as we sat marooned in traffic. 'It'll be quieter when half of them have buggered off to Europe.' A mournful silence. I could have been riding a hearse.

Cabbies' remorse? Maybe they too just enjoyed letting off steam in the referendum, without ever expecting to win? Now all they've got to moan about are Uber and the cyclists.

Meanwhile I was sorry to hear that your experiment with a staycation this year on an English beach was such a washout. July was a pestilential month, as if the country had turned its face from the sun as part of its decision to blank out Europe. It picked up later, though year by year our rainy summer season seems to be getting more established, and it looks as if global warming will give us more wet than warmth. Not a huge incentive to stay.

Though if it's any consolation the price of the sun down here in the South of France is the presence of a trio of armed troops overseeing our public beach, after the attack in Nice. One of them is a woman, who sits on a rock above us, like a mermaid in army fatigues with automatic at the ready, keeping her eyes skinned while her teenage colleagues gaze longingly at the bikini-clad girls. Glad somebody's got her mind on the job.

*

Enough politics, let's be practical. If you're thinking of moving from one country to another, four things are crucial: a job, a house, a health service, and education. So how do we stack up against others?

I've never known you or Robert to be overly concerned about your social or financial position. As a lawyer and accountant you're both what we grandly call professionals, though I haven't noticed you living a financially exuberant life. Just as well. As statistically middle-class folk you may be surprised to learn that your position is becoming less middling and more lower-middle than it was. That's because economic and social trends are nudging you further below the rich than you were, and somewhat closer to the poor – all relative, of course.

I can't write about the decline of the middle classes without thinking of T. E. Hulme, the English philosopher who was caught short in the street after a drinking bout and pissed against a wall. When he'd finished a hand tapped his shoulder: 'You can't do that here,' said the copper. 'Do you realize,' the philosopher is said to have responded, buttoning himself, 'that you're addressing a member of the English middle classes?' 'Beg pardon, Sir', said the copper and went his way.

On lawyers, I read something of which you would have approved, reminding people that the ones who pocket millions for dividing yachts and mansions between estranged Russian spouses, or getting guilty as hell celebrities off some sexual or narcotic hook, are a small minority. Nearly half of you earn around £40,000, and due to your public-service spirit you may come out below that. 16% of solicitors who do criminal legal aid business earn less than £30,000.

You may both do better abroad – it depends where you go. Here the lower range of accountancy incomes, I gather, is similar to yours. One of the many reasons I admire Robert is that he long ago decided that as a family man and outdoors enthusiast the upper reaches of the profession, with all they demand in out-of-office time and responsibility, were not for him. Having missed out on nearly twenty years of contact with the three of you through round-the-clock jobs as a diplomat, MP and minister, I respect his priorities.

But the point I'm making is about subsiding expectations if you stay in Britain. I know similar trends are afoot in the US, but then America is richer than us. I don't want to pry, but your joint pre-tax income I would guess to be not enormously over the London average, which is £54,000 for two. If things don't turn up quickly, a slow drift down could be on the way for many. Status may not concern you, but the money could. There's such a thing as a comfortable minimum, and it would not be fun to slide below it. Obviously we'd do what we could to help, but there's no guarantee that, post-Brexit, our savings will be what they were.

Twenty years ago two-thirds of the middle class owned their own houses, but now it's only half. You're in the right half, thanks to a little assistance with your deposit (don't mention it). What mattered for you about the house you chose was less the smartness of the area than the quality-of-life thing, and with its park and market and relative lack of traffic you assured us it was fine.

That was almost a decade ago. Today I can tell you that when you bought it a friend of ours who knows the locality referred to it as 'a brave place to live.' As Londoners elbow one another for space we've noticed that it's begun running down, not too gently. The gang fight in a street next to yours was a signal of the way things may be going. Robert gave us an appalled account of the old boy who was happily painting his windows when a round went through a pane over his head.

The main culprit got away, a policeman told Robert, because he couldn't give chase alone in case he was shot and the guy made off with his Glock pistol. Robert's view was that he should have shot the bastard himself, an un-lawyerly suggestion which suggests you have still have work to do on his animal instincts.

On top of that the change in the school catchment area near you has been for the worse, I gather, and on present form your boys are headed for one of those over-stretched places with umpteen languages that everyone talks about with a fixed determined smile, insisting they're hugely friendly places and wonderfully diverse. By which they mean fine for those with no option. Very English.

I've heard you play down this and other local issues, but with pre-teen children it's time to face the truth. Houses like yours in what were once traditional middle-class strongholds still cost middle-class money, but no longer provide middle-class levels of security and tranquillity. To think you live close to what used to be prime Mr Pooter territory, whole rows of solid, late Victorian respectability! Remember how you laughed when we found an imagined sketch of his house in an edition of *Diary of a Nobody*, looking like a larger version of yours? God knows how his diary might read after an evening stroll in your local park on a Saturday night today.

As for houses and emigration, the position is clear. Abroad they tend to be cheaper, but falling prices in Britain and the wilting of the pound could cut the premium that could once be made from exchanging a hilariously over-valued London semi for a similar, or better, place abroad. Another Brexit casualty.

*

It wasn't your fault, but I have to say that the inter-generational dust-up at that party you gave the other week took me aback. I know it was late, you'd been generous with the drinks, and the incident only lasted a few minutes, but to find 30s and 40s turning on us 60s and 70s like that, in raw, personalized resentment, is something. The wife of one of your friends heard that I'd been a Conservative MP, assumed I was a Brexit man (others have done the same…), and boy did she let me have it.

As Minister for Higher Education I was never short of abuse, and occasional expectoration, but the three of them didn't spit at me, they weren't students, they were young parents. Judith, I think she was called (she certainly wanted my head on a plate), took the lead. Cheap houses, grammar schools, free universities, a functioning NHS, guaranteed employment, good pensions and an open gateway to Europe – our generation had it all, and now the oldies were bloody well fucking everything up for us (her words), and leaving the country a shambles.

I was glad when Robert saw what was happening and sorted her out. Apparently her husband, an aspiring banker, had just lost his first City job. I'd never bought the idea of bitterness between generations, it seemed such an invented, magazine subject, but you felt it all right that night. Another poisonous emanation of Brexit.

Not that I don't sympathize, as I tried to explain to your impassioned friend. People her age were just beginning to resign themselves to the idea that they'd never be as well-off as their parents, when wham, along comes the threat of another recession, a low pound and visas for Europe, and the rest. And on top of that people their age could expect to inherit less as the price of their parents' houses decline and their savings came under threat.

'So you've buggered up your own lives as well as ours,' was Judith's final shot, before Robert prised her away. On houses she's got a point, I fear: talk about prices suffering a 'correction' is growing, as it were some kind of punishment, which in a sense it is.

The idea that the humblest three-up and two-down dwelling in some dismal, dodgy outer-London street is 'worth' a million dollars was always a delusion, a form of national megalomania in which everyone connived, but one people built their lives on. The honey-pot house was their pension, they planned their retirement around it, borrowed against it to help the kids, or for cars or holidays. God help us if the honey runs low, and payouts from the parental bank stall.

Enough pessimism. In trying to cover every base I'm making myself depressed, as well as you. Brexiteers say things will perk up in the longer term, and for once we want them to be right.

It's five o'clock, the afternoon heat's subsiding and I'm going for a swim, followed by a drink – though not the English papers. You told your mother not to allow your plans to spoil our holiday, and with that in mind (as well as the cost – a fiver for *The Times*!) she refuses to buy them. Sometimes I sneak a look, but when I caught sight of a headline on a newsstand yesterday – *Business Activity at Post Financial Crisis Low* – I wasn't tempted.

What is truly depressing however is the Brexiteers' forced cheeriness, and scrabbling about for crumbs of comfort. Now they're bigging up a possible future deal with Australia, no less: 1% of our foreign trade! It reminds me of a Soviet joke current in my time in Moscow: a Kremlin announcement following some disaster or other, saying 'the situation is excellent but not entirely hopeless.'

*

One good result of Brexit for us are signs of a slackening in the basement business. The owners, foreigners mostly, behave like rich peasants. Well-endowed with everything except civilized instincts, and oblivious of the notion of neighbours, except as someone to admire their wealth, they shatter the lives of everyone, and leave fractured and resentful communities in their wake when they sell up at a profit.

Are we permitted to name names? Sure we are. Racism directed against the super rich is fine, I imagine, so we're allowed to curse any Russian, Iranian, Chinese, Turkish or Middle Eastern bastard who digs out our streets and hollows out houses like environmental vandals from the steppes.

In some streets the houses are no more than depositories for cash. The owners put in a new floor or basement or extension in their personal Fort Knox the way you lob another million in the bank. The only good thing is that when the dust and drills, industrial-sized cranes and mining-sized lorries have gone, they don't live there. All you see is a forlorn-looking Albanian or Filipino guard.

Now you can hear the patter of cold feet, as the cranes and bulldozers stand idle. Which of course will have consequences for humble people lower down the property scale. This is what happens when the top of the tent gives way, and soon Londoners will be lamenting the departure of people no one's ever met. Come back, come back, we'll chorus when they've gone, and unemployed Romanian builders are sleeping in the streets and property prices founder around us.

*

If you stay, what can you look forward to on the health front? The four of you have been lucky to date, as have we, though as we get on we're beginning to perform our statistical function of putting more strain on doctors and hospitals than we did. I covered the subject in my letters to Guy, and today the pressures are worse than they were. As you can see from something I read.

Older patients are responsible for more than half of physical assaults on NHS staff in hospitals across England, and 4% of the assaults involved male and female patients who were over 100 years old. It's come to something when folk on the edge of the grave lash out at their physicians. It doesn't help that morale is bad largely for reasons neither they nor we are permitted to discuss (over-population), and with the doctors' strikes their ethos have reached rock bottom.

We disagree about those strikes, but the fact that they happened at all tells you a lot about where the NHS is heading. In the 1970s cemetery workers looking for a rise left the dead unburied, but at least they were dead. Whereas today our not-too-badly-rewarded doctors are prepared to hurry you to your coffin if they don't get more Saturday money. No wonder 100 year olds are fighting back.

Last month I almost added to their number. After a cursory examination I was explaining the background of my problem to a not over-sympathetic young woman (she was actually tapping her pencil), when she looked at her watch and said 'You've been here nearly twenty minutes.'

You don't tangle with doctors, do you, especially if you're a one-time Conservative minister and she's a steely-looking lady. So I didn't say 'that's because I have to explain the background every time I'm here, since I can never see the same doctor twice.' Not her fault, I suppose. You too are beginning to have trouble getting NHS appointments for the kids, now the population density in your area has soared, and are worried about what happens if you no longer have Robert's modest bit of private insurance, one of the few perks of his job, to fall back on.

As I gave up on the NHS after my last encounter (not for the first time), and paid to see a consultant, it struck me that, medicine wise, I'm in precisely the same situation today as I was as a post-graduate student on a British Council scholarship in Moscow University in the early Sixties, Khrushchev's time.

Whilst there I had a bad tooth. After I'd waited for hours at the University *Poliklinika* the tooth doctor, as they call them, a buxom lady, took one look and sighed 'I can't do anything about that now. Too busy.' Then a breath in my ear. 'But I can do it privately.' Like almost everything else in communist Russia private medicine was banned at the time. I took my aching tooth to her one-roomed flat that evening, she got out her gear from beneath her bed, purloined no doubt from the clinic, fixed the tooth and charged 100 rubbles, which being richer than Russian students on my British Council scholarship, I could afford.

In Britain today I operate in exactly the same fashion, because our system is basically Stalinist: free healthcare for one and all, centrally controlled, is a citizen's right, guaranteed by the state, comrades, and one we must all applaud. Just don't expect it to deliver.

I wait to see an NHS doctor, who tells me I need a specialist, and I say how long? I'm still a working man, I can't wait months, better give me the name of a private practitioner. So I pay my £200-£300 for my 40 minutes of his or her time, because I am better off than the average. And if you can't afford it, like the majority of the population, tough luck: you just wait and worry till your name comes up – or your number. Whichever is the first.

On the NHS, I would encourage you to expect no improvement. Patient numbers will rise exponentially, never mind immigration – the birth-rate and the elderly will see to that – and money will be finite. Assuming money is the cure, which it isn't. No one on either side of Parliament and virtually no one in the press or the profession is bold enough to say we should re-examine the system, perhaps by looking at France or Germany, where things appear to work better.

Why? Because our NHS is unique, God-given, a global wonder to be flaunted at the Olympic Games, no less, and even if it doesn't work it's our patriotic duty to fall on our knees before it. To change it for some superior foreign model (and I don't mean the American system) would be apostasy, and now we've decided that our 450 million fellow Europeans have little to offer us on this or anything else, the likelihood of any progress is sinking to zero.

*

So we'll stick to our two–nation health service as stubbornly as we shall to our apartheid education system. As an MP I had a stab at bridging the gap, encouraged by the educational philanthropist and all-round admirable fellow, Sir Peter Lampl, founder of the Sutton Trust. Described as a 'do tank' rather than a 'think tank', it does wonderful work to push social mobility up the political agenda.

In Parliament I was unsurprised to get a minimum of polite interest, and nil support from all three parties. Whatever they say, in a perverse way they are all contented with things as they are: Labour and the Lib-Dems are in hock to their teacher electorate, who in turn are wedded to the failed old comprehensive model, both of them relishing their grudge against the independent sector. As for the Tories, many have a limited interest in the matter, being privately happy with 'their' private schools.

Labour profess to think we should dispense with them, which would do away with many of the best schools in the country, on a variant of the dog-in-the-manger principle: we're not allowed to use them (unless you're Diane Abbott), so we won't let you. My scheme was to keep the schools but make them available to all, on an open access principle, which meant that well-to-do kids paid fees on a sliding scale, down to the poor who paid nothing.

You approved, I'm glad to say, and came to give a talk encouraging the sixth form into a legal career at the private girls' secondary Peter Lampl opened to all comers at his own cost in a mixed area of Liverpool. The scheme was a huge success, large numbers of independent school heads backed the experiment, but neither party wanted to expand it. Labour was hag-ridden, as ever, about selective entry (how else could it work?), and Cameron would never have wanted to upset the minority of private schools who preferred the old, socially exclusive system.

Do you remember the hilarious remark he made during the 2010 election, betraying how out of touch he was about the state/private problem? Challenged by an interviewer who said 'Your wife's rather posh, isn't she?' he shot back: 'Not at all, Sam went to day school, and she's very unconventional.'

Roll that around you tongue. 90% of listeners must have thought, day school? What's he on about? Does he mean a comprehensive? No, what he meant was that his wife couldn't be posh because, like his down-market friend Osborne, she didn't go to a £35,000-a-year boarding school, she went to a £20,000 a year private day school. Which makes her wildly unconventional.

Back to you. You've got children coming up to eleven, but for them independents are a non-option. Life has been good to Sarah and me, and we're still earning, but with three lots of grandchildren pending, not that good. It's the old story. Your boys have been scraping by in what sounds like a so-so local primary. But if you stay, when it comes to secondaries, in London you will have to fret and finagle. You could get lucky with a successful Academy, free school or Church of England outfit, but it's the usual problem: house prices in their vicinity vary accordingly, and in any case currently there are none near you.

Solutions to your health, house and education problems are readily available, providing you've got the money. The three of you were educated in independent day schools because in London our local state schools were lousy, at the time independents were cheaper (as were mortgages), and on our joint salaries we could afford them – just. I have to say that, for all the occasionally beneficial changes there've been in state schools over 30 years, if I were you and had the means, I would do the same today.

Let's tot up the money needed to save you a lot of headaches and satisfy your basic needs. For Guy I worked out that to have basic medical insurance, get a bigger mortgage for a house in a better area and send his two children to one of the less expensive private day schools he'd need something like an extra £38,000 a year, or getting on for £50,000 pre-tax. Today you can up that to £80,000, minimum.

Will Theresa May change the us-and-them ethos on education? After all, she has experience of working in a two-nation Cabinet, as one of the state-educated oiks. But vested interests on both sides are keen to keep it that way, so as with the NHS it would be risky to rely on progress in time for when you need it. As for grammar schools, she seems to have lunged in without enough thought – and, anyway, you and Robert don't agree with them.

It's the gambling thing again. People shrug resignedly and say that schools and doctors are a lottery. Brexiteers will tell you that eventually we shall be a richer nation, which will help with both. Eventually. And should their gamble fail, you can be certain that health and education will be a bigger lottery than before.

*

As an anti-Corbyn Labour supporter, politically speaking there's not a lot to keep you in the country. If things go on as they are we could be in for an implosion of Labour and a run of Conservative governments. As a non-leftwing voter I wouldn't be too unhappy, though I'd prefer a decent opposition, and my contentment with one-party rule would be qualified, for other reasons.

For some time now I've had a feeling that there's something oddly immature about a number of Tory leaders and their circle. Their behaviour over Brexit has strengthened this impression, and now I think I understand why. It was a biography of Tolstoy, believe it or not, that enlightened me.

Given a play to read written by George Bernard Shaw the old boy was unimpressed, scribbling the comment 'clever/silly' on the text. A sound judgement, in my view. Shaw was Irish, but we seem to be producing an entire generation of clever/silly people in high places in Britain. Gove, Johnson, and Andrew Roberts are just three who spring to mind, and I'm sure you've got your own candidates in Labour. Normally they do limited damage, but in national life our clever/silly performers and impostors are beginning to be a bane and a pain.

Increasingly, many of the people most prominent in our daily lives appear less than grown-up. It can't be 'the policemen are getting younger' syndrome, because I've heard you and others make the same point, independently of me. With their undoubted intelligence and education, how is it that so many privileged Brits seem so immature?

One reason is that their privilege is historical as well as social, by which I mean that they have experienced no wars or even national service to interfere with their frequently prolonged adolescence. Another is that in Britain cleverness is suspect, so you have to disguise it with wilfully eccentric behaviour, populist affectation or facile remarks.

Yet another is that social mobility is at a record low in Britain, which means that the clever/silly tribe can make their careers with minimal competition from below. With society broadly segmented into two social strata who barely meet, we can wind up with people in positions of power in politics or the media with imposing backgrounds and impeccable schooling, and sod-all common sense.

The gulf between them and the hoi polloi is filled by condescension, not in the sense of arrogance but its opposite: by the upper lot lowering themselves, ostentatiously and with a self-delighted smile, to common tastes. Cameron adores *The Smiths*, he assures us, especially *The Queen Is Dead* – so naughty – while his unconventional wife is frightfully keen on fun contemporary art. And naturally it's brainbox Gove, a neo-con who thinks it jolly ironic to yah-boo experts and keep student-type Che Guevara posters in his office.

Extended adolescence is catching. Did you notice the way BBC reported the little contretemps of our new Foreign Secretary during his first press conference abroad? A giveaway of the national ethos if ever there was one. Invariably it was done with an indulgent smirk at his jokey remarks, echoing Johnson's own, the message for British viewers being that foreigners wouldn't understand, poor devils, they don't do jokes.

Al Murray, the pub landlord, a bright fellow and a favourite, has a nicely self-deprecating line on the theme. The French have no sense of humour, it goes, because they've got a town called Brest and they don't think it's funny.

Something Guy wrote to me during the referendum has stayed in my mind. He keeps up with the press in the old country from Canada with growing incredulity. Seen from a distance the whole Brexit thing gave him a sensation not of opening to the world, but of smallness and introversion. His attention was grabbed by the following report in a serious Sunday paper about our Brexit negotiating strategy: *'One of New Zealand's top trade negotiators will fly to London to provide support for offi-*

cials in the Department for International Trade later this month.'

Talk about the wrong end of the telescope! I know what he meant: the feeling of everything contracting around you, pressing you in on yourself, like Gulliver being bound down by hordes of noisy shrunken folk. The Tories and their inflatable Churchill, Labour's miniature Lenins, and our puffed-up Brexiteers strutting the globe touting quick-fix trade deals we're not supposed to arrange before we're out of the EU in a couple years, inspire shame and embarrassment.

To us they may look like normal people, but these are stunted, parochial folk, in no position to walk tall in the world. I'm no parliamentary romantic, and the quality of the postwar generation of leaders has been subsiding in other countries: Sarkozy and Hollande are a bit of a comedown after de Gaulle, Pompidou, Giscard d'Estaing and Mitterrand. All I'm saying, I suppose, is that thirty years ago both the Labour and Tory front benches were more impressive.

You need to imagine, if you can, some of our British inflatables dealing with people like Putin or Obama, one a powerful and dangerous ruffian, the other a highly sophisticated leader in control of what he is thinking and saying. You can't. Their champions in the press seem incapable of seeing that, in the words of the poet Pope, a genuinely great man of diminutive size, some of what appear to us to be important national figures form a 'club for persons of modest circumstances of stature' – something Pope actually set up as a joke.

Self-puffery has become a national disease, and it isn't just politics. Remember James Purnell, former Secretary of State for Culture, announcing that in Britain a Renaissance comparable to that in fifteenth century Italy was underway? 'That is not an overstatement,' he said, 'it's exactly true.' An Arts Council Report on which his comment was based had announced that 'Britain was on the verge of producing the greatest art yet created.'

Nothing can be more vulgarly Philistine than this kind of adman's talk, and yet despite – or because of – his asinine remark, Purnell is now on a £300,000 plus salary at the BBC. Next it will be a gong, and being of modest circumstances of stature you can cram more Purnells and the like than ever into the Lords.

Sorry for the digression, though I'm sure you agree that however much our arts persons scorn our politicians, the two of them are part of our national culture, their failings or successes can be reflected in one another, and you have to look at them both together.

On the grown-up side, we share some hope for Theresa May, me from the One Nation angle, you from a more left-wing perspective. Think of the relief of someone not doing the jollies to amuse the plebs. Though if you decide to stay, you told me, it won't be because of her. The reforms she promises would take years, meanwhile she has interminable Brexit business to conduct with the deeply suspect team she's appointed, and a clique of Tory ultras invigilating her every step.

I know Messrs Davis, Johnson and Fox, as well as a couple of the EU experts they'll face, and I suggest you keep your expectations modest. It's not just 'a mess for a woman to clear up' Cameron has left her, as the cliché has it, it's an ammunition dump that could go up at any moment: the post-Brexit economy, Scotland, our EU negotiating team, the Tory Party itself.

Against that background, what price the May reforms? It's the opportunity cost thing, isn't it, the one people always forget. Because whilst you are doing one thing you're not doing something else, and that aspect of the Brexit cost will be enormous. Instead of developing and modernizing our society a stupendous effort will be needed to hold it together.

Unscrambling and reconstructing much of the country's external relations, not to speak of domestic legislation influenced by Brussels, could take years. How much time and energy will be left for reform? And remember there could be Tory ultras opposing that too.

Then there's the Prime Minister's health. I know as much as you, but I'm sceptical of people who say nonsense, in today's world you can do the most stressful job in the country while suffering from type I diabetes, no problem. So looked at in the round, when it comes to deciding to go or stay, May is a doubtful plus. I hope you're wrong, but I note something you said when we last met: that if her health goes and she has to step down, Johnson could have another bite at the cherry, and win.

The only fun there would be that, come the 2020 election, in theory that could pit Johnson against Corbyn. So then we'd have Laurel against Hardy, the Labour straight man against the Tory joker. As Henry Kissinger said when asked for his opinion of the Iran/Iraq war, 'pity only one can lose.'

*

Contemplating the turmoil in France on the TV news here has set me thinking about prospects for stability in Britain. One reason for staying, I wrote to Guy, was that unlike many another country the UK was 'stable, civil and secure.' For generations that's how foreigners saw us, though I find it hard to make the same point now.

There's still such a thing as English decency and civic sense – though as the country lurches about in the post-Brexit era, moderation is not what it was, and civility seems to be going out of the window as London swells exponentially in imitation of a Chinese mega-city.

Instead of stability we have edginess. Not the pretend, way-out, stagey sort we pride ourselves on, but the genuine thing, and living on the edge in real-life politics and economics is a lot less fun than in films or fashion. The tranquillity foreigners admired is becoming a seesaw stability, up one moment, down the next. Seventies down, eighties and nineties up, down again in the recession, followed by five years up, now down again, this time perhaps for an indefinite period. Simultaneously detaching ourselves from Europe and risking a break-up of the UK are scarcely the actions of a stability-seeking people.

Nor is there much hope of a stable population. The outers have dangled an immigration-free future before us, but even if it stopped tomorrow we would have an eleven million strong minority population by mid-century. It's an uncertain science, and the assumptions we make can be wrong: Chinese and Indian immigrants, for example, can have lower birth rates than the natives, whereas some Eastern European rates are higher.

Meanwhile the Muslim element is expanding, and on present trends in a generation the white British could cease to be a majority in the UK. Whether that prospect would be a plus, a minus, or of no importance, is for you to decide. Insofar as we're allowed an opinion, which in a sense we're not. Why? Because if all cultures are equal, any preference for your kith and kin must be prejudicial to others. All I know is that I won't be around, though my grandkids will.

Last, security. Compared with strike-bound, street-battling, terrorist-stricken France, in the recent past we've been relatively calm. Today I see little reason why that should last, and many why it should not. I told Guy that Britain could become a country of extremes – an extreme thought in itself, it seemed at the time, yet it sometimes looks as though that's where we're heading.

The way the Brexit-Remainer row is being pursued reflects this new insobriety. The most pessimistic commentators refuse to budge an iota from their doomsday scenarios, or admit they might have been a touch excessive. On the other side the remarkable Olympic victories of our cyclists, sprinters and hockey-players have been hijacked as proof that if Team GB can stand proud and alone in Rio we can take on the world, and show EU negotiators what we're made of. Usain Bolt will sort them out. Only an atmosphere of underlying angst and insecurity could produce such farcical attempts to buoy up the national mood.

The sad thing is that our increasingly nasty ultra-patriotic booster talk is so un-British – as Dr Johnson taught us. In Russia or China, the mildest dissent is branded treasonable, and here almost half the population with honest doubts about Brexit are increasingly labelled as anti-British. Dr Johnson spoke of 'plebeian patriotism', and if this were just the red-tops, you might shrug, but it goes higher. Should anyone ever read them I fully expect to have the same label slapped on these letters, along with the racist one, making me that unlikely creature, a racist anti-patriot.

Then there are extremes of wealth, of which you've seen more than most in your work, and which have grown absurdly, as have extremes of population (the highest density in Europe). As for political extremes, a decade ago a Labour party led by Corbyn would have been the plot of a bad political thriller. Startlingly vicious crimes, of the kind we used to shake our heads over in America, now seem prevalent here. And of course extremes of alienation among our various ethnic tribes as assimilation fails, entire neighbourhoods become mono-cultural, and no-go areas proliferate.

On this point I know you're more optimistic than me, yet you recognize that non-integration has progressed to troubling levels. The only people merging seamlessly from outside Europe, it occurred to me in a West End street, were the cosmopolitan rich – Iranians, Chinese, Russians, Saudis, you name it. In other words, folk who worship the same God and speak the same language – money – whose devotion to their religions (if any) is unlikely to be excessive, and for whom real racial intolerance would be to ask where their cash came from.

Charming, is it not, to see people of all races, colours and creeds mingling peaceably in Bond Street or in Harrods, while their children prosper in our best public schools, which will help them into Oxbridge and keep state-educated natives out. If only the Brits themselves could learn from these people's tolerance and manners, and embrace without question the newcomers crowding their run-down towns and cities.

On terrorism, to a family contemplating emigration, what do you say? Two things. One that the attacks in Paris, Brussels, Nice, America and Germany give us the nervous feeling that it has to be our turn next; the other that the danger will be there wherever you go, and it's not abstract, it's personal.

We were reminded of this when your younger brother rang us from Munich as the shootings were happening there in July, to assure us he'd taken shelter with his wife in their hotel, and was fine. It was then that we began fretting: we hadn't known they were in Germany at all. Your brother thought that hilarious, like the Jewish story about the son who wires his mother to say 'Dear Mother, start worrying, letter follows.'

On the UK, I hope you didn't find *A State of Fear* – the thriller about a dirty bomb attack in the City I published a year or two ago under the pen name of Joseph Clyde – too alarmist. (This assumes that you read it.) I wrote it because I don't like the idea that certain subjects are off limits as too disturbing, even when M15 are horribly aware of the risks of that form of attack and are flat out trying to pre-empt it. I know this because I've discussed these things with intelligence folk I worked alongside in my Cold War days, and can assure you that the kind of conspiracy I dramatized in the novel wasn't scaremongering, it's real.

It's late, I'm tired, but before I wrap up, a single statistic to keep us awake at night. Of the 3-4 million Muslims in the UK (we don't know exactly), a respected poll has shown that if they knew someone involved in terrorism in Syria only 33% would report it to the police. Which means jihadis would stand a fair chance of training and fighting there before coming back here. On the plus side, 86% felt a strong sense of belonging to Britain. How you square those two percentages God alone knows.

Having seen something of M15 (and it's much bigger now) I would subscribe to our national belief that we have good people. But to cover every contingency, when we know that all it takes is a single, screwball loner, and with a mere third of Muslims willing to tip them off about trips to Syria... What else can I say? Better leave it there.

*

If I've succeeded in putting you off staying you won't be alone. A recent global migration report claims that the UK has the highest number of professionals leaving the country, for better weather and improved quality of life amongst other reasons, to which Brexit may now be added. Since 23rd June there've been 300% more computer searches by Brits seeking to emigrate, the majority looking at Australia and New Zealand. I accept that alarm may have subsided during the dog days of summer and self-consciously up-beat reporting in the UK press, but I doubt whether it has gone away.

The latest poll suggests that a quarter of adults had considered emigration, a figure that rose to 43% amongst the young. Even allowing for a large element of letting off steam, and the fact that only a minority of people have a realistic choice of settling abroad, that's still quite a number.

I've yet to hear of any preferences from you or Robert about where to go. I know you both love France, and like your brothers you're fluent in French after my five years at the Embassy in Paris. Dual passports might be handy in the more insular Britain of the future, but I have to say that as a destination, France is not looking good. Economically they are mired in a mind-set of maximum welfare and job protection, and security-wise, with almost six million Muslims even less integrated than in the UK, things look grim.

Master Gove promised us that Brexit would liberate Europe by example. In the case of France, by that he could only have meant that Brexit would give heart to the fascist-faced, Brussels-hating, Putin-adoring National Front leader Marine Le Pen, who has been promising an In/Out referendum over there. And if the French put Le Pen in office and voted out, her closest friends would be in Moscow. So another clever/silly remark by Gove, though since I've been involved with Russia and France for fifty odd years he could always write me off as another know-nothing expert.

Fortunately, he's been proved wrong. Appalled by the uncertain Brexit aftermath in Britain, French opinion not only declined Gove's invitation to throw off their chains, it's shifted towards Brussels, leaving fascist-face Le Pen looking as silly as him. So horrified were they to see us adrift on the ocean wave that they've swung too far in that direction, by my book, favouring a directly elected European president and a centralised finance ministry. Such is the power of our non-example.

I know you loved our French years and hanker for another spell there, though settling in France would be a different matter. The human rights business is well developed, after a slow start, and they're keen on attracting bankers and accountants like Robert from our shaky City. Yet as I suggested to Guy, much as I enjoy the country, to live and work and have friends in France, by and large it's advisable to be French.

Guy's still fine in Ontario, as you know, but after a disappointing stay in Montreal he reported that what happened there is a parable for some of the post-Brexit dangers London faces, writ small. He emailed me a smart piece by the Canadian writer Tyler Brûlé. Montreal used to be a sophisticated city, the Canadian says, the commercial and financial capital of Canada, but hankered endlessly after a French future and an EU link. Following several referenda on sovereignty and independence, people went on having conflicting views, the place began to feel unsettled, and international interest shifted to Vancouver and Toronto.

The 1995 referendum in Quebec on whether to be in or out of

Canada was a close-run thing – like ours a 51% affair, except it was for in. But that didn't settle the matter. The narrowness of the margin told its tale, and the uncertainty and rancour it engendered in the city took its toll. Not a direct analogy with London, of course, just a warning.

Personally, I'd go to America. I can see it working for you too, were it not for the malign shadow of Trump, leering out at you as if from some horror movie. As I write, thank God, he's on the slide, but who knows? Unlike you I'm not thrilled by Clinton, but the sight of America putting a mentally less than stable candidate for the White House back in his box would be worth a little Clintonian smuggery. If he gets in all bets will be off, and there'd be an exodus there too I imagine. Uncanny, the way we Anglo-Saxon brothers have worked ourselves into a state of crisis together. A poor portent for global stability.

In the English-speaking world that leaves Canada, Australia and New Zealand. Out-doorsy enough for Robert, though maybe a little too much so for you. A matter of taste.

An alternative to emigration might be small-town English life. Again, you wouldn't be alone: 'white flight' from London, as we must be careful not to call it, is increasing, but people leave for more positive reasons too. In the Home Counties, as we cosily refer to them, what's not to like? The houses are bigger, the chances of seeing a GP better, and the drugs and knife-carrying quotients in schools lower. I know you've also been thinking about the suburbs, and scouting round a couple with Robert.

The trouble is that such places have not been immune to the wave-making effects of a tumultuously growing London. In the worst examples they're becoming a pullulating excrescence. Poorer families, including immigrants, many on benefits, have been pushed in that direction, reducing everyone's 'quality of life' – their own included – and resulting in a run-down look and that desolating 'nowheresville' feeling.

There are now more people in poverty in outer than in inner London, with consequent effects on council budgets. Then there's the matter of getting a job, or resigning yourself to commuting. Not that it makes houses that much cheaper, as the younger white flight brigade are apt to discover when they look for places to re-construct the East End communities they grew up in. So I see little appeal there.

Sorry to speak in stark simplicities, but when we're talking about you and your children's future politically correct gentility is best forgotten. I just don't see you settling into a humdrum part-time job running a Citizens' Advice Bureau, or Robert finding a niche in a small financial company. In the end you and he are Big City people, and that's where you belong. Where that city might be is the problem.

*

Something else you said after the campaign stayed with me: 'these are historic times, everyone tells you, but it doesn't feel that way, does it?' We certainly didn't hear any speeches that will be remembered, or feel we were in the presence of historic figures, but then you get the same feeling across the board. We blink in incredulity when we are told that Her Majesty's Secretary of State for Foreign and Commonwealth Affairs and the Leader of Her Official Opposition are who they are. Just as we do when assured that Tracey Emin, she of the untraceable talent, is a Professor of Drawing at the Royal Academy of Arts.

Or there is Catherine Ashton, elevated to the Lords in return for low-level unelected service to the NHS, and until recently for five years High Representative of the European Union for Foreign Affairs and Security Policy, subjects on which she was as innocent as a newborn. I remember your particular annoyance about Ashton, on the grounds that the over-promotion of women is bad for the sex, and that she was given the job by male foreign ministers in the EU who didn't want anyone knowledgeable or experienced usurping their powers.

These are all Pokémon people, virtual reality figures implanted in our collective brain by the media and politicians. Yet it doesn't mean that talent has drained from the country. When the Brits do something well they do it superbly, as a random array of brilliance shows. Scientists who have discovered things, know things, but do not overstate their importance because they are also cultivated people, aware of the limits of science in our lives. Raymond Tallis, a neuroscientist and highly literate fellow, is a fine example.

Then there are our best historians, who don't push ideological lines, don't do correctness, and know how to communicate with the reader. Dominic Sandbrook, Michael Burleigh and David Reynolds are examples, but there are more. Or there are superb non-conforming actors and comedians who don't mouth political banalities and whose names resound in the world. Or our extraordinary Olympic athletes, or articulate football commentators who know the game inside out because they've played it. All of these dwarf the celebrity artists and politicos.

Charlatans, rogues and inadequates exist the world over, as do the credulous imbeciles whom the media persuade to take them seriously. Why do our own examples seem worse than others? Maybe because you have the feeling that we used to be better than this. Think of the post-war period – another time when the electorate gave the country a hell of a shock. A month after accepting the German surrender Churchill, a national leader voted the greatest Briton ever, launched into the postwar campaign of 1945 with an 85% approval rating – and lost. (As did the referendum bookies who predicted a 90% chance for Remain.)

Yet there the parallel stops. Think of Labour then. In postwar government it struck a positive, forward-looking note, promising an impoverished country a new beginning: social security for all, the NHS and nationalization – not yet a dirty word. Today primitivist Labour (your word, not mine) is focusing ever more narrowly on the politics of envy and class revenge. Austerity and immigration have left the electorate rancorous, disillusioned and bloody-minded, so negativity will strike a chord with many.

In 1945 people had a sharpened sense of history, and of cause and effect. Not any more. In our amnesiac, attention-deficit culture, an understanding of even the recent past no longer plays. In 1939-45 people had been genuinely 'all in it together,' as the social mix of the pilots in the Battle of Britain reminds us. Today the words raise a sour laugh. The inherited wealth and privilege of Tories like George Osborne who resuscitated the phrase are not their fault; their absence of social imagination is.

There is no comparison between someone who had to borrow a year or two's school fees during the recession years and the millions whose post-inflation spending power has fallen by 10%, and will take years to recover. The war also gave rise to a sense of 'never again', reflected in an openness to change. Now the pressures from the base are negative: no Europe, no bankers, no immigrants, and for Scotland, no English.

Is the country just tossing about in the post-Brexit swell, or has it lost its moorings completely, destined to drift – or be swept – down-river? Maybe I'm being too negative, though at least I haven't compared the popular mood in Britain today to Germany in the 1930s, something you told me that Robert Harris, one of your favourites, had recently done.

Your mother said you sounded a bit down when you spoke with her on the phone yesterday. I suppose my scribbles won't have helped. I know I haven't exactly accentuated the positive, as the song has it, but then the country is hardly in a whistling mood, is it?

In my anxiety to cover every eventuality, maybe I'm guilty of accentuating the negative. So let's go back to what I said in my first letter, to restore the balance. 'I do not believe you should make your decision on the basis of the referendum alone,' I wrote, 'and have no solid advice to give on whether Brexit will pan out for good or ill. In the uncertainty it has created nobody can know.' Many letters later that's what I still believe.

Before he went I warned Guy against getting into a state of mind where you develop a kind of fascination with decline, and I repeat it to you today. Now and again it's worth standing back, forgetting our worst fears for a moment, and thinking how things may look to others. If Brexit is a huge gamble, for all my misgivings and yours it follows that given time it could pay off, as gambles can. If you throw everything up in the air you can't exclude the possibility that it comes down in a better order. It's early days, we're not irretrievably doomed, and some things could still come right.

Now I'm beginning to sound like our professional Brexit boosters. But there *will* be new opportunities, there *is* such a thing as British vitality and there *are* enterprising, energetic people around, frequently immigrants. So there's a chance that life post-Brexit may settle down sooner than we fear.

Nor can you entirely exclude a balanced agreement on EU emigration, in return for access to the Single Market; there are plenty of people in France and Germany who would welcome limitations on the inflow there too. Rightwing Tory absolutists would go crazy, but they have no parliamentary majority. In time the Conservative party could come together, giving May the chance to establish herself as a Tory reformer, while Corbyn auto-combusts (he's keen on creative destruction), and a modern-minded Opposition appears. Hard to envisage at present, I grant you, but in the longer term conceivable.

Meanwhile (and here we're well into the realms of wishful thinking), in a few years' time the EU could find ways of progressively withdrawing from the Euro, so as to avoid a collapse of the currency and the EU with it, at which no one but Putin and our own anti-Brussels obsessives would cheer. But that's another – and admittedly improbable – story.

*

I recall you asking, not entirely in jest, whether we planned to stay in Britain ourselves. It's not the country's best moment, but I bear it no animosity, why would I? As your friend Judith forcibly reminded me at your party, England has been good to me: a direct grant and Cambridge education, free, meritocratic access to careers as a diplomat and politician that I gave up voluntarily, when I chose, when I decided it was time, and a steadily rising standard of living. How could I bear any resentment against 'the system'? Because of the leg up it gave people like me the three of you had an easier start in life.

But now things are likely to get tougher, and it's because this remarkable country has done so much for me that signs of a self-willed national shrinkage pain me.

Obviously we'd prefer you to stay, but then we're interested parties. The decision is for you alone. Fortunately, you're very much your own woman, always have been, and react badly to the kind of people who helped put you in this position writing off anyone expressing post-Brexit anxieties as anti-patriots or gloomsters.

Here I've set out some facts as I see them, a little over-coloured here and there, but you'll make the necessary discounts. What seems certain is that rough waters may be ahead, that could take time to calm. The risk period could be long, and there could be advantages to sitting things out abroad.

With Guy I inclined towards stay – not that he took much notice – but the horizon looks darker now than then. What more can I say? Obviously we'd miss all four of you terribly, but everything depends on how you yourself feel about Britain, and I sense a deepening malaise. To quote Cyril Connolly, there comes a point where it's better to feel *dépaysé* (disorientated) abroad than in your own country, and that's how Robert and you have been sounding. So if there's somewhere that attracts you, with huge reluctance, I suppose I have to say: go.

But before you make up your mind finally, I am attaching a copy of what I wrote to Guy. I assure you that what I wrote then is still highly relevant.

Love to all, Dad.

September, 2016,

South of France

Dear Guy,

You may be surprised to find me writing to you from France when we could have waited till I got back from holiday and talked things over in a pub. You'll be even more surprised that what began as a letter has come out at some two hundred pages. I shall explain.

When we had dinner at your place before we left, you said something Sarah and I affected to take calmly but which knocked us sideways: that you and Catherine were thinking about emigration. Something about the way you said it – a sort of studied defiance – made us think you didn't mean it. Talking it over on the way home we decided it was a way of letting off steam after what has been a tough period. Having your eight year old son kicked unconscious a hundred yards from your home is enough to make anyone give up asking where things are going, and start thinking about living somewhere else.

When Billy was out of danger we were confident you'd feel better about things, and it would be the last we'd hear about emigration. Obviously we were wrong. When I talked to you on the phone before we took off, and you told me the brain scan had come out OK and that Billy was home, in the euphoria of the moment I said in that case we assumed you would still be in the country when we got back. You said you would, but that your decision to emigrate had been pretty much taken. All that remained to be settled was when you would take off and where you'd pitch your tent.

It wasn't the best news for us to take on holiday, I have to tell you. What took us aback was your casualness: it was as if you'd rolled out a map and were debating where to spend the summer. It's a low trick to cite your mother's feelings, but I'll do it anyway. It took her time to adjust to you and your brother and sister leaving home, though given that the three of you stayed till you were twenty-six, twenty-eight and thirty she ought to have expected that sooner or later it might happen. But abandoning the parental nest is one thing: taking off to a different forest, something else. I'm glad you asked for my advice, even if you say the decision's been taken, because I was going to give it anyway. I still hope that before doing anything irrevocable you'll spare a moment to scan what follows.

*

I can see your incredulous smiles as you open this packet and see the stack of paper. 'Ask your dad a simple question,' I hear Catherine saying, 'and he comes up with a bloody book.' I have excuses. Firstly, abandoning country, friends and family is not a simple matter. Secondly, as you'll remember from our holidays together, unless I'm scribbling something when I'm away I get bored and restless. Third, every holiday has its undercurrent of anxiety, this time it was you who provided it, and given enough leisure people tend to fret about things more than they should.

We're staying with friends, but whenever we're on our own we have our worry session about you. The friends as you know are Alain and Giselle, anglophiles both: when we said you were thinking of emigrating they cried with one voice, like a chorus in an operetta, *mais il est fou votre fils.* So there you are: in French eyes you'd be crazy. When we mentioned that France would probably be one of the countries you considered moving to, they said you were certifiable. Their son Philippe, you may remember, has just left France to look for a job in Britain, where he'll join 300,000 of his countrymen already there.

In coming to your decision I hope you haven't been over-influenced by anything I've said; if so it would be a first. You may have heard me grumble from time to time about where the country's going, but as a father and an ex-politico, that is my function. Yours is to be optimistic, and to find you leap-frogging me in your scepticism is unsettling. We've spent many a year fencing and parrying on this or that issue, with you taking the line that I'm too hard on the country and me suggesting you should be less indulgent. And now this. You know how it is when someone who's dismissed everything you say about something suddenly agrees with you, then pushes your argument further? Your first thought is: maybe I've got it wrong?

The suddenness of your conversion is what worries me most about it. I had my criticisms of the old place but I never said emigration was the answer. It sounds kind of drastic, over the top. Un-British. But you get to know when your children are serious about something and I sense you are very serious about this. That's why we decided we owed you considered advice. Jobs, schools, languages, houses, taxes.... Have they thought this through, we asked ourselves? Easy enough to say he's had a bellyful of Britain, but where will he go? God knows there's a lot wrong with the country, but there's plenty wrong with the world.

As we went through it together I started jotting down notes for the letter. Then I put the book I was beginning aside and started fleshing out the notes. You caught me at an opportune moment. As you know the book is about the Chinese, ancient and modern, so my mind was already running on national types when the question arose of whether you might have seen enough of yours. Meanwhile we've resisted the urge to ring you every couple of days to check that you weren't selling the house and booking passages God knows where. This involved a certain self-restraint, so you can look at the two hundred page letter as the bottled-up result.

I'm sorry if it's come out a bit state-of-the-nation, but then that's the reason people emigrate, isn't it? In a way this was a fresh field for me: I've been too busy to give the nation much of a thought since I gave up my seat in the Commons nine years ago, and your decision forced me to think about how things look for the first time since then. There's nothing like the condition of England question to get the juices flowing, and once I got going I found myself attacking the subject with a certain relish.

Should you go or should you stay? I began with my prejudices – who wouldn't? – but when I got down to setting out the pros and cons it began to seem a many-sided question. Instead of just offering advice I found I was arguing things through with myself about how the future might look to different generations, yours especially. And so the letter outgrew any available envelope. With some exceptions which she'll communicate personally, Sarah has authorised me to say that what follows represents both our views.

*

What struck me first was the irony of the situation. Here I am, a terrible cynic in Catherine's eyes, being asked by people thirty years younger whether the time hasn't come to give up on Britain. Irony number two is that according to surveys for millions of people Britain remains the most desirable place to live. I don't just mean Poles or Pakistanis: Americans fed-up with Bush and his free-wheeling capitalism and Frenchmen cheesed off with over-regulation are among the many who allow their eyes to drift longingly to our shores. Half the world seems ready to run any risk to get into the country, and here you are saying you can't wait to get out. So my first conclusion is that someone somewhere is getting it wrong.

In our conversation over dinner you said you no longer saw much of a future for you or your children here. You've never said anything like that before. In fact, I always thought of you as a little over-inclined to romanticise the country. I remember you quoting John Osborne, to the effect that to be born English and heterosexual were the two greatest gifts of God (Catherine may frown at the heterosexual bit, but will have trouble disagreeing in your case). So it's quite a turnaround. Amazing how swiftly the self-perceptions of the British can flip. Maybe it's all that quirkiness and eccentricity.

We think of ourselves as the sanest of folk, but the way our stock has vacillated in our own eyes during the last twenty-five years doesn't say a lot for our stability. In the late Seventies (you will not remember) the place felt like something between a salvage yard and a cemetery, except that even the dead lay unburied, on account of a strike. Institutions crumbling right and left, the trade unions rampant, massive inflation, the government abdicating power – it felt as if the whole country was in the grip of a depression. When things began looking grim Arthur Koestler had written about the suicide of the British nation, and it looked as if this was it.

But Koestler had a theory, remember, that Britain was a cross between an ostrich and a lion: which is to say that when we get tired of keeping our arse in the air and our head underground we're capable of pulling it out with a Metro Goldwyn roar. So it was in the late Seventies. We peered over the edge (this is the suicide, not the ostrich), stepped back, volunteered for treatment, and were whipped into sanity by Mistress Thatcher. It's undeniable that in the Eighties and Nineties the country came alive, though looking back I sometimes think we over-dramatised the recovery. To listen to our noisiest Little Englanders the salvage yard blossomed into a renaissance state, a Venice of the North that was not sinking but floating on an endless surge of prosperity. And boy did we let people know it.

Now the trumpets of self-satisfaction sound a trifle muted. People keep up a perky air, but you sense an apprehension. I cannot recall a moment of such uncertainty about the future, or such a determination to avoid thinking about it. Will our *risorgimento* prove to have been no more than an interlude? Are we heading back to where we saw ourselves not so long ago, as a nation on the slide? There are different opinions. I've got two myself, and I'm never sure which side I'll come down on, though given that we live from day to day that's not surprising. Not long ago I was thinking, what's so wrong? There hasn't been a terrorist attack for a year, the stock market is at its highest since it was at its lowest, and we've got the Olympics (to the great joy of Alain and Giselle, who are convinced they'll cost the earth and be a security disaster.) Next thing you're blinking at a report about the scale of our individual debt – £4,000 per person and a world record – or seeing the unemployment figures inch upwards, or reading about some appalling terrorist plot we escaped by the skin of our teeth, and begin thinking we're riding for a fall.

It's not just me, it's the mood. Maybe the feeling of insecurity generated by the Seventies has never gone away? That would explain why we took to talking ourselves up so extravagantly. Rarely have a supposedly reticent people been louder in their self-praise than the UK in recent years. The up/down economic cycle? Licked. The arts? More renaissances than Michelangelo had hot breakfasts. Fashion, sex, food? The French come here to learn. London? Greatest city in the world bar none, and that means ever. I know there are scraps of truth in it all, but braggadocio on this scale tends to get its comeuppance, and on bad days you have a sense it may be round the corner. Is this what it felt like when Kipling wrote his Recessional? 'For frantic boast and foolish word.... Lest we forget.' The year was 1897, a nice round century before Labour came in with its frantic boasting about Cool Britannia and the rest. Did it *smell* in 1897, I wonder, the way things have begun smelling today? That curious combination of fruitiness and mustiness, like an overripe melon?

The boasts go on but doubt is in the air. You're not the first to talk to me about emigration. People have begun throwing the word around in conversation, it struck me recently, in a sort of threatening manner, as if warning an unseen authority that if things go on like this the time may be approaching when... well, when they've had enough. Of what they never quite say – with the obvious exception.

'They've hijacked the place, we'll have to leave now.' My cabbie conversation began with the congestion charge, but from the state of the traffic it's a short leap to you know what. He'd rehearsed his spiel so often it had become a creative genre, with colourful inventions: 'The government's sending all our kids to University so the immigrants can get the jobs for themselves.' You think you've heard everything but that one was new to me. Not that he was discriminating racially: he was into the East Europeans as well as the Pakistanis. 'You've got to verbalise' was his closing remark, and so he had, if only for his health.

'I don't know why I live in this country' a complete stranger said to me in a store last month. Habit I imagine, like most of us, I felt like saying, in cynical English fashion. As always when someone speaks to you out of nowhere I didn't know whether a reaction was required. Seeing me raise an eyebrow the fellow – a businessman I'd guess, quite young – gestured towards the front page of the Evening Standard. The headline was about the police chief Sir Ian Blair warning we could face years of terror, and the photo was David Beckham wearing I can't remember what. I don't know which had got to him; perhaps it was both. The combination is sufficient to drive any rational man abroad.

'I see what you mean' I said, and we exchanged smiles. Funny how our national reserve breaks down when we're having a moan. Having had it I looked around the store with a questioning eye. It was a new branch of Waitrose, wonderfully run, with polite, well-trained staff, who'd come to us (as they say) from around the globe – everywhere from the West Indies to the Philippines via Iraq and Bangladesh. The customers' voices included Russian, French, Iranian and American, and everyone seemed to be buying extravagant amounts of food and drink. Multiculturalism in action, prosperity spreading. What's wrong with this, you found yourself thinking?

Well something must be wrong, to judge by the emigration figures. Now that I've checked them out I suppose we should have been less astonished by your decision. If you go you'll be upholding a long tradition. The British have topped the emigration league for centuries: twenty-five million people since 1600, getting on for half the current population. In the Eighties it tailed away as we became richer – we even got some boomerang migrants back. After that the scales began tipping heavily in the opposite direction, with millions coming in.

Now there seems to be a sharp pick-up in people moving out. 54% of your fellow countrymen – a record – are attracted by the idea of living somewhere else, and the numbers actually leaving have doubled in the last few years to several hundred thousand. In 2004 there were 350,000 – not a lot, till you remember that in three years that's enough to fill a town the size of Birmingham (I'm not saying Birmingham would be a loss). We've had big shifts out over the years, and a couple of big shifts in, but there doesn't seem to be a precedent for what we've got at present: high levels in and out. You could put it down to new migratory patterns, as globalization picks up, except that there's a surge of emigration in other countries with immigration problems too. In Holland – a place that on the road to any particular disaster always seems one step ahead – emigration is running at four times our level, proportionately, and overall migration flows have become negative. Apparently there's now a net outflow in Germany too.

And the typical British emigrant is getting younger. Mostly they used to be retirees heading for the hills in France or the coasts of Spain, but now the average age is down. A quarter of people aged between 18 and 25 say they'd be happy to leave the country, and one in six of those upping sticks and going has a degree – the highest figure amongst emigrants in the Western world. Why they're going is harder to establish, for the same reasons that it's difficult to gather reliable statistics about sex: probing too closely into people's feelings about their country is like asking them how often they make love. People tend to lie. The compilers of academic reports are scarcely more trustworthy. 'Quality of life' is said to be the main reason people are going, a catch-all phrase. And should anyone make the mildest reflection on the speed with which the population is changing, they get marked down as racists.

Researchers do their best to show that people are leaving for positive reasons, and it probably does have something to do with a more outward-bound attitude by young, aspiring business folk: bankers risking their necks in Russia or property wide-boys out to make their pile selling Spanish villas to the aforesaid elderly sun-seekers. Only a minority say they're going because they don't like what Britain has become – a favourite euphemism – but I gather they're franker with the relocation agencies who specialise in emigration packages than they are with the pollsters. In private people have begun edging onto cabdriver territory, saying they can't go on living in a place they no longer recognise. 'It's not our country anymore.'

If this means tens of thousands of racists are heading for the ports, in a sort of ethnic cleansing in reverse, I suppose we should be grateful. But I doubt it's that simple, and the fact that you're considering joining the exodus suggests it's not.

*

Now that a decent interval has elapsed, and Billy is out of danger, I feel I can speak freely about where I think the problem began. I'm sorry if some of what I'm going to say sounds harsh, but it's preferable to the awkward silences we've had so far. Clearly what happened can only have reinforced your instinct that it's time to leave the country, and if you do I don't want any feeling between us that too many things have been left unsaid.

Five years ago, with a helping hand from us and your dad-in-law, you were moving from your rented flat to your first house. You asked us to take a look before you decided it was the right place, and Catherine's father came along as well. Dickie and I, it will not have escaped you, have views of the world that began at widely different points and show few signs of converging. In the friendliest possible spirit, I would call him a kind of liberal-minded squire belonging to another era, and were he not such a gentle soul he'd call me all manner of things.

Before we got together Sarah and I did a bit of snooping around the neighbourhood, to get the flavour. Afterwards we all met at the house and agreed it was ideal. On the neighbourhood – silence. Except for Dickie, who went on about what a wonderfully mixed area it seemed; jolly, I seem to recall, was his word for it. It was a tricky moment. There were other people interested in the house, Billy and Sandra were bounding about, and you and Catherine and her father were keen to go ahead and make a bid. I didn't know what to do. I felt I had a duty to say what I thought, on the other hand Sarah had warned me about playing the party pooper.

You have to agree I behaved well. Too well, in retrospect. I said nothing about the council estate on the other side of the main road, which we'd explored as much as we dared, or the fact that it seemed inhabited by young men in cowls, though of no monkish disposition. Nor did I say what I'd discovered about the second-hand furniture store round the corner, the one with the piles of cheap mattresses on the pavement. We dropped in there because it was coming up to Catherine's birthday and your mother – always on the look-out for sensible, home-building presents – went in to enquire about a chest of drawers she'd spotted in the window. I followed and got chatting with the owner.

The chest turned out to be fake Georgian, wood-wormed and laughably over-priced. The mattresses (I gleaned from the owner) were for immigrants and asylum-seekers, Albanians and Somalis mostly. Apparently the council was overwhelmed by the numbers flooding in and was paying out housing benefit, no questions asked, to anyone who'd put a roof over their heads. The result was a brisk business in stuffing the decaying flats over the shops along the main road with immigrants, six to a room.

Putting the hoods and the mattresses together – arbitrarily I admit – on no interpretation of the word did the implications for the area seem jolly. We had a little taste that very day. Seconds after we'd parked the car a bicycling monk rode up and stopped, with a swaggering skid, to check it out. Didn't even wait for us to get round the corner. It was his carelessness about our feelings that got to me. Talk about dissing people. Leave it, said Sarah, but of course I didn't. It's people leaving it that makes them so bloody cocky I said, in responsible citizen mode. So back I strode.

The boy was taking his time itemizing the contents of our car, peering in, cool as you like, to check whether the radio would be to his satisfaction. I asked what the hell he thought he was doing. He looked at me, as if peeved to be interrupted, and said he was thinking of smashing my fucking face in, that's what he was fucking doing. Remembering in a flash, not the whole of my life, but a number of newspaper articles about middle-aged males lying bleeding in the gutter after coming between a young thief and his work, I forbore to insist, and we disengaged. For a strange moment it felt as if I was the interloper and he was the law. Which I suppose in a manner of speaking is the case.

Something else I held my tongue about that day was the local primary school. You probably don't remember, but I asked Catherine how many languages there were there. Dickie must have misheard, or (being an innocent countryman) misunderstood. Before she had a chance to reply he chipped in and said what did it matter, he'd done French and Latin at his prep school from the age of eight and they'd never been the slightest use to him. There was a silence. I was about to re-phrase the question when Sarah caught my eye, and we left it at that. If I sighed too loudly or shrugged too ostentatiously, I offer a retrospective apology.

There was another reason I felt it wise to be silent about your choice of locality. As you've reminded me on a number of occasions since, it was Sarah and I who suggested you look at the area. We'd lived in a flat about half a mile away when we were first married and had always admired the little Victorian enclave. A friend of ours – a BBC type – had a place there and we'd house-sat for him a couple of times when he was on holiday, got to know the area, and liked it. It crossed our minds that we might buy a place there ourselves once we'd saved up the deposit, though luckily nothing came up.

I say luckily because there seems to be a Sod's law whereby the faster a middle-class enclave goes up in the world the more inexorably its immediate surroundings decline. It's begun happening enough for the press to invent a word for it: de-gentrification. Something else I kept quiet about that day. I had no wish to depress you by pointing out how much the area seemed to have changed for the worse since we'd first known it. Now that we've reached a moment of truth, I will.

There'd been scruffy tenements and council houses on the other side of the road thirty years ago, but they were decent places, not the hellholes they are today. And your island of respectability was more respectable than it's become. At the time it had villagy touches. A cluster of shops, butcher and fishmonger included, gave it a local atmosphere. There was a post-office where people met and talked in the prescribed fashion, and if you stood around long enough and it wasn't raining you stood a small chance of seeing an ambulating policeman. A knife-grinder called at the door and people gave him knives that weren't blunt, just to keep him calling, and friendly Irish builders attended to people's houses when they weren't attending to their thirsts in the corner pub.

In the late Eighties a restaurant opened: poncy food at West End prices the vertically mobile locals were nevertheless eager to pay. From what we remember the area was a quiet spot. The most trouble the inhabitants encountered were a few drunks hollering outside the pub on a Saturday night, when their team had had a good day. There was the odd act of disorder, but what the hell: at that time a mugging or car theft was still rare enough to give people a little urban thrill.

The residents were a fertile bunch, and the local school had a good reputation: the kind of state primary young professionals boast about sending their children to, before the more discreet transition to the private secondary sector. Best of all was the triangular stretch of grass, locally ennobled into the 'village green.' I seem to remember telling you how our BBC friend, an arty fellow, got up a petition to the council for permission to build a duck-pond at householders' expense; an extravagant notion the council killed off by asking, reasonably enough, who would maintain it? With his licence-fee mentality our BBC friend hadn't thought of that. To complete the semi-rural picture, just across the road there was a run-down garage, manned by a pair of brothers, who would do you a decent repair job at a reasonable price, providing their technical ingenuity – limited to spark-plugs or exhaust-changing – was not over-stretched.

Over those three decades things have changed rather radically in the wrong direction, have they not, notably in the last few years? Changed to the point where the urban village we knew has become more like a frontier town. The border is notional, though everyone knows where it runs (the main road), and who lives on either side. Previously it had been leaky, with a few working class folk on your side and a couple of professionals on the other. Now it's absolute: the cycling Cistercians have taken over the tenements and the yuppies have snaffled the village. The difference between you is simple but decisive: they are the masters of their territory, whereas you are not.

None of this will be news to you, but I wanted to tell you how I see it. It's not a happy picture. The garage has expanded into a kind of trading post, the only place where the communities come face to face. The staff (Arabs I think) exercise due vigilance. When they take your money you can see them keeping an eye out over your head on the kids from the estate, as diverse and multicultural a bunch of delinquents as you could wish never to set eyes on. The most troublesome were the whites, the Arabs told us one evening when they caught a kid with half the shop up his jerkin. One of a problem family of Irish Tinkers, it turned out. A month later we saw them together, a trio of teenagers at once villainous and pathetic, with their hair cropped against lice and their pasty, ill-nourished faces. I imagine you are acquainted. Not the kind of youngsters you'll want knocking around your street when they're eighteen, assuming they haven't been locked up by then.

The villagers long ago began barring and alarming and five-lever locking their houses, and are burgled just the same (twice in three years in your case – nothing to boast about by local standards). The green can still be pleasant on a sunny Sunday, one of the few times it's safe to take the kids there, providing they've done a good job of cleaning up the vomit and drugs detritus after Saturday night. Recently (you tell me) the spot has been renamed 'the Sunni triangle', which gives the flavour well enough, but is defamatory to Iraqis: it's Somalis who've taken the area over, notably the space outside the pub. Which is an advance on the Irish, you tell me, to the extent that they don't get pissed and sing on a Saturday night, if only because they're busy dealing drugs.

The fishmonger has gone the way of his tribe, and the last time we called in at the butcher for your Christmas turkey, and complimented him on his meat, he said we should enjoy it while it lasted because he wouldn't be there much longer. He spoke colourfully about his reasons, as butchers do. The post-office meanwhile has been taken over by Indians: no one else would have the stoicism necessary to keep going after four hold-ups in five years, the last two armed. Even the knife-grinder appears to have been contaminated by the decline in local morals. Your faithful artisan turned up late one evening, Catherine told me, gave you a sob-story about being ejected from his flat the next day, borrowed £50 and was never seen again.

Ten months ago you had your first shooting, just across the frontier, which meant that the village made the papers. A bit of urban glamour you could have done without. Turf war, apparently, black on Kosovan – or was it the other way round? Not that it matters: somehow the fact that they're not specifically gunning for you doesn't do much for your sense of security. Lucky the duck-pond idea didn't take off: five minutes in there and they'd have been shot out of the water. Sorry to be facetious, but then that's the English way of dealing with the unsayable, isn't it? Because the truth is that for you the last few years have been a mounting disaster, culminating with the attack on Billy, and it was a mistake to move into your urban village in the first place.

You can't say you weren't warned – though not by me. Remember the story you told me about finding one of the boys from the estate pissing in the street? When you made the mistake of protesting (no one likes being interfered with when engaged in his natural functions), he finished his business, buttoned himself at his leisure, turned and said: 'What you doin' livin' round 'ere? Whitey fuckin' cunt, go back where you belong.'

I'm afraid the smart-arse black guy has turned out to be right. You'd better go back where you belong, wherever that is, because as far as I can see you've come to the end of the line. You've stuck it for nearly five years. I know your motives sprang from noble sentiments, particularly over the multi-lingual school, and I applaud you for it. Now I applaud you for your realism in deciding it's time to move. But abroad?

*

Assuming you go what sort of a country will you be leaving? The point about Britain (we used to be told) was that it never aspired to be vulgarly modern or showily prosperous: that we left to America. And it wasn't shamelessly hedonistic or snobbishly cultivated either: that was for the French. So what were we about? Well the main thing about Britain was that it was stable, civil and secure. Our instinct for moderation and our reticent emotions were qualities that gave the Englishman's existence a certain sweetness. It also drove people mad. That was why D.H. Lawrence (another favourite of yours) spent a lot of his life abroad. In 1927, you'll remember, he came to England on a visit, couldn't bear it and got back on the night-ferry to the Continent within days. What drove him away was the reticence, the moderation and the yearning for security: *pokiness* was his term for it, by which he meant small, knock-kneed and maddeningly inoffensive. The only thing to be said for Britain, he wrote, was that it was mildly warm and safe.

What would he say if he visited us today? The reticence has gone all right, especially about sex. It's taken us years but finally the Brits have got by heart the Lady Chatterley message: forget any qualms about adultery, class barriers and the rest, and have it away when and where you want, al fresco if that appeals. I have a hunch Lawrence wouldn't care for the result. If he came here today the preacher of 'phallic consciousness' would be appalled to discover that the Brits had taken him at his word, and that every newspaper and TV programme was winking and tittering and smirking about pricks and willies every living moment of the day.

Finding everything coarse, overblown and feeble-minded he would probably do exactly what he did three quarters of a century ago: write a devastating article for the papers and climb back onto his boat. (Curious how all our writers spend as little time as they can in Britain – Lawrence, Wodehouse, Greene, Joyce if you can count him, and people like Salman Rushdie or Martin Amis today – though it might be going too far to say it's only the bad writers who stay)

Post-war we enjoyed another kind of security: the secure and unshakeable conviction that we were going to the dogs. A cosy declinism was our steady state. Going to the dogs was something you became accustomed to, and in a curious way enjoyed. Broadcasters, commentators, academics and fiction writers made a living out of it. When we lost at cricket or football, the pound fell or the export figures were dire, people felt a kind of bitter satisfaction.

The running-down of Empire – a process on which the sun never seemed to set – the tattiness of the buildings, new as well as old, our genteel impoverishment relative to Europe and the United States, the failures of the nationalised industries – these were utterly dependable facts of life, satisfying in their way. Declinism was a kind of home-grown version of communism, offering similar compensations: equality of misery and a dank security. Yes there was the Bomb, but the point about the Cold War was that it stayed cold, and the very awesomeness of the nuclear threat was a steadying factor. There's nothing to steady things now.

*

Today we're no longer the country we were, and for that we should be grateful. But are we the country we imagine ourselves to be – prosperous, dynamic, creative and the rest? In the Seventies we saw ourselves as run-down stock. Now it's as if the whole place has been bought out by a venture capital company. As partners in the enterprise we must all talk up the shares, and we've been doing plenty of that, but the closer you look at the company's accounts the more you realise that venture is the word.

The craving for security has gone all right. Now everyone plays the market, and it's high wire stuff. Everywhere you look – the economy, the house market, immigration, terrorism, climate-change – there's an eerie instability, a feeling of living on the edge. These are not risks we've calculated: they're risks we're locked into, like it or not. Our bets against the future are those of a person with no alternative but to keep on betting.

How did we come to hoist ourselves on this tight-rope? Partly it's because after decades in the doldrums we needed to get rich quick, like gentlefolk down on their luck, and partly it was the leftovers of national ambition. After all those centuries of empire we find it hard to lower our sights and become a semi-retired nation, so we've developed a swash-buckling streak, like a reckless widow. You saw it in the Falklands (a closer-run thing than people imagine), it's there in Iraq, and you're seeing it in the attempt to grow the economy hell for leather by mass immigration. There's a bit of the old death or glory mentality in it, which helps to make Britain a stimulating place to live – so long as you don't think too much about the day after tomorrow.

I hear Catherine saying this is all too downbeat, but what I'm trying to get across is that pessimism and optimism are out of date. In a number of ways, not least immigration, we're living out the biggest bet in our history, and there can be no upbeat or downbeat about it because nobody knows the odds. The merest glance at the national scene shows that huge uncertainties hang over every aspect of our lives. Have we really got over the up-down cycle, as Gordon Brown keeps trying to persuade himself and us? Not if you follow the behaviour of the economic moron in the street, with his manic borrowing and spending. Not if you glance at the property market, which looks a bit like the Thames at high tide in winter: swollen to within inches of its banks.

Will immigration be a source of dynamism and cultural enrichment, as the company's prospectus promises? Or of tensions that could explode in the streets the moment we hit turbulent economic weather? Something else no one knows. And what are the chances of more terrorist strikes? Rather depends on who they've got in the country, and we don't have a lot of information about that either. Never mind. Compared with the stark inevitability of climate change the risk from fundamentalist Islam is second order stuff. After what we've seen this summer it looks as if God himself has noted that a temperate climate is no longer in tune with the character of the British people, and decided to give us one more prone to extremes.

No wonder we've taken to gambling, big time (we now spend a billion a week, twice the figure a few years ago). A game of double or quits is what the life of the nation has pretty much become. But don't worry, they keep telling us with worrying insistence: the underpinnings are sound. Maybe they are – whatever they are. Or maybe Britain is like one of those houses with a view over the sea that look idyllic – till the camera pans wider and you see that what appeared to be a most desirable residence in a superb location is perched a few feet away from a crumbling cliff.

*

The question for you is how this new precariousness, this living on the edge, will affect you and your family. Economically you could be vulnerable. As you may have noticed you are exactly the sort of person whose balls Gordon Brown is squeezing year on year, so deftly you could almost mistake it for a rough caress. Catherine earns the same as you, but then your job is more secure than hers. Her part-time radio journalism will have its ups and downs, but your chemistry lecturing will be steady. Teaching has always seemed to me an excessively self-sacrificial way of life, but then that's your choice, and I respect it. You've always had a selfless streak, which is just as well since the rewards of your career are unlikely to be of this world. What I am trying to say is that there's no point in disguising the fact that on present form you're never going to be well-off, or even what they call comfortable.

I'm being plain with you because there seem so many unrealistic expectations around. It can come as a shock to young, middle-class folk to discover that for all their degrees and our much-trumpeted prosperity they're probably going to end up poorer than their parents. A strange thing when you think of it. People our age were supposed to be the never-had-it-so-bad generation, brought up on cod liver oil and orange juice concentrate in a shoebox off the North Circular, in a country all blitzed to hell. And you were to be the fortunate beneficiaries of the world's longest period of peace and prosperity. The way things are going it looks as if it's going to be a trade-off between generations: your youth was more enjoyable than ours – more freedom, more money, more sex – but you could still end up having things tougher than us. Until, that is, our disappearance comes to your assistance – too late in most cases, now that we're all living to an inconsiderate age.

Compared with the present generation in many respects we had it easy. Forty years ago, no matter how miserable your background, a kid with talent and ambition could have a superlative education, free. You got into grammar or direct grant school, you went to University on a grant big enough to keep beer and soul together, you came out with a degree that meant something, and you got a guaranteed job for forty years with a pension at sixty. The equivalent person today would have no choice but to attend a comprehensive of the kind where cowed and demoralised staff are reduced to pleading with pupils to leave their weapons at the door, and to sit up and pay attention to the comic books or TV series by means of which they're attempting to teach them.

If the kids have talent they could be lucky – it might be spotted and encouraged. Or not. The risk factor again. And if they aspire to anything beyond the Big Brother culture they'd be wise not to show it. Even if they make it as far as University it will be unlikely to be one of the best. Which will not prevent them emerging fifteen or twenty thousand in debt, a sum they hope rapidly to recoup by finding a well-paid job – at a time when employers are coming to believe that university degrees are conferred with the same discrimination as confetti. On the other hand, if the only work they can find commands a low enough salary they don't pay anything back. So the only way you can have a free university education in Britain today is by getting such a rotten job on the back of your worthless degree that you're poverty-stricken for the rest of your life. And should the non-paying job be in a big city, youngsters from modest backgrounds will have trouble affording a roof over their heads without a helping hand from their parents, who by definition will be unable to oblige.

As a member of the lower-middle class, what would have been my fate today? I would certainly never have got to Cambridge. I know all the arguments against selection – Jesus do I know them – just as I know that the people who flaunt their egalitarianism turn out with remarkable regularity to have enjoyed an expensive education, and to send their children to remarkably similar schools. The advantages we enjoyed didn't stop there. After university your mother and I both began our careers in the public sector (I as a Russian specialist in the Foreign Office, Sarah restoring pictures in the Tate Gallery). Had we wished to stay where we were (neither of us did) we could have enjoyed jobs for life with an indexed pension. Today the jobs are less secure, and so is the pension.

In those halcyon days (I'm getting into my stride now) you didn't even need money. Should you feel short of capital (we had next to none), on the back of your secure employment you simply got a mortgage and you bought a house – any house – and lo that house grew and it prospered mightily and it brought forth fruit. And with the help of inflation your minuscule mortgage wizened and shrivelled and a decade or so later had pretty much vanished. Your only problem was whether to sit on your gains, sell up and spend them, or buy a larger house, at a cost that was affordable because of mortgage tax relief.

Why am I reminding you of all this? Not to rub it in, but because in some ways ours was a golden era, and I don't see it coming back.

*

Before Billy was attacked, whenever we made troubled noises about the way the area was going, Catherine used to tell me I was too hard on your local villains, and should remember how deprived they were. My answer, you may recall, was to ask who had deprived them exactly, and of what? Having seen a little of the world I can assure you that their living conditions, while less than ideal, are a thousand percent improvement on those their parents have endured. And whilst we are competing in the deprivation stakes – a favourite English pastime – may I enter a bid for my deprived years as a postwar child in Dagenham? Now that I've left politics I have fewer opportunities to pull a bit of inverted social rank, and I've never had a chance to pull it on Albanians and Somalis.

I suspect I may have bored you with this before, but not Catherine, so I'll bore her now. I lived as a young child in Dagenham because my father had done a bunk, my mother was homeless and my uncle, a Ford worker, took us in. He lived with his wife and three kids in a small house on an estate. When I went back recently, for the first time in more than fifty years, it was by accident: we were coming home after a trip to Essex and I called by on a whim. Why hadn't I been back before? There was no reason to go. My sister and I hadn't spent our entire childhoods there, and it seemed somehow indecent to snoop on a previous life in a working class area to which I had only fleetingly belonged.

Remembering the flimsy, Jerry-built houses, I thought I might be wasting my time, and that the estate would be gone, but it was there all right, still with its evocative street names (First Avenue, Second Avenue...) The houses looked better than I'd expected, but then as the old boy who answered the door at the one I'd lived in told me they'd been mostly sold off, tarted up and extended. They certainly needed that. When we lived in ours there were eight people for three box-room sized bedrooms: one for my uncle and aunt, one for their three children, and the smallest – just room for a bed big enough to take my mother, my sister and myself – for us. At the time I was too young to notice, but the atmosphere in the house was not happy. I remember my sister and I sitting on the curtained-off stairs listening to our mother rowing with my uncle's wife, a vociferous woman who was not enthusiastic about taking in relatives off the streets.

The school was still there when I went back, and the pub; there was even a whelk stall, with whelks. From what I recall of our estate in the 1940s it was a disciplined place. Everyone had a job at Fords, we ran around in the streets and alleyways, the primary school was serious, and if you stepped out of line there was always someone handy to give you a whack. At school the sons and daughters of the working class were taught in much the same way as their social betters: they sat in rows, in silence, with a teacher and a blackboard before them, and they learned.

The difference between now and then is not that things are easier in terms of space and food, which obviously they are: it's that if you live on estates like that today, you stay there. Thanks to good state primary schools there and elsewhere my sister and I didn't. She eventually got into Wycombe Abbey on a scholarship, and I got a place at Latymer Upper in West London, in the years when it was open to people without money. When a liberal lady accused me on some radio programme years later of betraying my roots by going to a direct grant school, I forget what I replied, but whatever it was Sarah suggested that it was over-vigorous. I consider it rather good of me not to have smacked the bitch up on the spot – an expression we would never have used in prim, 1940s proletarian Dagenham.

It was a few months after my visit that Barking and Dagenham gave the BNP a big vote in the local elections (no connection). I can't say I'm surprised, though the part where I'd lived was a bit of a white enclave: when we'd gone for a drink at the pub after calling in at my former house I saw only a single, rather sheepish black, who appeared to be keeping close to the door. I told the landlord I'd lived there years ago and said I supposed there'd been a lot of changes. There's been changes all right he said, and looked away, with a sort of set look to his mouth. I'd meant the big job reductions at Fords a few years ago; he meant something else.

The speed and size of migration into the Dagenham area as a whole (I've since learned) have been extraordinary. If you wanted to test a com-

munity to destruction this is the way to do it. 'Close-knit' is what everyone calls a working class area when they're being smarmy about the proles.
But the thing about close-knit folk is that they don't easily make room for
strangers, let alone foreigners. I don't like to think of a community of
which I have pleasant memories going rancid, but there's no doubt it has.

The places of my childhood seem to be in the news. It caught my eye
the other week that two young Asians had been beaten and stabbed to
death by a gang of thirteen others in Fircroft Road, Tooting, after a public
brawl. Fircroft Road Primary was my second school, after Dagenham. By
then we'd graduated from homelessness to a half-wrecked house nearby.
My sister and I roamed about the neighbourhood freely, aged eight and
ten, on the Tube, the buses, the streets, in a way I don't think you'd let
Billy and Sandra do now.

Which brings me back to your delinquents. They're better housed than
we were, probably better fed too. They've got TVs and maybe a car, and
they've certainly got more money. And yet I don't give much for their
chances. Of course high rises are a disaster, but yours are not all that high,
and in the end it isn't the housing that matters, or even the discrimination:
it's the culture, innit? One or two youngsters may fight their way out,
though it won't be easy. On current showing I imagine the rest will fester
and decline, and drag your area down with them.

Prejudice? Sure I'm prejudiced. Against the kind of people you hear
dodging and weaving and smarming and pretending things are other than
they are. It's an incorrigible prejudice I have, and it comes over me whenever the worst sort of Englishman puts on that superior moral smirk of
his and looks down his droop-snoot nose, as if to say tut tut, we're getting just a tiny bit racist, aren't we? At times like that I begin to understand your urge to get the hell out of the country. For if an Englishman is
no longer at liberty to say out loud and in all honesty what he sees before
him, in the way dear old Dr Johnson would have done, what's the point
of remaining English?

*

It will be no news and absolutely no comfort to you to hear that your part

of town is not alone. Will the natives notice or care when they wake up
one morning not too far hence and find themselves a minority in their
own capital? Catherine said they'd feel no different from today, because
by then the new wave of immigrants will have settled down to being as
British as you. (Which implies there might be something good about
being British, but we'll let that pass.) Do you believe it? I don't know whether I do or not. The whole thing seems too extraordinary to envisage.
No one has ever done anything like we're doing, so there's no experience
to go on.

Richard Rogers, the architect who heads something called the Urban
Task Force, doesn't seem to share Catherine's optimism. I read the other
day that he believes that the inner cities are in danger of being abandoned to the underclass. Seems to me a fair assumption, except that the suggestion appears to be that the white middle classes are guilty of derelic-
tion of duty by getting out. What is becoming more difficult to explain is
why anyone should stay. It's very sad, and may get a lot sadder, but I don't
see how we can get very far in 'reclaiming our inner cities' when no one
is allowed to discuss what everyone knows, sees and thinks about what's
happening there.

It's easy to blame government hypocrisy, though a bit of hypocrisy is
as essential to politicians as it is in family life. There are necessary conven-
tions. There can no more be any question of a politician stating openly
that there's a link between crime and immigration than you can get up at
a family Christmas and say that your mother-in-law is a mean-spirited old
bitch. (Imagine if someone did: '*Is the honourable gentleman saying that all
immigrants are violent criminals? If so I think he should withdraw.*' God how little
I miss the Commons…) Public lies – usually lies of omission – can be a
public necessity. I should know: as a diplomat and politician I was obliged to tell a couple. The trouble is, as you and Catherine are discovering,
you cannot live a private lie.

'But it's the same all over London' the urban sophisticates tell us. It
certainly is. The only difference between our relatively sedate area and
yours is that the origins of your troubles are mostly black. To judge by the

thieves and drunks we see around here, ours are largely white. It's a rare Sunday when I can go for the papers without crunching over broken glass from the Saturday night break-ins. Quite pretty in late Spring, all those diamond-like fragments of car window sparkling amongst the falling cherry blossom. I can't say the same for the occasional pools of vomit, or the dumped takeaway cartons. Still, I shouldn't exaggerate. If you're careful not to leave so much as a plastic bag in the car, remember to triple lock every door and window and set the alarm before going round the corner to the shops, keep your head down and your eyes about you (it takes practice), and avoid looking anyone in the eye, you can get through whole days without trouble.

'What are you beefing about? You should see what goes on where we live. You just have to be realistic and take precautions' is the usual comeback. It's an odd reaction, isn't it, all this boasting about how my crime rate's worse than yours, and anyway there's bugger all you can do about it? There they are, all over the capital, eyes in the back of their heads and fingers on their panic buttons, saying not to worry, it's the same everywhere, you just have to accept it. The sense of powerlessness is amazing. You can see how people get used to wars. Though in one sense it's worse than a war, because this is a conflict where one side has all the weapons and the other takes what's coming. So there's not a lot of point in complaining if – like you – you're hit. You live in a war zone, what did you expect? Object that this is a completely abnormal way to live and they'll get you for cowardice. (Can't take it, eh?) Leave the capital altogether and they'll do you for desertion.

In a war it's vital to keep up morale, and in Britain you do that by keeping mum. That's what we've all been doing, isn't it, you and Catherine and Sarah and I? Pretending that ignoring all this ugliness and anger and danger is the way we hardy urbanites have learned to live. And no one wants to appear intolerant, least of all racially. So we get the 'It's the same all over' shrug. That's not what minorities say: they can have crisp views about what should be done with urban bandits, whose most frequent victims they are. Sometimes you get the impression that the only people who have the sense to be indignant are the migrants from Teheran or Calcutta who came here under the misapprehension that they were exchanging urban jungles for a civilised life. Though after what happened to Billy, it seems as if you and Catherine have begun speaking up too, if only in private.

*

While you waited at the hospital that day I went and reported the attack at your local station. The result? 'It's the same all over' or equivalent. Shrugging resignation. And when authority shrugs it's time to worry. *My advice to your grandson, Mr Walden, is just don't go there* – meaning the green. *And keep to your own side of the road* – meaning the frontier – *because over there it's not just kicks to the head, it's knives.* It occurred to me that sarcasm was in order ('Thanks officer. Your words are a comfort'), but in retrospect I was glad I refrained. It turned out that the station covered an area where one of the would-be Tube bombers had lived. Which gave you the feeling that every moment you'd spent describing how your grandson had been savagely attacked was a criminal waste of police time. Because while you are whining on in your middle-class way about a routine head-kicking, some maniac could be priming his fuse.

Who attacked Billy? He was playing on the green. Catherine rushed out when he screamed, you said, and got a glimpse of the guy running away. Not long after she said something to me that has stayed in my mind: that it was a pity he hadn't been white, because then she would have felt less guilty about hating him. I have to say that this seems to me a little convoluted. When victims begin behaving like defence lawyers for the accused, we are in trouble.

Imagine the real lawyer in action. *What time was it?* Early evening. *So it was getting dark?* A little. *Was it wise to let a young boy play outside in the dark?* It wasn't dark, it was twilight, and he was in view of the house. *Twilight means neither light nor dark. Maybe that's why you chose to believe the attacker was black?* Actually I rather hoped he was white.

Fantasy, of course. There'll never be any trial, will there, even though Catherine is sure who did it because she's seen him since at the garage. A trial won't make Billy safer, or any of you; maybe the contrary. You testi-fy publicly, you get a conviction, he's given some piddling penalty – and his friends live three minutes from your house. No, the last thing you want is justice. So you decided not to tell the police who it was. At least I assume that's what you decided. We never really talked about it, the four of us together, because race is the new sex: too embarrassing to discuss openly, especially with your parents.

Catherine's feeling seemed to be that we couldn't speak honestly about these things because if we did in some way she'd be giving in to our pre-judices. That hurt a little, I admit. Prejudices we all have, but I think I can lay claim to a little experience too, which is the opposite. I can see the case for self-censorship, for being careful what you say, because once you've allowed a situation to develop in which fear of racial tension becomes endemic you're walking on eggshells. (A white society treading eggshells. A ghostly image.) In this respect if no other we have retained our natio-nal reputation for reticence. The trouble comes when you reach the point where a lot of little reticences tot up to one big lie.

To say one fears for the future if you stay where you are would be an understatement. Billy is eight, Sandra six. The security position is not going to get better. Assuming they attend local secondary schools, what are the chances that they'll grow up without incident, or contamination? I suppose I should say they'll have to learn to take care of themselves, acquire a bit of street cred and the rest of it, and you are supposed to agree. But that kind inter-generational agreement disguises a lot of pho-niness, doesn't it? I'm no big fan of street cred, and I suspect that, with two children approaching adolescence, neither are you.

It makes a kind of demented sense, but it's bullshit, isn't it? Street cred has a credibility problem. And what's all this 'respect' everyone goes on about? Kicking hell out of people if they don't show they're afraid of you? When the Prime Minister tells the country that what we need is more respect a million hoods and skinheads will nod in agreement. I don't think Blair gets it. Bit short on his street cred, I would say. Ali G is closer to the mark.

Have you noticed how the ones most inclined to boast about their sons' and daughters' urban sophistication are those whose children play at street cred during boarding school or university holidays, and are given enough money to give them a taxi fare back from the areas where they've been slumming it? These are the ones who smirk at the fears of the poor bastards whose children are obliged to do their credding each and every day of the week. *My children go to the most frightful places, and never seem to have any trouble.* How to be one up by being one down. Very English.

I'm not sure you ever heard much Tom Lehrer, in particular his *The Old Dope Peddler*. It dates from the Seventies and it goes:

> *He gives the kids free samples*
> *Because he knows darn well*
> *That today's little innocent faces*
> *Will be tomorrow's clientele.*

We used to think Lehrer's songs hilarious, but I don't think he'd write that one today. It wouldn't make sense, because now we have kids doing some of the peddling (including, you tell me, at Billy and Sandra's school). And it isn't funny.

*

We've been away a couple of nights to stay with some other friends in the Luberon. All very exquisite, though since we last saw it years ago the area has acquired a celebrity patina that puts a glaze of fashion on every stone. Not that you don't get the same thing where we're staying, though here at least it's all a bit of a joke, and the house is so wonderfully authentic. Anyway we're happy to be back.

Looking over what I've written after being away, two things strike me. The first is that for someone who's trying to get you to think twice before boarding the next plane I'm not doing much of a job. The second is that I haven't got very far before talking about immigration. You wouldn't know, because you don't read a word I write, but I've never discussed the subject before. Why? Partly because most of the public debate has been on such a name-calling or edgily evasive level you hesitate to become involved, and partly for the selfish reason that immigration has never done any harm to me. Till Billy.

The evasion gets to all of us, doesn't it? When I started writing about it instinctively I found myself thinking I must keep anything I had to say to a minimum. Then I thought, why? Censorship in totalitarian countries, I understood when I lived in Russia and China, was not in the last analysis enforced by the state. No government has enough powers for that, and in any case they didn't need to. The state makes clear what the line is, spreads a little fear, and censorship becomes a voluntary code enforced by citizens themselves. It's creepy to watch a kind of nervy totalitarianism of opinion developing here. Sure you have the right to say what you think, even if it's against the grain; it's just that people no longer avail themselves of the freedom. Everyone's so apprehensive, so busy throwing sidelong glances, that a straightforward statement of fact about immigration begins to sound like publicity material for *Mein Kampf.*

Assuming you stay, immigration will condition your lives in a hundred ways, for good or ill, not to speak of those of the children. Already virtually everything you hear on the radio or TV touches on it. Watching the British news the other night I made a mental check of the stories: marches by British Muslims against Israel, Rumanian slave girl traffickers, bad news from Afghanistan and Iraq, more scandals at the Home Office. Except for one story about cricket every item was concerned with terrorism or immigration. And we're not supposed to think about it.

It isn't just the news. If you're honest about it, what we call our rapidly changing society affects almost every aspect of your daily lives: the way your children are taught, whether or not to move house, whether to travel by Tube, problems over the broadcasting schedule at the station where Catherine works (keeping an ethnic balance), your difficulties in getting to see an NHS doctor. I'm not saying race and immigration are always a problem, let alone *the* problem: I'm saying they're a rapidly growing preoccupation. Even where they're not an issue the racists and militant anti-racists are intent on ensuring that that is how they are perceived. I don't see why we should go along with that. We're supposed to be a nation of individualists, aren't we, so how about we set aside what the race merchants of Left and Right tell us and decide for ourselves what we think?

As someone with cosmopolitan instincts, till now I've never fretted too much about it. My only interest lies in what kind of country my children will live in, assuming the three of you stay. If people more patriotically-inclined than I am are happy with the way things are going, or too nervous to complain, why should I worry? Yet now I do – and not only because of what happened to you. I'm a lapsed politician whose interest in public affairs is limited, but at the very least you feel you owe a debt to a society that has done you a lot more good than harm, and it's extraordinary to watch your country walking into the future with its ears stopped up and its hands over its eyes.

I remember Catherine saying when I alluded, with the utmost delicacy, to the ethnic component of the school after it rose dramatically, that it didn't seem to her a helpful approach. As you see from the fact that I remembered the remark, I rather resented it. Reality – unhelpful? But that was three years ago, and to judge by our more recent conversations Catherine has begun giving rather more thought to the subject herself. I have no wish to sound triumphant, though as Bob Monkhouse said, they laughed when I said I was going to be a comedian, but they're not laughing now.

The Englishman is usually all a-sweat and a-tremor about social class, in fact he's so morbidly conscious of it that he's taken to denying it exists. Now he's got race to worry about too he seems likely to become a very sweaty sort of person. What's the immigration etiquette? What can you say, and what can't you? The idea that grown-up people like us should contemplate the transformation of their capital city in silence, refraining from comment and pretending that everything is for the best in the best of all bright new multicultural worlds, seems to me a gift to the far right. Boxed, wrapped, and done up in bows.

The fact that we've never been much good at extremist politics (compared to their Continental equivalents our fascists and communists were not just short on numbers, but blithering amateurs) doesn't mean those that way inclined might not have another go, and recruit some of those nervy, sweaty-palmed people to their cause. And we should remember that the reason we threw up less than our quota of political extremists in the past was because we avoided too many extremes in society. The risk now is that, even in dozy, tolerant England, things might reach a point where over-abrupt changes evoke an extreme response.

People pretend to be relaxed about it, but they're not. In a relaxed society it would be possible to speak openly and honestly about what might be an optimum balance between natives and immigrants, English and Chinese, Brits and Bengalis, or about the long-term implications of a swelling number of Muslims in a country with a contracting (and in most cases non-practising) number of Christians. But you can't. For one thing it would mean talking openly about birth rates. When it comes to Northern Ireland you're permitted to observe that, given the tendency of Catholics to reproduce more than Protestants, eventually they look like being in a majority. With Muslims it's become bad form to say they have the biggest households in the country, an average of 3.8, because someone will say it's racist to talk about them breeding like rabbits, even if the rabbit word never entered your mind.

Even Catherine seemed unhappy when you mentioned immigrant birth rates at dinner once. I said nothing at the time, but it seems to me a perfectly legitimate subject for reflection. The fact that 57% of births in the capital are now to mothers who were born abroad says something about the kind of city in which you'll soon find yourself living. To deny that fact is to deny the right to think about the future. You can welcome it, throw a fit, or say that in the long term it won't matter because we'll all get along fine. The thing you can't do is to ignore it.

Much as I love and respect her I don't grasp Catherine's logic: how can she dissociate what's happening with Billy and Sandra from the wider picture? The percentage of the children of minorities in primary schools has risen from 11% ten years ago to over 20% today (more in some parts of London), and speaking a different language at home has increased just as sharply. To note these things is not to wish Bosnian or Pakistani infants any harm, or deny them an education. It's simply to recognise that massive social changes are underway.

At this rate of expansion it's reasonable to wonder how many minarets will be mixed in with the spires in ten years' time, to the benefit of the skyline perhaps, though not necessarily to the cause of religious toleration. Or how many boarded up churches and pubs there'll be, of the kind I've seen in ghettoes in the North? On the other hand, with the pubs closed and Muslim families by and large more stable than our own, maybe there'll be a little less street cred about, and a bit more civility? If there's no change in the way some Muslims treat their wives there'll certainly be a lot more docile women.

On the lighter side all sorts of novel perspectives open up. It's amusing to speculate on how our national character and appearance could be improved by inter-breeding. We can look forward to a lot of good-looking mixtures around, and who knows, one day the average Brit could have the culinary imagination of the Chinese, the conscientiousness of the Pole, the patience of the Indian and the spirituality of the Muslim. Unless we end up with the violence of the Albanians and the drunkenness of the Russians.

The darker side it is not permitted to discuss. A test of how far we've gone in self-censorship is that any article in the press that is clearly truthful stands out like a page three picture in a church magazine. In a Sunday paper we got last week a piece describing the breakdown of the local identity in the author's native Woolwich following waves of immigration leapt off the page: 'Now it appears to me fragmented, with different ethnic communities existing side by side, sometimes uneasily, sometimes violently and always with a sense of nothingness in the air.' Sorry to say so, but his description fits the position across the road from your urban village rather closely.

That sense of nothingness I know and recognise. The first time I came across it, believe it or not, was living in a diplomatic ghetto in China. There it was a kind of blandness that, apart from boring the pants off everyone, did no one any harm, so it didn't matter. The nothingness matters all right if you live in an ugly, piss-poor neighbourhood, where whatever character there once was has been replaced, not by people playing happy racial families, but by a wasteland brought about by a random multiplicity of cultures, with violence hovering everywhere. It's a feeling you're beginning to get in non-communities all over the country.

Could it be that – timorous English souls – we're over-reacting to change? 'In our swollen, polyglot cities we are all cultural mestizos' Salman Rushdie has written, rather grandly. Rushdie of course has chosen to live in New York rather than London, with his Asian model wife, and as usual he's talking about himself. Being an upper-middle class immigrant educated at an English boarding school and Oxford makes it easier for him to play the Brahmin on such matters. The trouble is that in some of these polyglot cities the natives are beginning to feel rather overlooked. It is after all they who are being called upon to surrender, in a matter of years, a type of citizenship that made sense to them for centuries, in favour of one that, however theoretically desirable, remains untested at the human level.

There's no problem for Rushdie, and little for me. But not everyone rejoices as much as they should in the prospect of becoming a mestizo, if only because a fair number of them would be hard pushed to say precisely what it means. Finding yourself exhorted to be something you don't understand can be irritating. It would be fun to see him spelling out to the lads in the pub in Dagenham why they should abandon their way of life and become cultural half-castes. Of course it's monstrous of them to want to stick with what they know, but then the world's like that. And they haven't had quite as much spent on their intellectual grooming as Salman.

*

It's a bit of a surprise to find myself sitting half-naked in a cloud of anti-mosquito vapour (it's getting towards evening) with the temperature at 33 in the shade, sounding off about immigration. It was Billy, I suppose, who got me going. Like a near miss in an accident it's only when the danger has passed that you get angry about the situation that brought it about. And the greater the difficulty of laying the blame on any individual the more frustrated you become. When you get the sense that everyone is side-stepping the question, the better to make you feel morally at fault for raising it, all you want to do is provoke them out of their righteous complacency. I know Catherine has susceptibilities on the subject, so in case she reads this, which I naturally hope she will, let me clarify a few things.

In an ideal world I'd be happy to see a large number of foreigners enter the country, on the understanding that a similar number of natives left, assuming anyone could be found to take them. The reason I'd prefer stable numbers is that ours is a small island and I'm feeling increasingly boxed in by surging humanity. Naturally I'd need sole charge over who came and who went. I'd leave the natives in the majority, including in the capital, if only because they have certain historic claims on the place, and have not made such a bad showing of things in their country over the last millennium or so compared with what other people have done to theirs. Also because I don't believe you can cobble together a nation out of random samples of the world's population and hope that it will stand for something distinctive, let alone preserve social peace.

Immigrants whose social and religious attitudes were least likely to cause mayhem would, unsurprisingly, be high on my list. Consequently, I'd be shy of including adherents of faiths which make intolerable demands for themselves while preaching intolerance towards the beliefs of others. And I'd be in no hurry to add to the bandit population by importing people from notoriously lawless cultures in Eastern Europe. So one way and another I'd be a little choosy about who I let in.

Anyone who thinks that selective immigration – like selective schools – is an abomination contrived by the Devil should remember that countries who have long been in the habit of sermonizing the rest of us, like Canada, have been practising it for years. An English-speaking Chinese computer engineer with a hundred thousand dollars to his name had a rather better chance of making it to Ottawa than a penniless, uneducated mullah who spoke not a syllable of the language. The ultra-tolerant, ultra-democratic Brits, on the other hand, are above making such arbitrary distinctions.

Purely for myself I have no reason to oppose immigration. Like other reasonably comfortable people I'm amongst the first to benefit. I have a particularly high opinion of Indians and Chinese, which I suppose is a form of discrimination itself, but to hell with it. What I believe is based on what I've seen and read in a life of travel (in another fifteen years I'll be able to add 'and I'm too old to change my mind.') I can't claim to have been equally impressed by Middle Eastern cultures, of which I've also seen something. Nowhere else in the world have I observed such hypocritical regimes, and nowhere rivals their corruption. Basing myself on a similar mixture of observation and experience I also prefer the Americans to the Canadians and the Scots to the Welsh, but I'm pretty relaxed about it. Should anyone have the reverse preference, they're welcome to it.

Saying you're opposed to mass immigration is of course pointless, because you can't oppose a fait accompli. Apart from closing the stable door and battening down the hatches (as an Indian stand-up might put it) there's little to be done. We've reached a point of critical mass where in human terms it's ceased to matter whether you were for or against what's happened. The fact is that it's happened, and all you can do now is make the best of it. It's like a couple deciding they don't want another child, then having a fit of absent-mindedness, as a result of which the baby appears. What are they supposed to do? They can argue about whose fault it was and tell themselves to be more careful in future, but that's about all. The one thing they can't do is take it out on the child.

About ten times a day immigrants walk up our front path. Mostly they're delivering junk mail for luxury products, from Pilates practitioners to oil portraits of yourself or paintings of your house – in other words things they'll never be able to afford and you will never need. Alternatively they're selling themselves as cleaners, gardeners, builders. Most are male and all of them seem to be between 20-35. Indians,

Pakistanis, Afghans or East Europeans (for some reason they're almost never black) they have a pinched, weary air but a dogged expression. And however new they are to the country someone has obviously told them that the first rule of canvassing and leaflet-dropping is to close the gate. (We prefer it open).

I assume they're mostly illegals, who are being exploited. Looked at in the mass it's hard to avoid the view that the best thing for them and for us is that they should return whence they came. But there they are on your doorstep, and meeting their eye as you encounter them on the path, as you sometimes do, hesitating over whether to hand you their nonsense or not, things become less easy. It's pointless to hold a grudge: what would you do, in their position? The same thing happens when some down-at-heel character on the street hands you a card advertising gyms or hairdressers or restaurants. You've never in your life bought anything in this way and never will, but you take one and bin it, just to help run down their stock, so they can claim their £10 for a day's work, or whatever pittance they get. (Remember what Dr Johnson said when he was asked why he insisted on putting a penny in the hand of a beggar boy on his doorstep? 'To enable him to beg on, Sir.')

So in personal terms, unless it's criminals you're dealing with, it's hard to be harsh. On a larger scale our feelings cease to matter. Demographically the die is cast. Of course we have to tighten controls, but if not a single illegal immigrant or counterfeit asylum seeker enters the UK in the future the millions of migrants already here and their descendents will swell the population to extraordinary levels.

For you there would seem to be just one point to consider: what are the downsides and what are the benefits? But even that's a pointless question, to which there can be no clear answer. All we can say for certain is that newcomers from the entire globe are bringing to Britain youth, energy, talent, ambition, resilience, entrepreneurial zeal, artistic ability, the promise of an even more tightly packed country than we have already, more public expenditure, huge educational problems, a startling level of criminality, a massive increase in the security threat, and cultural, religious and social tensions which may or may not prove containable.

'So what you're saying is that Powell was right?' Catherine would never stoop to that, but someone might, so I'll say a word about it.

The idea that Enoch saw the future all along is gaining adherents – many of them silent – by the day. Much as we have a duty to revere the distinction of a man who once taught Greek in a provincial Australian university, it's absurd to see Powell as some far-sighted prophet. He was a romantic nationalist of a malevolent disposition and what he said about race was almost completely wrong. As he was about pretty well everything else. Remember that we're talking about a man one of whose half-crazed theories it was that our true friends were the Russians and our real ene- mies the United States. It's easy to see why he believed it: as a poisoned patriot he resented America's usurpation of Britain's role in the world. Put his anti-Americanism and his Paisley-ite stances together and you arrive at some truly barking notions, such as his conviction that the CIA was behind the assassination of Earl Mountbatten.

He was right to point up the dangers of uncontrolled immigration, but then no one has ever been in favour of that. Far from foreseeing the future Powell, the Protestant Holy Joe, whose voice in Parliament always sounded to me like a ghost trapped in a sepulchre, and whose ancient mariner's eye made even Tony Benn seem sane, totally missed the point: the religious source of the problem. This despite his biblical erudition, through which the world was to learn to its surprise that Christ was stoned by the Jews rather than crucified by the Romans.

His warning, on the basis of a relatively small number of West Indian immigrants, was that immigration would result in tides of blood. West Indians have indeed spilled a fair bit of blood in Britain, mostly their own, and their self-inflicted social problems are horrendous. But our terrorist threat does not originate in the Caribbean. Being a bit of a religious nut himself Powell was ideally placed to overlook the danger that immigra- tion from countries with fundamentalist beliefs and failed cultures would be the problem. In one respect, however, he proved far-sighted. For it was Powell, as Health Minister in 1962, who began the policy of boosting

NHS staff by recruiting nurses from the Caribbean.

*

Apologies for the digression. Another example of how the subject can stir you up. Back to the present. Speaking for myself I'm happy to see the country's stock enriched and diversified, though not in the way we're called upon to believe. Enrichment does not happen if you have less of one thing and more of another; that is substitution. It means that as well as one thing you have another. I do not see how more knowledge about immigrant cultures, welcome as it is, will make up for knowing who you are yourself. A nodding acquaintance with Ramadan or Diwali will not make up for a total eclipse of knowledge about five thousand years of European history.

I don't feel bound to rejoice in diversity for its own sake, any more than most immigrants do. If I were to go up to a Korean or a Philippino in the street and say, look around you, all this multi-culturalism, isn't it wonderful? Let's celebrate our diversity together! – there would be one of two responses. Either he'd see me as a patronizing bastard, or tell me what he thought about the blacks, the Chinese, the Pakistanis. (What is the definition of proletarian internationalism? ran an old Russian joke. Answer: it's when the whole world joins the Georgians in knocking hell out of the Armenians.)

Catherine may think I'm overdoing the risks, but I don't think so. My fear is not that your English identity will be submerged, or that mayhem is guaranteed. What concerns me is the unpredictability of a random situation, that has come about entirely by chance and oversight. For a country that prides itself on its sense of measure it's astonishing what we have done. Should you continue to live in any large city you and your children will be caught up in a vast experiment which no one ever planned and which – should it go wrong – cannot be reversed. And because we're conducting the experiment blindfold, so as to be scrupulously impartial, no one can say with the slightest scrap of authority whether or not it's likely to succeed.

If you're beginning to think I'm giving a disproportionate amount of attention to immigration I would agree. My excuse would be that there's been a disproportionate silence about it, and that it's going to play a disproportionate role in your lives. We've got to stop pretending there's no problem. Unprecedented migration rates are causing tensions across Europe. Here there's a slight tendency at the moment for people to go around waving their hands merrily and saying 'If we celebrate our multiculturalism it will be lovely.'

Sorry, but I've just pulled a cheap politician's trick: I didn't say any of the last three sentences. I was quoting Trevor Phillips, our race equality watchdog, warning against smugness and complacency about the degree of integration. I can see the attractions of complacency, mind you: think about it too long and the whole business becomes depressing. We've got a problem about class, but at least we can joke about it. You don't hear many jokes about race or religion, partly because they're not allowed, mainly because it's stopped being funny. 'A light class comedy' you can have. 'A light racial and religious comedy' doesn't sound right. Ali G sent up black culture a treat, to the point where everyone was doing the voices, but I doubt he'll try his hand on Muslims. Imagine if he did, and everyone started going round taking off imams. I don't think so.

*

I was never very struck by Trevor Phillips, but it seems I was wrong. Coming from where he does it takes guts to tell the truth about multiculturalism. Each race is equal and has an equal right to preserve its culture, the theory tells us, but that's where the cant begins. As a rule the natives do not believe that the Somali culture is equal to their own, and nor do many educated Somalis, if only in respect of its treatment of women, not to speak of its failure to produce anything resembling a civil society. That, after all, is why so many come here. I see why we must uphold the idea of equality nevertheless, as a tribute to the dignity of each culture; otherwise the racists creep in. (Martin Amis got it right the other day when he described multiculturalism as a polite fiction which has become a luxury). But don't let's fool ourselves. While we're all busy celebrating diversity each community does its damnedest to keep to itself, and prospects for integration lie a-mouldering in the grave.

The English are wonderfully well-suited to multiculturalism, in its perverse sense of separate development. Why? Because we're experts in exclusivity, in schools, in clothes, in addresses, in social classes and in clubs. And one man's club is another man's gang or ghetto. So when it comes to the downsides of multiculturalism there's no lack of native customs for immigrants to build on. And when we go on about the virtues of assimilation, there's never been a lot of that between the inhabitants of million pound Georgian terraces and those of the Peabody Buildings round the corner. So what do you expect?

Do I believe in a gradual breakdown of barriers? Obviously I believe in it, but on present form I don't see it happening. Like our race relations boss, I'm afraid what we're going to see is a crystallization of divisions and a proliferation of no-go areas. In East London and the Midlands it's already happened. The solution? Except for the kind of commercialised coexistence that happens in oases like Notting Hill, Brick Lane or other prosperous areas, I don't see one. If multiculturalism turns out to be a kind of apartheid in disguise, and assimilation is portrayed as tantamount to imperialism, what hope can there be of solutions? The solution is not to have the problem.

*

Meanwhile people like you and Catherine are unlikely to sit around waiting for the day of universal harmony to dawn. Those who are able will move from mixed neighbourhoods to smarter areas of town or to predominantly native suburbs, loudly applauding multiculturalism as they go, to disguise their retreat. We can moralise about richness and diversity to our heart's content, but by and large racial groups tend to prefer their own company to that of others, the natives included. And the natives are taking to the hills.

Not so long ago I recall Catherine denying that white flight exists. But it does, we're going to see more of it, and if you depart these shores the two of you – the unlikeliest racists I know – will become a part of it. You won't be alone. Two million people – getting on for a quarter of the current population – left the capital in the decade between 1994 and 2003. (They've been more than replaced). Who are these people, and why should they suddenly up sticks and leave the hippest, the most exciting, the most cultured, the most cosmopolitan and dynamic place to be?

You won't find out from the press. They write about people moving out of London, but a disingenuous puzzlement infects their investigations. Vast numbers of people quitting the capital? Whatever can be happening? Could it be the stress of city life? The crowded streets and under-performing schools? Or is it the price of houses, the sense of insecurity, or simply the exorbitant cost of living? Or perhaps it's the call of nature, as the yuppies of yesteryear throw up their City bonuses and head back to the plough? No mention is made of the ethnic composition of the leavers, so you could be forgiven for thinking that black Londoners are tiring of life in Haringey or Brixton and setting up smallholdings in Wales, or that Asians have exhausted the pleasures of Shepherds Bush and are taking to the open road in search of space and solitude.

You can understand why the press finds it hard to tell the truth. 'White flight', an American term, sounds brutally frank to our prim, evasive ears. When Migrationwatch published some startling figures on the subject the Joint Council for the Welfare of Immigrants did not contest them. All it said was that they were 'not helpful to a good climate of race relations.' In a way I see their point. If the population of London is a third or more ethnic it's hardly agreeable for two and a half million people to be told that an increasing number of natives would prefer to leave the capital altogether rather than live next to them, or share their schools. But what are we to do? Pretend it isn't happening? Suppress the figures?

In some ways, of course, 'white flight' is a misleading term. It's not just a case of one group fleeing contact with another. Nor is it invariably due to hostile feelings amongst the natives: you two are evidence enough of that. The segregation that is proceeding across the country takes place more often than not without fuss, and when the natives melt away ethnic folk are unlikely to feel 'deprived' by their departure. The truth is that if you and others like you go a fair number of people in your community will be happy to see the back of you and your whitey, middle-class ways. The most worrying form of racism, it could be argued, is that which proceeds by tacit consent.

I know we're tolerant compared to others, though I'm not convinced that makes us so much better than them. When the English say (with the smallest tincture of surprise) 'they're just like us', they mean exactly that: that following detailed and prolonged observation they've come to the conclusion that Asians or Africans think and function very much as we do. But having made a display of your liberal-mindedness it doesn't follow that you have to *live* next to them, socialise with them, send your children to the same schools, or see much of them at all. That's how we contrive to keep our liberal consciences and eat our cake. It's how we combine racial tolerance with ethnic segregation, surface fraternization with separation.

Silently, squeamishly, the natives are disengaging, and the lines of ethnic mini-states are forming around us. That is how the English behave on matters of class, and that is how, in their majority, they'll behave about race. It can be entertaining to watch how individuals go about it. In recent times a series of eminent folk in the arts and media have abandoned NW1, a traditional liberal enclave of great charm and even greater house prices, for less exotic parts. Caught in the act by the press they cite the changed nature of the neighbourhood, in this case Camden. Everyone knows how and why Camden has changed, but you'll not hear rich liberal notables telling you as they pad away to more sedate, pale-faced places. One of our less attractive national qualities, natives and immigrants will agree, is our infinite capacity for hypocrisy.

Catherine will say that there are plenty of decent folk trying to lead decent lives on the other side of the tracks, but of that I don't need to be persuaded. It's always been the case, regardless of ethnicity, and the only reason one hesitates to say it more often is a fear of sounding condescending. The official line is that with the help of such people boundaries will melt in time. The official line could scarcely be anything else. If I were Home Secretary I'd be saying the same, but my hopes would not be soaring. Defeatist, I hear Catherine murmuring now. Well, it isn't optimistic but then neither is the situation.

Forget immigrants for a moment, and consider a single fact. Of all the countries in Europe the underclass the British have spawned is the largest, the least literate, the most drunk and drugged, the most anti-social, the most violent and the most stubbornly unresponsive to treatment. That's why our jails are bigger and fuller than theirs. Add to this the fact that nowhere else in Europe are the disparities between the upper and lower reaches of society so gapingly wide, the gulf in educational opportunities so vast, or the record of social mobility so miserably low.

Hence my question for Catherine. If we've failed to assimilate a large section of society who were born in this country and in theory share our faith, our customs and traditions, how likely is it that we shall be able to assimilate millions of new arrivals, whose chief characteristics can include poverty, lack of education, unreformed religions, backward political cultures and a legacy of colonial resentment towards us? I don't think this as defeatism, I see it as realism. Of course there's no necessary link between immigration, poverty, low educational aspirations, unemployment and crime – though saying that doesn't get you very far. You might as well say that it's not necessary to be an Albanian to be involved in the Soho vice trade, or to be a Somali to be a criminal – sentiments with which Albanians or Somalis would unanimously agree, some of them violently.

People fret about the rigours of Muslim life – compulsory prayers, the segregation of women and girls, the brain-washing side of religious education – and they're right to worry. But we'll worry even more when the younger generation makes the break and adapts to British values and customs, because we've got a fair suspicion of what sort of British values they'll be. In the Muslim case I fear that what we're going to get – and are already getting – is a parallel underclass, complete with a ready-made gang mentality. The worst of their culture coupled with the worst of ours.

A mixture of discrimination and self-imposed insularity could leave them secluded in ghettoes of underachievement and joblessness, ready-made additions to the yobbish tendency, whose vowels, attitudes and general brutalism many are happy to emulate. So the blame is not entirely theirs. There's something curiously contagious about English bolshiness. Its ability to leap cultural gaps is awesome, and the speed with which so many inner-city Asian youths have adopted that peculiarly English air of immemorial resentment (the endlessly aggrieved expression, the withered vocabulary, the aggressively furrowed brow) isn't encouraging. You look at them and you think, for this they've come half-way round the world.

Then there's reverse assimilation – the attractions for young underclass whites of the most violent kind of young black lifestyle. We're resigned to the fact that there are too many young blacks in our prisons, but we're beginning to see a disproportionate number of Muslims too. Often they may be victims of the rigidities of a religious culture which, when it falls apart under Western pressure, leaves anarchy in its wake. Madrassas at ten, drug-dealing at twenty. (Something similar happened with the fall of Russian communism: totalitarian order before, and a moral vacuum afterwards.) So that's something else to look forward to, if you stay.

*

The odd thing is that there are probably more immigrants in our area than in yours. I don't live in England any more, I live amongst an agglomeration of foreigners, and it doesn't trouble me. In the course of a normal day sometimes I don't come across a single native, apart from some of my friends. Increasing numbers of Americans, French, Arabs and Iranians are moving in. The street sweeper is Ukrainian, with one of those rawhide faces you see in peasants selling vegetables in Moscow markets. When I asked how long he'd been here and how things were going he said fine, with the Slav's fatalistic shrug. Though everything was going to hell in his native country – and by the way did we need any *uborka* (housecleaning)? At least he's learning the art of enterprise, if only for his wife.

The newsagent is Korean, I think: small, sharp-witted and ultra-polite, particularly with tiresome old ladies who pretend not to understand what he's saying. Our local is staffed by a closed-shop of Australians. Our NHS doctors are Indian, Chinese or other, and I'm usually the only white native in the waiting room. The expatriates and immigrants around here do not strike me as being of the needy type, and when I'm told I can't have an appointment for a week I confess to base thoughts. Of course I can always take my custom elsewhere, which I'm sometimes obliged to do, and pay my £150 for my twenty minutes of a consultant's time.

The Homebase where we go for garden staples is a league of nations in the making. If you want to observe a comedy of immigrant manners these are the places to go. The assistants are mostly roisterous Caribbeans, the check-out girls demure Indian and Pakistani misses, and the customers frequently East Europeans straight off the plane, soulfully putting a place to live together as cheaply as they can.

I hear prim voices saying I shouldn't be noticing all this, that such thought are dangerous, as if the merest reflection on what you are seeing around you could send you reeling towards the BNP. Can it be wrong to observe that people look different, and have customs, attitudes and histories that influence their behaviour for good and ill? You never know where you stand. One moment we're told we all have different cultures and traditions, which we must respect. But when we observe that the French are like maniacs behind the wheel, while Indians resemble the drivers of hearses, or that there is such a thing as an English temperament, which is not the same as the Chinese, we're guilty of stereotyping. We must be colour blind, they tell us – and at the same time celebrate the differences we're not supposed to see.

Our parking attendants – one per resident it sometimes seems – are uniformly black. They hunt in pairs, either to allay boredom or out of fear of some of the more high-handed ladies who berate them in schoolmarm voices. Our builders are Polish or Albanian. Their boss says he'd never again employ any Irish, because the Irish get drunk, turn up late and don't work. As a former publican and an Irishman, he must be allowed his opinion. Sure enough the Poles and Albanians turn up at eight, unhungover, and go about their work in a sort of brisk, jogging motion. The main difference with English builders, however, is that they don't make you feel you are imposing on them by giving them work and paying their wages.

Everyone praises the Poles for their diligence and reliability, but that is to miss the point, which is the redemptive side of human nature. Think of it: these are survivors of a communist culture where vast state enterprises were over-manned by indolent, unmotivated, inefficient and drunken workers, otherwise known as heroes of socialist labour. Like the Russians I used to see taking their tea-break on building sites when I lived there, their most impressive skill (I still don't know how they did it) was to knock the cork out of a bottle of vodka by bashing it on the end. Then they'd gulp down the entire bottle, followed by a chunk of bread. I don't know how they did that either.

As far as I can see the local Catholic church is patronised largely by South Americans and Philippinos, many of them nannies or house-keepers. On postmen I can offer no generalization since they change their ethnic origin too frequently. The gym people are Czech or Australian or African, and the swimmers fighting me for a lane in the pool range from Japanese to South Africans to Middle-Easterners. The Japanese give way, unlike the Boers, who behave much as they did over apartheid: plough on, heads down, till they hit the wall. The Middle Easterners, mostly women, are more trouble. You can see where the Boers are heading, whereas these largish ladies flop about in oversized costumes that appear to date from the era of the bathing machine, and are clearly allergic to water.

The staff of virtually every local shop is ethnic. Iranians stand in front of their premises and seek to entice people in, in a way that is normal in much of the rest of the world but is seen as embarrassing and importunate by the Brits. The offence is limited because a good two-thirds of passers-by are non-natives. There's rarely a white face behind the counter of my local bank, any more than behind the wheel of the bus. Banks are famous for the way they drill the personalities out of their staff, and it's curious to observe how national mannerisms and even accents can be submerged beneath a homogenizing layer of institutional training. Their customers are mostly un-restructured versions of themselves: voluble

Nigerians with massively complicated international accounts, serene, sharply-dressed Iranians, and women with black robes and pallid faces, so oppressed-looking you're surprised they've been entrusted with the cash.

A notice has just gone up warning customers withdrawing large amounts of money that they could be subject to the attentions of thieves waiting outside. A friend told me that his builder had been relieved of the £5,000 he'd taken out to pay his workers. The robbers – one spilled yogurt over him while the other grabbed the cash – were white, and sounded English. So at least such natives as remain are actively involved in the community.

People seem to rub along all right, and it's rare that you see anything that could be construed as a racist incident. Yet every day there's some scene or nuance of behaviour redolent of ethnicity. Recently I saw two posh native schoolgirls in a shop where the assistant was Chinese. Though only about fifteen they were taller than him, and as they left one giggled to the other, in a voice loud enough for him to hear, 'Isn't he *sweet*.' It's a myth that the Chinese are expressionless: the look on the guy's face would have sparked the Boxer Revolt.

Normally it doesn't trouble me, but there can be times when your minority status works against you. Not long ago I was on a bus where the seats upstairs at the back had been commandeered by a group of black girls and boys shouting and cursing and playing a radio at top volume. Language-wise they were going it, especially the girls, but no one turned a hair; turning a hair might single you out for attention, which is what we were all avoiding. I was about to ask them to tone it down when it occurred to me that, apart from an elderly lady, I was the only native on the top deck, and the boys were a tough-looking bunch. If they're going to cut something up, I decided, better the seats than me. Bowing to the will of the majority I sat back and enjoyed the music, whose virtue was that it helped drown the screams of *motherfucker, prick* and *cunt*.

Catherine tells me that, confronted by a similar situation, you were braver than me. Coming home by bus at one in the morning there was a big black guy in a hood behind you, eating some high-smelling food and playing his music, loud. Apparently you swung round and asked him to turn it down, then waited for the knife in your neck. Instead the music stopped, and the guy said 'Sure man, we all gotta live together.' Sweet or what? Just don't make a habit of it.

There was a time when we used to be embarrassed by the Brits abroad; now you find them sticking out like sore thumbs amongst the cosmopolitan mass in their own country. The other day I was waiting in a queue at the Post Office. Guilty of holding things up was a middle-aged woman with a loud Chelsea voice. She'd failed to get to grips with the switch to chip-and-pin and was arguing with the Indian clerk who'd been unable to make her card work: *Don't you understand? It* has *to work! I've got no money! Try it again. My pin number is 7350 (shouted extra loud) – the last four numbers of my telephone number. I wrote it down you see to remind me and kept it in my wallet for safety, but my wallet was stolen.* The Indian treated her with studious courtesy, but she was losing it. *This is intolerable. Who are these people? Am I expected to have no money for the rest of my life?* The sight of the native behaving stupidly and offensively, and the more recent arrivals waiting to take her place at the counter, was somehow evocative.

*

Speaking of ethnic traits, I had a wonderful example of French insolence last week. In anticipation of my birthday Sarah persuaded me to treat myself to some fancy new prescription sunglasses she recommended. Off I went to a high-class optician and waited amongst the smart clientele. Maybe I looked a little shabby by contrast, anyway when it came to my turn the man asked me what I wanted while reading a letter. I suggested he finish his letter, so he could listen. No reaction. 'Stand there' he said when I told him, pointing to a place where he could test my sight. 'Now here'. At one point I began to laugh: 'If you're trying to alienate your clientele you're doing a great job.' Pointless. He was so rude he didn't even recognise insults. It was as if I'd commented adversely on the weather.

He got on with his measuring, issuing curt instructions, which I obeyed. One reason I didn't walk out was that he was a real case, and therefore funny. More importantly, he was super-efficient at his job. He took much more care than an optician would in Britain, gave good advice in his take it or leave it manner, and the glasses were ready the next day. 'Thanks' I said with heavy emphasis. A nod. No smile. No 'Merci à vous Monsieur.' What can you do?

*

One of the biggest arguments against excess immigration, I sometimes feel, is that it brings out some nasty characteristics of our own, not least our tendency to sanctimoniousness. You see it most often in the arts, where the drone of multicultural sermonizing is most insistent. Melting pots can stimulate creativity, everyone tells you endlessly, and isn't that wonderful? Well it's certainly good to know. Think of it: Holbein was a German and Van Dyck was from Flanders and they settled in England and being in England had an influence on their work, which in turn had an influence on English painters. And you want me to celebrate? The fact of the matter is that melting pots can indeed bring out new flavours, and as America has shown they can also boil down to a sticky residue of nothing. Think of those indiscriminately mixed herbs and sauces they serve over there with every meal, so as to make it, like, ethnic.

The pretence that a blend of cultures is necessary for great art is rubbish: Dostoyevsky, for one, was a far-right, nationalistic Slavophile. It's true that Picasso made inspired use of African sculpture (the usual example given), though he managed it without having much to do with Africa, or being tolerant towards anyone, least of all his wives. On the other hand he appears to have got along fine with the German officers buying his work during the occupation. (As Dali said of him: 'Picasso is a genius. So am I. Picasso is a communist. Neither am I.')

So while it's good that there's a lot going on various communities, I don't buy the official guff about art and ethnicity. Sounds to me like yet another form of racism inverted. The natives, after all, have produced some worthwhile stuff over the years. But the whole argument is too primitive to get into, so I won't.

*

Why do *you* stay here if you're so critical of everything, Catherine asked me once. I've forgotten what I said, but now I think about it the answer is that I'm not being critical for the sake of it, just pointing up a few truths that have been neglected. Britain still has a lot going for it, for people like us at least, otherwise we wouldn't be here. To begin with, the vitality of the British art and publishing industries gives Sarah and me work. Another reason we stay is because you have to live somewhere, wherever it is you develop ties, not least with your family, and I've seen enough of the world not to have illusions about life elsewhere.

For us London at its best can be like living in a dozen foreign countries at once, with a lot of the benefits and fewer of the inconveniences. The occasional stabs of claustrophobia we overcome by frequent travel, for business or holidays (America, Russia, China, and France so far this year). That of course is a middle-aged, comfortably-off view. Though if I lived with young children in a mixed, dicey area on a smaller income, and couldn't travel as frequently as I do, I can honestly claim that I'd be saying exactly the same thing. While thinking something very different.

When we lived in America I found myself wondering why, with the number of ethnic people London has, it doesn't feel more like New York? Now I think I know the reason. The USA is historically an immigrant country, and for all the pious hogwash people have begun writing about how Britain has always been a land of immigration, that has never been the case here on remotely the same scale. As in the arts, an industry has grown up dedicated to reminding us of the benefits immigrants and asylum seekers can bring to Britain. The assumption is that we had no idea that the Huguenots from France built those Norfolk churches, that Disraeli was a Jew or that Brunel was a Belgian.

No one needs to be reminded that, left to itself, Britain can be a self-satisfied culture, replete with patrician attitudes and inclined to live off the past whenever it can get away with it. The wave of Jewish refugees from Hitler alone gave us a much-needed cultural and economic boot in the backside. (It used to be said of Russian Jews emigrating to Israel that if they got off the plane in Tel Aviv without a violin case, that was because they were concert pianists.) Examples include Sir Ernst Gombrich who transformed art history, Lord Weidenfeld who brought an international dimension to parochial publishing, or the boss of what used to be GEC, Arnold Weinstock, whose accomplishments included running the smallest HQ of any major company, and declining to employ me as a (clearly supernumerary) consultant on Chinese and Russian affairs. Without them and more of their kind Britain would have been a poorer and duller place.

All this is true, edifying – and not strictly relevant to the point, which is that there can be little comparison between what happened in the past and what's happening today. The number of Jewish immigrants was as nothing compared to the level of newcomers in recent years. By the 1930's, after decades of Jewish immigration, there were about 200,000 in the East End – about the same as a single year's (official) immigration now. Nor did they bring social problems. They lived amongst themselves but were not fenced off, with as much difficulty in adapting to the British way of life as Disraeli. They did not put a strain on the social security budget, inflame religious tensions or concoct bomb plots, and their women were as avid for advancement as their men. As a community they were smart and successful. One can see why Mosley's fascists took against them.

While some of these things are true of some more recent immigrants, some are not. But it's the figures that are overwhelming: nothing comparable to what's happening now has happened since the Anglo-Saxon and Danish invasions a thousand years ago, relative to population. Another difference with the USA is that immigrants to the UK today aren't coming to settle a half-empty land, till virgin soil, build townships or extract oil and gold and iron from the bounteous soil. They're squeezing into the nooks and crannies of cities in the most intensively populated land in Europe – a country with twelve times more people per square mile than the United States. It may surprise the Bangladeshis and Pakistanis who come to live in South East England to know that they're emigrating to a place more densely settled than India.

A final, crucial difference between us and the USA is that the people we see as minorities went there to be Americans, and that is what they have become. Our immigrants do not necessarily come here to be British, and a sizeable number seem in no hurry to adapt to native ways. Instead they regard the country that has opened its doors to them as a pagan, alien, decadent culture, ripe for destruction.

If they're coming to such a rotten place purely for materialist reasons, you have to ask how holy is that? Alternatively they have come with notions of islamicising the nation, by violence if necessary, or more often by tacit support for it. A small handful we are told, but that is all it takes. Fanatics we do not need, even a handful. No one went to America with the aim of bringing it down, and nor did immigrants have a backlog of colonial resentments, nurtured over generations, in their baggage, since America had not been a colonizing power. For these and other reasons our problems of assimilation will be far greater than theirs. Insuperable, perhaps.

*

Though do not despair. What I'm saying is not so much a prediction, as an apprehension. And if it's true that the whole thing is a gigantic leap in the dark, it follows that the outcome is uncertain. Which means that Catherine could turn out to be right and I could be wrong. Maybe she's backed the right horse, and Peaceful Assimilation, the rank outsider, will come up on the home stretch and the great blind bet of mass immigration could turn out for the best. I'm patriotic enough to see that if anyone can pull off a miracle in this area it's the British. Fears of 'the other' could be muted by closer acquaintance. All those eager and acquisitive workers could have a galvanizing effect on the economy, in which case the costs of assimilation will be outweighed by the benefits. Who knows? Maybe Britain will one day become the model of race relations we claim it is already.

Here and there you can see it happening. Simple observation shows people of all races working together on public transport, in shops, in schools, in hospitals, on building sites. Workplace association isn't integration, and amicable co-existence isn't cultural assimilation. But it's something. It's not the occasional riots or racist crimes (and last year there were more racist murders of whites than the other way round), the discrimination or the tensions that are the most striking aspect of what's happening. What's truly extraordinary is how relatively smoothly things have gone to date. One wonders if any other society could import such a vast array of cultures in so short a period and avoid turmoil.

Our tolerance may have a lot to do with apathy (the great William Hazlitt described English tolerance as 'indolence of disposition'), and some of it is tinged with fear. But it can be genuine. The British have many faults. They can be arrogant, complacent, intellectually lazy and bleatingly egalitarian, but they're not by and large racist. Or, to put it in a more nuanced way, they're not violently and intuitively hostile to foreigners. Anyone who doubts this general truth should look at attitudes in countries such as Russia and China towards blacks or Muslims. (Expressing utter astonishment after a visit to Britain recently, a Russian I know said with pride that Moscow would be the last white city in Europe).

Maybe the experience of living in a tolerant society will weaken the power of extremists quicker than we think, and hasten a belated reformation of Islam. Perhaps we've seen the worst of the terror attacks, and the police will get a grip on criminality. And Muslims could inject a dose of moral seriousness, family values and spiritual depth into a cynically irreligious, hedonistic culture.

I think of the sharp, intelligent foreign faces I've seen on university campuses, not all of them out to subvert the culture that's given them their chance in life. I think of people from the Middle East who provide us with brilliant surgeons as well as bogus doctors of surreal audacity, or of high-octane Muslims less interested in cultivating their grievances in sour, self-imposed ghettoes than in making it big in science or the City. You can even put a positive gloss on the massive electoral frauds we've seen in places like Birmingham. I can't imagine the natives going to all that trouble to rig a local election when only a third of them turn out to vote, so I suppose it shows a level of engagement with the democratic process.

There are ways in which Muslims could bring us benefits as well as trouble. Religious indoctrination cuts two ways: either it fouls you up for life, even after you've rejected it, or it can raise your intellectual game. (Until she went all arty and batty Jeanette Winterson, brought up by religious zealots, was an English example). The second generation of Muslims will be attracted (or if you like corrupted) by Western culture and the brightest of them will tire of ghetto thinking. 'You love life, we love death' is an unappealing sort of future. The more successful they become the less prickly they will be. In commerce Muslims can be a dynamic force, when they're not hamstrung by the Islamic prohibition against interest, and ways round this are currently being devised. (One of the reasons the British and Americans were so prominent in business and industry, remember, was because the early Puritans found a way round the Biblical ban on usury).

Similar hopes could be voiced about the black community. Contrary to stereotype they've begun making a mark in business as well as music, sport and fashion. Then there are the Eastern Europeans, all those faraway peoples of whose outstanding talents (and vicious criminal gangs) we till recently knew little, thanks to the iron curtain. And if there's one thing we can depend on it's that the Chinese will continue to be Chinese.

That's enough optimism for the moment: I'm not sure who I'm trying to convince, you or myself. Maybe it's because I've just read that the Rumanians and Bulgarians are due to get free entry into Britain. Not to work of course, but then the average hit-man or prostitute smuggler doesn't go through the formality of applying for a work permit. We have the Russian mafia, the Albanian vice trade (Kosovan if you ask Albanians), and the Turkish drug trade, but if you think that's bad wait till you see their Bulgarian brothers. Their gangland is run by a piquant mixture of the boxing and wrestling fraternity and former security service agents so nasty that their KGB brothers used to delegate their messier operations to them, such as the (attempted) assassination of the Pope. We do a good job of nurturing our own criminals, but with them there are rules. When home-grown mobsters beat someone to a jelly they leave him in the gutter for the ambulance to pick up, in the accepted way. When a Rumanian gang beat up a rival not long ago, and the ambulance came for him, they climbed into the back and bludgeoned him to death.

Never mind. If things go well London could emerge as the greatest, most prosperous and most cosmopolitan city in the world. A little rowdy on the criminal front, but that may be one of the prices we have to pay for the vitality that immigrants bring. So there you are: an alternative reading of the future that would be a positive incentive to stay in Britain.

You'll expect me to add a prudent disclaimer, so here it is. The problem with the optimistic scenario is not that it's impossible: it's that it's the only one we can bring ourselves to face. We're obliged to behave as if the most hopeful outcome is the most probable, because the alternatives are too bleak to contemplate. If ever we needed optimism of the will alongside pessimism of the intellect, it's on immigration.

*

One good reason for your quitting the country, it occurred to me, is that there's a good three-quarters of it you never use. Like most Southerners, for you holiday travel in Britain tends to be a way of escape from anything that's typical about the way the British live. Which means avoiding Northern and Midlands urban centres like badlands and hop-scotching from one oasis of gentility – Bath, Harrowgate, York, Edinburgh – to another.

When was the last time you saw Liverpool, Manchester, Birmingham or Newcastle? Have you or will you *ever* see Bradford, Nottingham or Leicester? Sarah and I have been trying to think of anyone who goes to these places, unless family connections or business oblige them, and have come up with a blank. If you lived in Paris you might well choose to spend a weekend in Lyon, Bordeaux or Marseilles, and a New Yorker would go happily to Boston, Los Angeles or San Francisco for a vacation. 'We're off to Birmingham for a weekend break' doesn't ring true. (Vivienne Westwood, an honest woman I've always thought, recently admitted that till this year she'd never been north of Scarborough).

Not that Southerners have a down on these places. On the contrary, they affect to have an up, forever telling us how completely out-of-date our perception of them is. The North has changed utterly, they say, with an upsurge of creativity everywhere from Gateshead to Bradford and new galleries and bridges and theatres and orchestras by the dozen, and isn't it all wonderful? Most commendable. Just one thing: how come that, except to write the article, like everyone else the people who make these claims never go? It's the old story of English cant and condescension. They patronise these places in words but not with their presence. Patting people on the head while looking absently over their shoulders is a national vice. Not that I'm implying that Northerners are any shorter than us.

And while Southerners pat away, our Northern brothers, more realistic about these matters, are heading South. So many young people are queuing to get out that in twenty years' time 60% of the remaining population will be over forty-five – an astonishing figure. The BBC is foremost in the Northern propaganda drive, but what happened when it announced that it was thinking of moving 1,800 of its London employees to the Manchester ship canal at Salford? General insurrection, put down with the help of massive re-location payouts.

And what did we see when David Cameron and Michael Heseltine launched out on a trip to Liverpool? It was a national event. Pictures of our elegant beasts were everywhere, posed against a background of slummy houses, and the commentaries said how good it was of them to go. Two rich politicians, one retired, take a first-class train ride to spend a day in one of our major cities and are lauded for their pains. One Nation and all that, what? For a similar gesture at a similar stage of her career Thatcher would scarcely have got a mention, but then who was she? A lower-middle class Midlander, whereas an Old Etonian Southerner purporting to interest himself in Scouse issues, now you're talking.

There's no end to the deference of our countrymen, I sometimes fear. Throw them a few crumbs from on high and they peck them up, gurgling with gratitude. You're garlanded with praise simply for doing your job, and would-be Prime Ministers get credit for troubling to visit parts of the country they aspire to govern. You don't get that sort of easy accolade on the Continent, though you did in totalitarian states: 'Yesterday, comrade Brezhnev demonstrated his solidarity with the people by visiting the town of Novosibirsk.'

*

Shortly before coming on holiday, as you know Sarah and I *did* go North. I can't say it was entirely voluntary: Sarah had to look at a couple of pictures in Manchester, and having seen little of the territory since my ministerial days I thought I'd tag along. We stayed on and cruised the area, not difficult because of the multiplicity of motorways, and the way one town blends dispiritingly into another.

On the way up we called in at Birmingham. Afterwards we drove on in silence. There seemed nothing to say. My after-image of the place is of an old woman in the centre wandering through the desert of roads and underpasses, like someone searching after a war for the remains of what had once been her city. The difference with the Birmingham bomb site is that it's mostly new. You have to give high marks for trying – God how they've tried – but to no avail. Monuments of urban ugliness of the last five decades affront the eye at every turn, the latest of them (the new shopping centre) even more meretricious than in the past. We'd thought of dropping into the museum but had to give up the idea: there seemed no way to negotiate the traffic system. A pity, it's a great gallery.

On the way out we drove through the ethnic suburb of Handsworth, thinking naively we might have a curry lunch, but couldn't find a restaurant. No natives, no demand. There didn't seem to be any pubs either – mostly they were disused and boarded up, like the churches. No demand. Birmingham had seemed oddly empty; here there was an air of teeming desolation, the long straight road through Handsworth a continuous traffic jam. Curious how there's no poverty so complete they can't afford a jam. It's the kind of place where you don't see a lot of people laughing: even our smile at the *Have Faith Car Wash* sign, where someone had inscribed *Nuff Faith* at the bottom, felt illicit.

The most striking thing was not the size of the immigrant community, but its exclusivity. Not a white face in sight besides our own, which when we enquired about restaurants did not seem noticeably welcome. I've felt more at home in many a foreign country. Another ghetto, afflicted no doubt with ghetto thinking. The sight of it inspired Sarah with an aesthetic theory of terrorism. The trouble with such squalid, beaten-up places, she thinks, is that their new inhabitants could never develop an affection for them, or for Britain. So that living there would alienate the moderates and make the dangerous ones even more alienated than they were before.

It was the chief imam of Birmingham, I recalled, who declared after the 7/7 murders that there was no proof Muslims were involved. And to think that people used to look to priests for instruction and enlightenment. The population of Birmingham, as I've said, is about a million, so if the country grows by another seven million, as we are promised, it would be the equivalent of seven more Birminghams, with seven more chief imams. Nothing to be said.

Next, we call in at Stoke-on-Trent, for historical reasons. The town was our earliest environmental catastrophe, because of the depredations of the pottery business, and we thought we'd see what had happened since. Desolation. As always in such places it's the attempts to prettify them that are so tragic. The hideous, cheap new buildings, the puce-painted shopping centre, a piteous public market in a dismal modern square, with burglar alarms like piped music. And everywhere the obese, ill-looking inhabitants, victims of the hereditary effects of pollution it seems, as well as of their eating habits. It's not just the buildings, it's the people who look as though they need reconstituting from scratch.

Still no Indian restaurant. Instead we had lunch in a café advertising home-made pies. The sight of chips as thick as your fingers, and the rich, dark, glutinous gravy gave me a moment's nostalgia for my Dagenham years. Sitting there amongst the chalk-featured, smoking mothers and their children with faces the colour of unwholesome bread, feeling we were slumming, I was reminded of the reverse situation described by George Gissing in the 1890s. Dining in a restaurant he once saw a working man who was obviously treating himself. After a while the man became so flustered at the complexities of the business (side-dishes, cutlery, transferring food from serving dish to plate) he eventually asked the waiter to wrap up the entire meal, paid and departed. I ate up all my gristly meat and gravy-soaked starch like a good Dagenham boy, and guiltily enjoyed it.

We drove on. Scenically the route was distinctive if nothing else. There are vantage points on the motorways in the North and Midlands that afford an uninterrupted, horizon-to-horizon panorama of urban and industrial squalor old and new, of an ugliness you will encounter nowhere else in Europe. Even the fields look worn out, residual. Of course things are better than they were, in patches, sometimes a whole lot better, but how can any serious revival take root in such a disheartening wilderness? Maybe we should rope off the entire area and lease it to the Chinese, as they leased the New Territories in Hong Kong to us. There'd be a satisfying symmetry to that. It was the Chinese who made a go of Hong Kong, under British rule, and maybe the same trick would work here.

Time is getting on, so we drive straight to Manchester, avoiding the motorway, so we can see a bit of the outskirts. The suburb of Shirley is prim, prosperous, and exceedingly white. A few minutes down the road is the less genteel Sparkbrook: messy, poor-looking, and almost entirely black and brown. Should you be colour-blind you can tell when you're passing from one to the other because of the blitzed pubs and churches. The churches – lumbering, frowsy, nineteenth century – are not much of an architectural loss, but it seems a shame about the pubs. At least people must have laughed there.

*

As always Manchester is an agreeable surprise, a prop to your patriotism after the surrounding towns. All those sturdy, upright nineteenth century buildings: a tall town for a big people. The crucible of the manufacturing world, is what it's telling you, and don't you forget it. It's good to see the vast university evidently thriving, with its students from across the globe got up in identical gear: trainers, chinos, concerned air, mobile phone. I remember being impressed with this place when I was Minister for Higher Education. It has a Northern seriousness and solidity which will infect its graduates. A lot of the immigrants who'll give the natives a run for their money will come from here.

Needing to be in the centre we choose a new hotel, which is fine except it could be anywhere: check-in girl Asian, lobby attendant black, car-parker Czech, breakfast waiter Baltic. I do not understand what the indigenous inhabitants do any more. You so rarely see them at work. The sad thing is that when you come across a native receptionist or waiter, with their eleven year minimum of free, compulsory education, they're almost invariably dimmer. As employees their only advantage seems to be that they speak the language, more or less.

Theoretically they're supposed to be concentrated in skilled, high-tech jobs, leaving the menial jobs to immigrants. In government, when anyone said we were running down our manufacturing skills, I used to say 'Nonsense. Look at the British aircraft industry, a world leader. Think of the quality of the technicians doing those jobs.' I'm glad I don't have to field that sort of question now that BAE have just sold off its stake in Airbus, and thousands of high-skilled jobs will go to France and Germany. A lot of them, I gather, from around Manchester.

We had a good walk round, enjoying the relative space and lack of traffic, before making for the gallery where Sarah had to see her pictures. It's less well-stocked than I remember, except of course for the Pre-Raphaelites, a taste I look forward to never acquiring. How did we ever get from the glowing health of Constable and Turner to this ghastly, sanctimonious, mawkish stuff? In the same way we went from the lusty Georgians to the moralizing Victorians. All those pictures about honest-to-god labourers and pining women, where the message seems to be that *work is good for you, love too when it is pure.* Well said, so true.

And their appalling literal-mindedness: paint a leaf perfectly from nature, they thought, and what you get is a perfect picture of a leaf. But you don't: you get a waxwork image, a lifeless imitation with no value added, a soundless echo of the real thing. You certainly can't accuse them of painting their women from nature. Where did they find such freaks?

*

We'd intended to go out for a drink before dinner, but the hotel bar looked so raucously inviting we had one there. It was new and swanky, with those gaudily vibrant colours you get in provincial towns self-consciously kicking over the traces. We'd been thinking of seeking out a characterful pub, and here it was: raw-looking faces putting away large amounts of liquor, and emitting lots of noise. Encouraged by all this modernity I asked for the drink I wanted – an Old Fashioned. The barman, a native, nodded as if he served them every hour of the day, and set to work manufacturing my order.

From a bottle of Jim Beam he took a measure of bourbon. Next he fetched a glass and some bitters, then an orange. From it he cut some rind, taking care to leave a bit of pith. And for the next fifteen minutes, eyes down, oblivious to everything and everyone, he made the drink. This involved pouring a few drops of whisky onto orange peel and, using a glass pestle, mixing it in. Bitters, bourbon, peel, grind. Like some demented apothecary on and on he went. He must have performed the same operation twenty times. To begin with the customers round us got annoyed. When the barman, intent on his grinding, took no notice they quietened down, mesmerised it seemed by the deliberateness of his movements.

I thought of telling him not to bother, there were so many customers, just give me the bourbon and a chunk of orange, but that would have been to insult his Mancunian manhood. And by then I was seriously looking forward to my drink. Which turned out perfect: that sour mash taste richly imbued with rind of orange, not too sweet. When I told him it was the best I'd ever had he looked grimly contented. As if to say, any time.

An episode like that should not be without its moral. The fortyish barman, we decided, had been on a course to update his skills in anticipation of the opening of the modern bar. All part of the new Manchester. In the past the application he put into my drink would have gone into the drilling out of some sensitive piece of machinery, with *Made in Britain* stamped on it. He must have seen we were effete Southerners, and an entire tradition of Northern manufacturing was at stake.

Everywhere you saw examples of a determined cosmopolitanism at work in this rootedly local culture. A guide book in our hotel room boasted that Manchester had a coffee culture. The evidence? A picture of... Starbucks. An executive in the firm's HQ in Houston or wherever pinpoints Manchester on his map of operations, and the city that led the world before the US got started is awarded its Starbucks coffee house, and is mighty proud of it. A million Continental bars have served millions of coffees since the dawn of modern times and up pops Manchester with its Starbucks, boasting of its coffee culture.

And of its sex. In the last few years Canal Street, the homosexual quarter, has done what Berlin and San Francisco and the Marais in Paris have been doing for many a decade, yet it sees itself, and is written up, as a gay wonder of the world. You want modern, we'll do modern. This is the spirit that went into the fifteen-minute Old Fashioned and the corporate coffee. How could you explain to Mancunians, exploding with pride at being right out there on the edge, that Canal Street is not challenging convention, it's following it, rather late in the day, as provinces do, and that by making a song and dance about a couple of gay bars it's revealing itself as rather, well, provincial. Handy as they are for mopping up labour in a service economy, it seems unlikely that Manchester can rebuild a world-class future on non-illicit sex.

This is old-fashioned chapel country at heart, so even gay hedonism has its finger-wagging, preachy side: gaze upon the extent of our sexual emancipation and thank the Lord, amen. You feel like saying, relax pal, no one minds what you do any more, so there's no need to make a big deal of it. But with Puritans inverted, which is what the English increasingly are, there's nothing to be done. If you told them nobody cares you'd be taking away what matters to them most: their sense of transgression. Making a big deal of it is half the fun.

*

I'm sure there's been a renaissance in Manchester cooking too, but you learn to be wary. Advised by a Manchester friend of a celebrated Chinese restaurant, there we went. Full. I pleaded with the young manager in Mandarin, he asked where I'd learned it, I told him, and for extra effect – we really were hungry – added that I'd spent two years in China during the Cultural Revolution. It worked. He described how his parents had been 'struggled' by the Red Guards, and found a table. I asked how many Chinese there were in Manchester. Too many he said, and a lot of the younger ones were rich layabouts with sports cars. Which rather undermines my theory of the Chinese as the eventual saviour of these parts.

Too many or not, there wasn't a solitary Chinese at the tables – normally a bad sign, though not here. The food turned out to be more sophisticated than the customers. Next to us a middle-aged guy was standing in his seat regaling his table with how much he'd drunk the night before, and they were egging him on. The contrast between this boorishness and the dignity of the manager in his tuxedo, looking on with his sweet and sour expression, was sad. You can't take the Brits anywhere, not even to a Chinese. And the ugliness of their clothes. The mystery of a country that spends its entire life shopping and getting into debt, and at the end of it all manages to be so stylelessly dressed. Only the Brits could invent the drabbie hedonist. And only we could turn out some of the best stylists around, then export them to Continental fashion houses, which is what we do.

A distressing scene on the way back to the hotel: shrieking fifteen year old girls falling down drunk in the street, mini-skirts rucked up over unappetizing thighs. You can't call them legless because all legs is what they are. Watching them get up and stagger on was comic: two steps ahead then flat on their faces, like the baby in *The Simpsons*, except these girls had bottles rather than a dummy. Screaming women's voices went on late into the night. I've seen the same thing in Newcastle. And Birmingham. And Aylesbury. I've never seen it in Hong Kong, New York, or Paris. Why does it happen so much in Britain? We of all people ought to have evolved a sane view of sex and alcohol, but we never have. It's the boo/hurrah, Puritan/anti-Puritan thing again. We're always either condemning something or cheering it on, banging on about the evils of drink or boasting about how we went out with the boys and got plastered. The centre doesn't hold because in drink and sex there's never been one. Everything is out of kilter, and as with homosexuality, so with booze.

It's the bragging that's so boring, the more-shit-faced-than-thou one-upmanship of the Brits, whether it comes from the sloshed slags of Manchester or Bollinger-popping Oxford students. Personally I don't mind if people drink themselves to death or copulate like dogs in the street (their street), so long as they don't sermonise me about how tolerant and open-minded and fun-loving and original they are. Not minding is what real liberalism's about, but the Brits, forever pointing the finger, don't get it. Maybe one day we'll learn to drink like normal people, though God knows how many years it will take.

Look at you, your brother, and me. On booze we all did the same: two generations and absolutely no progress to show. I was a jazz drummer at university, it was too early for drugs, there was a dearth of girls, so it had to be drink, and we felt obligated to down it by the gallon. Morning mouths like the bottom of a baby's pram. I remember a pitiable sense of accomplishment, and I hated it. You and your brother, I'm sorry to say, were no improvement. The nudges, the winks, the 'just going for a few jars.' The delicious sense of sin. The idea that you were defying the Gods by downing a beer.

It's worse than the drinking I saw in Russia, not in quantity but because there they had an excuse: they were drinking to die and had every reason to do so (the men still do, by the way, at 56 on average). British drinking, amongst other things, is an attempt to loosen up, but it doesn't work, and we end up transferring our earnestness to the bottle. That's why I was so much in favor of opening up the pubs. The banalisation of booze is our only hope.

I know I ought to deplore the hedonism and vulgarity that has replaced the primness, but I'm not sure I can. You look at those leggy young drunks and you shrug. There's absolutely no future in blaming girls like this. Ours used to be a culture of parsimony and repression, now young people are relatively rich and free. What else do we expect them to do when they have the money and the leisure and the commercial and media incitement but to go out clubbing, binge-drinking and copulating? Compose Latin verse? What would you do in their situation? What would my generation have done, if we'd had the freedom, the cash and the girls? Enjoy, like these poor bastards are trying to do. You should only get indignant over things you can do something about. This is how it is, for civilizational reasons, and nothing's going to change it.

Of course it's primitive and ugly, but why are we surprised? It's the penalty of progress. The truest thing that's been said of contemporary Britain is that the Left has won in culture and the Right in economics. Put them together and a pigging-it life-style is what you get. Egalitarianism plus the market gives you the lowest behavioural denominator, plus the highest regard for cash.

So I find I'm no more fazed by the Manchester slappers than I am when I see Russians lying drunk in the snow in Moscow. (The ones they dig out dead next morning are called 'snowdrops.') The difference is that in Moscow you don't see young girls falling down on the streets: even in the new Chicago, there are standards. Though however much you try to shrug it off you find yourself feeling sorry for the girls. Everything that used to regulate their lives has gone. The old working class, the church, school discipline and the family: the parents of almost half the population are likely to be separated or divorced, and with these girls the figure will be higher.

We took the Peak District road out of Manchester. It's a few years since I've seen it, but it's as imposing as ever. And unspoiled. When the Brits set their mind to preserving something they do it right: in Italy the equivalent place would have been a mess of encroaching houses, built on bribes. The more ugly and intense urban life becomes, the more soothing the serenity of these places. Sarah, however, was uneasy: to her it seemed inhumanly bleak, and fenced off like a crime scene. She couldn't get it out of her mind that this was the landscape of the Moors murders.

*

Bradford next, and the biggest hole you've ever seen. Not the town (this is not on the Stoke on Trent scale of things), but the construction work that meets you as you come in from the South. The plan is for one of those gigantic new supermarkets where Northerners in state employment and on national wage rates (a quarter of all workers in the communised North) can spend the money they save on housing costs. The town itself is less of a hole than I expected, though the centre, of course, is hideous. The most tragic image was an echo of the same scene in Birmingham: this time the lost-looking figure was an ancient, bearded Pakistani with a plastic bag picking a path through a desolate stretch of smashed-up concrete, like an Afghan in the ruins of Kabul. On the outside there are handsome old buildings, trees and parks. Bradford Grammar school, the size of Buckingham Palace, looms like a lost world.

The reasons for the race riots a few years back soon became obvious. There's been a large ethnic presence here for decades, in the cloth trade, and Asians occupy many of the rather solid-looking, stone-built terraces and council houses. The worst slums we saw were white, on the town's perimeter. In ten years time the problem will be solved by the simple expedient of an Asian takeover. Five years after that, if you're still here, you could be listening to excited media discussions about whether or not they're entitled to introduce Sharia law in Bradford. Not wife-burying or stoning to death, just some minor curtailments of English liberties. Will the English, keener to show how tolerant they are than to uphold there own principles, allow it? Never mind. They say the climate round here is especially favourable to growing rhubarb. So there'll always be a future.

*

Leeds, our next stop, was a pick-me-up. Imposing and evocative architecture. Not bad modern stuff. The kind of waterside conversion you see everywhere from Docklands to Boston Mass, but well done. A smell of money about, much of it from the legal profession, so it's extra strength. Also a whiff of civic pride, as the economy grows at the Chinese rate of

9%. 'The Knightsbridge of the North' the town boasts. Its first mistake: never identify yourself by reference to something else, especially when your precinctified shops are reminiscent less of Knightsbridge than of King Street Hammersmith, Kensington High Street, or pretty much any other shopping centre in any large town you care to name. All you see here is all you see anywhere: Boots, Dixons, Halifax, HMV, Jessops, O2, Russell and Bromley.

Why go on having names at all, when the shops and the products are much the same? If high street standardization continues at this rate, and everything becomes a near-monopoly, you could reach the stage when capitalism begins to resemble a kind of advanced communism. In which case we might as well do what the Russians did: have shop signs that read meat, vegetables, fruit, clothes, shoes, chemist. The British grumble about it, but I don't think they mind, otherwise it wouldn't happen. They like the familiar in all things. Why do French high-streets look more invitingly individual than ours, with rents small shopkeepers can afford? It didn't just happen: a law was passed in 1973 to keep the big monopolies out. The culture demanded it.

Still intent on our Indian meal, I ask a policeman for the ethnic quarter. They don't have one, he tells me, looking away and ahead in the way policemen determined not to betray untoward emotions do. In this case, the hidden emotion appears to be satisfaction. Leeds is not as other towns are, I think he's saying, we are not Birmingham or Bradford. He must have thought I'd meant ghetto.

Leeds does have its Muslim quarter, however, and later we were to hear some of them complaining about racism on the World Service ('Angry young Muslims'). I'm sure there is some. We didn't learn how much because no-one was invited onto the programme to contest the complaints, but there you go. Since the British do tend to go in for a lot of self-flagellating about race, in depriving the country of the chance to defend itself the Corporation are only projecting an objective image. It doesn't *want* to defend itself, it wants to kick itself. Why would honest folk like ourselves want to defend ourselves when we are so evidently guilty as charged? Curious when you think that the World Service is supposed to encourage foreigners to feel well-disposed towards Britain.

Having made his point the policeman comes up with a restaurant, which turns out to be an imposing-looking, Taj Mahal sort of place. Closed. We end up in a self-service Indian up three flights of stairs with all you can eat for £6. A real find. The only customers are Indian families so the kids are under control and the food is excellent. The nuances between Indian English and Indian Leeds English would be material for a University study, I reflect, listening to their subtly variegated accent, and it's probably cooking.

Later we try to see inside the splendid, neo-classical town hall. You can't, there's a function. On the lobby ceiling Victoria and Albert are welcoming figures from Asia, Europe, Africa, America. Peoples of the world, come to Leeds. The policeman might not be happy with that. Or the World Service. Outside the Town Hall, as if to demonstrate their anti-colonial credentials, the imperial guardian lions on either side of the entrance have muzzles worn away by pollution. Now they are big pussy cats guarding against – what?

'From gloomy, polluted and sooty to young and trendy' says a promotional piece on the town. Which doesn't show much pride in the past for a place that was world-famous for its textiles and engineering. That's why it looks so handsome today, despite misguided efforts here and there at a 'makeover'. The municipal art gallery is certainly doing its modernizing bit. When Sarah asks after the gloomy, sooty Old Masters it turns out they've been locked away, in favour of a display of off-cuts from a Saatchi show.

Elsewhere there's the usual new contemporary gallery, housing the usual old stuff. It's the sex and coffee thing again. The left-behind Brits scurrying to catch up. It's taken us a hundred years to get the joke about Dada and Duchamp, and now we've got it we can't stop re-telling it – with killer explanations. What's so sad is the thought of provincials being excited at their own little daring. All this naughtiness must make the local aldermen feel frisky. They think they're coming out on the side of modernity, but the problem with brave new Britain is that it's so painfully passé. Someone should tell the locals that the Russians had artists running about Moscow naked with pictures on their bodies before the First World War. Which makes their frightfully subversive gallery look pretty timid, as well as a century out of date. Never mind, what you don't know you don't care about, and council tax payers are not going to march on the pussy-cat lions asking why they have to cough up tens of thousands of pounds for a display of dated, derivative, talent-free sub-Duchampian tat.

Contemporary British art has become a bit like Boots or the Halifax. You can't get away from it, it's part of the urban landscape. Sarah tells me there are cellars-full of irreparable contemporary junk in the major museums of London, the detritus of decades of indiscriminate buying. When the capital finally tires of it a lot more will wash up here. All those witless, laborious installations and the rest will look thoroughly in place alongside the plonking, moralizing Victoriana.

In the nineteenth-century room, children are lolling about creatively on cushions dumped on the floor, while their mothers chat. No-one except us looks at the pictures. Should one resent this conversion of a temple of art into a play-group? I find I don't care. The pictures in this bit are pretty absurd, and the kids have to play somewhere. Just don't make any more art, there's a dear.

*

For relief from urban sameness we came back on the Fosse Way, dodging the motorway and its hellish panoramas. The long stretches of traffic-free road through truly green and pleasant land calmed the nerves and soothed the affronted eyes. Viewing your own country like an ethnographer is an estranging process. What are you to say? That while some places seem to be prospering, vast stretches of the Midlands and the North are a no-man's land of urban desolation or meretricious modernity, which could explain why a worrying number of Northerners are drifting south? Or do your Southerner's duty and rabbit on about renaissance and rejuvenation?

Your sympathy for their problems is framed against an admiration for the past. It's not sentiment: the independence of character that helped make them (and us) is still tangible. But how is that independence to be exercised today, in their sovietised structures? In many ways their future isn't in their hands. It's in those of China, India and the rest, who'll soon be making many of the things they make here to the same standard at a quarter the price. Nor will the Asian business brain be content to rely on British financial services for ever, whether it's Leeds or London. And the idea that the second coming of the North will be based on garden centres in Liverpool (Heseltine), art galleries in Gateshead or casinos everywhere (Tessa Jowell) is risible, as well as cynical.

There are pleasant enough places, which a bit of global warming could brighten up, but with the best multicultural will in the world I find it impossible to envisage a genuine rebirth of Northern towns, their culture, their supremacy. Maybe I'm wrong, though I doubt it, and in any case it scarcely matters. One of the charms of the North is that, like China in the time of Marco Polo, you can say what you like about it and no one can contradict you, because apart from a trip to Durham and a holiday in the Lake District they haven't been there for years, if ever, and have absolutely no intention of going.

Why this provincial detour? Because in deciding to make the journey it crossed my mind that one option for you would be to go North and settle in a small, pretty town within reach of some superb Yorkshire countryside and a University where you could work. But if you did you'd cross large numbers of young people migrating in the opposite direction, so in all honesty I can't advise it. The creativity of the North in the eighteenth and nineteenth centuries was as solid as the steels and engines and technical wonders it produced. The cultural renaissance they talk about today is three parts phoney.

To live in some small town up there would be a form of escapism, life in an oasis. Because the truth is that aside from some parts of Manchester, Leeds and a couple of other places, too much of the North and Midlands is a Sahara freshly made, or in the making.

*

Thinking about where you might move to if you stay, and where we and you have lived to date, it occurred to Sarah and me that our family is a representative sample of what's happened to housing since the war. Both of us narrowly escaped being bombed. Sarah's parents had a place in Kensington which was lucky to survive – the other side of the street was blasted. When her father came back from the Middle East they moved back in, and she had a great time boating on smashed-up doors in the water-filled craters that were all that was left of the houses opposite. The house where my mother lodged before being evacuated was reduced to rubble shortly after. And the only reason she was able to afford our first house in South London after our squat in Dagenham was because it was sold off as war damaged; with a bloody great crack in the back, it cost nothing. A tenant paid for the mortgage.

Then came the days of controlled rents. The first place Sarah and I had when we were married was one of those 'fixtures and fittings' jobs – flats where you had to pay exorbitant sums up front (ours was £1,500) for rotting carpets and curtains, just to get a foot in the door. Once you were installed, you were in clover. The place we had was in Kilburn: three rooms and a studio, £6 a week. Even then that was cheap.

Next came the great leap forward. Rent controls went and houses in down-at-heel areas that had been in multi-occupation were being bought up by what are now called young professionals. Ours, as you well remember, had a colossal garden. We all lived there for thirty-two years when we were not abroad, Italian fashion, till your late twenties, and sold it a couple of years ago when the three of you eventually left home, partly so as to put roofs over your heads. Another symbol of the times.

Even our houses have been turned into venture capital companies, and for the moment business is thriving. Like millions of others you've made money from yours just by living there. Ours is an odd life, isn't? You may not be able to rely on schools to teach your kids to read, let them out on the streets after dark or get to see a doctor when you do and they're mugged, but you can always stay at home, bolt the door and count your house price gains. Did you see that in 2004 the average householder made

£47 a day? Which means you probably grossed something close to £100, ie £36,500 that year, the rough equivalent of the £50,000 salary you've yet to earn.

When windfalls like that are possible it would seem to make sense to stick around. Unless of course you decide that in a country where surreal profits can be clocked up without lifting a finger something is amiss, and that the sensible thing to do is to sell up and do a bunk before the whole pile of cards keels over. Another side of everyday life in sober, feet-on-the-ground Britain which turns out to be a colossal gamble.

*

I seem to remember someone saying in the Thatcher era (was it Thatcher herself?) that with house prices as they were cash would henceforth cascade from generation to generation. I have never been able to get my head round the economics of this. How can it be possible for each generation to make a mint on their houses and to pass it to their children, and so on down the line? If that were the way to get rich every country would do it. What happens of course is that the gains of one generation are at the expense of another. The money parents make on the back of rising prices will be needed by their children if they're to have any home at all. So the cascade of wealth is likely to shrivel to a trickle, with almost half of it trickling into the Chancellor's mouth.

The surreal side of things comes out when you translate the notional gains into other currencies. I don't suppose you realise that at the current rate of exchange you are a dollar millionaire, the sort of money that could buy you a pretty swell place in Los Angeles or San Francisco. (Another incentive to hop it). It's the psychology that intrigues me. The fact that people say the housing market has slumped because it's not rising two or three times inflation tells us a lot about the workings – or vacancy – of the national mind. It's the effortless thing again. The British feel they have a right to their annual housing fix, not because they've earned it but because (as the ad says) they're worth it.

So what do I advise, specifically? Your neighbourhood is rough and getting rougher. Your school has lost its reputation, rightly, and is unlikely to retrieve it. All that survives is the fantasy that you live in a village, which in the crazy world of housing means you could still sell at a fat profit. It's sad to have to think this way, but the nation that used to boast that their homes were their castles – the inviolable core of English family life – have made them into a tradable asset, no more. Only a minority of people (I see from some survey) buy their first house as somewhere they actively want to live. The rest have no feelings towards it. Now that partners are increasingly inclined to 'move on' after a few years, and invest in someone else, the same mentality is creeping into marriage: home and spouse as tradable assets.

In your case I know you've grown into the place and feel attached to it, despite everything. For all that, this is one market you really can't buck. I've no idea what's going to happen, any more than the next man, but on instinct I'd put the arguments for taking your profits and getting out as somewhere between strong and overwhelming.

*

Have you seen one of those aerial pictures of Europe at night? The Continent has clusters of city lights, with broad spaces between. We show up as a series of white blobs, with a few dark rural patches. What you see from the air is what you get on the ground. England has 383 people per square kilometre – four times as many as France and twice as many as Germany, and it feels like it. London and the South-East are nearly twice as highly populated as the Netherlands. But breathe freely while you can, because they're talking about a huge growth in the number of households, and over a third of the new building that is going to be necessary is on green field sites. So the aerial photos of the future will show England as one continuous refulgent mass. Pretty from the air, less so on ground level.

I see that Ruth Kelly, the weird-sounding rich girl (rich enough to do a flip and work for David Cameron, if only she'd get her populist accent right) says we're all 'too protective of our own space.' We probably are, in the same way she'll be protective of her inheritance. And if anyone has a right to feel protective about space it's the boxed-in Brits. How will people exist in the cities of the future? Buried alive, a lot of them. Within a hundred yards of our house four basements are being dug out, or extended, in search of ever more square footage. One goes down thirty-five feet, roughly the height of the house.

Until a couple of years ago I never thought of flats or houses in terms of feet per person, but the experience of moving further into London and helping you and your brother to buy places has brought me smartly up to date. Now my entire world is mapped out in yards, feet and inches: I struggle to leave a yard between me and the person in front on the pavement, I calculate the cost of accommodation in pounds per foot, and I park in inches.

The Great Wen, they used to call London when there were a couple of hundred thousand people. Not nice to have your capital compared to a gigantic cyst, but when the population reaches eight, nine, ten million in a decade or two, and we're heading towards Mexico City, the feeling could recur. Never mind what race they are, it's a question of numbers. 'The future belongs to crowds' wrote my favourite author, Don DeLillo, and I have a feeling that crowds are not your thing. How will you feel about living in a South American-style megalopolis? And if the natives are getting out before the big squeeze has really begun, how many more will go as the crowd takes over? Farewell to the urban middle classes, as they become horizontally as well as vertically mobile, and welcome to Richard Rogers' underclass capital. Catherine won't like me saying it, but if you go you will be running before the tide.

The shrinkage of space, already begun, has a long way to run. The house you bought was a third the size we bought at your age, though our income was no higher than yours, and we had no one to help us buy it. Unless Billy and Sandra's incomes are very much larger than your own, their homes seem likely to be a third smaller still. Amazing to think that till recently Briton used to be the most generously housed country in Europe. People with the same or bigger incomes on the Continent lived in smaller spaces, even when their countries were twice or more the size of ours. Partly it was a historical thing: if there's one thing the British can do it's build houses for living, and our prosperity right through the eighteenth and nineteenth centuries and into the twentieth left us with a huge stock of enviable Georgian, Victorian and Edwardian homes. Even the much derided 1930s terraced semi seems idyllic when compared to the Parisian's exiguous flat, measured (as we are coming to do ourselves) in square metres (*We live in a sixty metres* you hear them say).

All those suburban villas in a sub-Norman Shaw style, with their two poky receptions and three pokier bedrooms, and their poignant memento of the countryside in the shape of a patch of grass outside the back door, have their dismal aspect, but not half so dismal as bringing up children in blocks of flats. Now that rather civilised style of English living appears to be on the way out, and like every other change in Britain it's happening at dizzying speed.

Suddenly we've begun building fewer houses than anywhere in Europe, and those we manage to shove up are of dwindling size. Everything in the country except the number of its inhabitants seems to be contracting by a third. In the space of two years the proportion of apartments to houses under construction has gone up by about 30%. A three-bedroom house built in the 1930s is a third larger than one built today, and our residences for dwarves are increasingly close together. Now the Urban Task Force has recommended a rise in the density levels from 12 to 16 homes per acre – another shrinking by a third – and there's talk of the high-rises coming back. One way and another it looks as if we're on our way to Hong Kong-style cities. When I lived there I saw the way workers lived in bunk beds, a dozen to a room. Recently I've seen immigrant labourers here living in not dissimilar conditions.

*

Have you ever read the scientist and environmentalist James Lovelock? If not I think you should. Few people are both saints and scientists, but he is one, and when I met him at dinner not long ago I asked him about all this. The sensible solution, he told me, would be to give up thinking in terms of town and country altogether, build on the available space, and have national parks in lieu of a countryside. You might say that is pretty much what we've done, and are doing.

Our tight little island, Byron called Britain, when the population was a quarter what it is today. The fact that it's common knowledge that mice get nervy and neurotic when they're caged in over-crowded conditions hasn't stopped us doing the same to ourselves. It's a tribute to the English sang froid that we remain as cool as we do, while undergoing gradual suffocation. An alternative explanation is that we're not so much mice in a cage as cattle in a pen, and that our ability to shuffle about disconsolately or queue up passively is evidence not so much of civic-mindedness than of a bovine resignation to life in a herd.

Have you noticed the feeling of freedom and well-being you get when you first drive off the ferry onto un-crammed roads on the Continent? Makes you feel like an old sweater that's been pulled out of a mildewed cupboard to let the wind blow through. Wonderful to pass in and out of towns without those terrible linking suburbs that suck the soul out of otherwise attractive places. And the nerviness *is* beginning to get to us. A friend with a weekend retreat told me that returning to London was becoming a greater strain by the week. As soon as he hit town everyone seemed even more pissed off than they'd been a week before. To plunge into the turgid, rancorous mass after a couple of days amongst tranquil rural faces was becoming more unpleasant each time he did it. Recently my friend has begun spending more time in the country.

The increase in un-British excitement, aggressiveness and aimless anger is mainly of course on the roads. Nine million people, I read, suffer from traffic stress syndrome – anxiety, nausea, sleepless nights, depression. And traffic, of course, is due to increase massively with an increased population: in Bristol by 14% in the next four years. How depressed will people feel when there are twelve rather than nine million sleepless drivers about, with fewer of them insured? It's true we still kill less people on the roads than the French or the Italians, though one of the reasons may be that we can scarcely move. When things grind to a complete halt no-one will be killed at all.

*

One of the many things I learned as a town-bred MP for a rural seat was how very little is left of country life. Obviously there are lovely places. A beautiful landscape is pleasing to look at, and to walk or ride in, but that is not country life: it's living in the country. Country life means local people working the land and producing and consuming its products locally, the way that is still done in France. Apart from some good cheeses, fine beef and lamb and excellent apples in Britain there are few products to excite the palate, or the eye. Mostly what we have down on the farm are primary products in industrial quantities, stored in industrial-looking hangers.

For this and many more reasons, for all the tranquil faces I wouldn't recommend a retreat to rural parts. I can see it might hold attractions for you, but Catherine might be restless. Country life in the full meaning of the words has gone and will not return. That's why we fantasise about it, with our lovingly recreated farmyard scenes in the latest Jane Austen movie, TV series like *Pictures of England* fronted by David Dimbleby trying not to sound elegiac, and our sadly immortal Archers. Now there are even fantasy fox hunts.

What we have in lieu of rural life are a number of generally elderly folk who with the earnings from their city houses have retired to a make-believe Arcadia within supermarket reach. For peasants we have the remnants of the rustic poor grubbing run-down lives amongst rusted cars and overgrown smallholdings in not especially attractive country environments. For gentry we have new-rich Russians, who after taking over mines or oil wells in Siberia are taking over the Home Counties. And of course we have the stars. When Joanna Trollope announced to the world that she'd moved from the Cotswolds, she said it was because the countryside had become infested by rich celebrity townees. A touchingly naïve remark. Why would a celebrity want to live in anything approaching genuine countryside, assuming there was any left? They want the country to be like London with larger lawns.

You could of course look at it the other way round, and say that the entire nation has become so centralised and compressed and homogenised it's like one big village. The thing about village life is that everything assumes a shrunken intensity, and as the density of British life builds up sometimes it feels like being in some grossly over-crowded village pub on a Saturday night. The villagers spill onto the green, half-pissed and gossiping away about the doings of the notables, watching and gawking and nudging, on permanent lookout for a Name. So what do you reckon to that singer having it off with the bassist then?... Isn't that that cookery feller from the telly?... Ooh look there's that David Cameron. Likes his pint dunnee?

Wherever you end up, at home or abroad, I'd recommend somewhere more roomy and serene. Do what the rich do, so far as you can: escape the throttling mass. For earlier generations the problem people had was time: either they died in wars or of disease at twenty, or of old age at sixty. You're going to have a much longer run, but your problem will be space to run in.

*

All this expansion of numbers and shrivelling and contracting of space looks like bringing big changes in who lives where. The way things are going in ten to fifteen years' time London will end up as a three ring circus, without the laughs. The wealthy of all races will live in the inner ring – Belgravia, Knightsbridge, Kensington and Chelsea – as they do at present. (The truly and monumentally rich, too insecure to live in London at all, will escape to mansions in commuterland, where their wives and their daughters and their Aston Martins will be safer.)

The outer ring will consist of the more salubrious suburbs – Wimbledon, Richmond, Barnes, Dulwich, Belsize Park, Hampstead, that sort of place. Between the inner and outer circles will be the multicultural ring, where every race except the natives will be plentifully represented. (This is where you are.) Some will cohabit peacefully, others not. To date we've had Somali-Caribbean, Turkic-Albanian, Sri-Lankan, black and Muslim, and Muslim and Jewish tensions. The list can be extended. Some parts of the multicultural ring will be slums, some enclaves of respectability, others the kind of exotic places (Brick Lane or equivalent) that natives from the inner and outer rings will absolutely adore to visit from time to time, like tourists in their own country.

The rougher parts of the multicultural ring will be ghettoes of crime, poverty and racialism in reverse, the kind of places where even bohos looking for ethnic thrills will hesitate to set foot. (In the capital as well as the Midlands such areas exist already.) As the population builds up and white flight progresses there'll be enormous changes to the housing structure. The retreat of the young professionals (which you seem set to join), together with the surge of births, will result in vast areas being sold off to landlords who will turn whole streets from owner occupied houses back into flats. So postwar London could come full circle – without the rent controls. Over time your 'village' could well be bought out by 'buy to rent' investors and revert to multi-occupation.

As the population rockets there'll be big money to be made by squeezing more people into vanishing space. Manufacturers of plasterboard and four-by-two will benefit from a boom in partition walls. A six-roomed terraced place housing a family of four, such as yours, will become a nine-roomed house consisting of three flats, and the inhabitants doubled or trebled. Aesthetically the results will not be pleasing. Houses that have been lovingly renovated could crumble, landlords being generically less likely to mend walls and fences and maintain facades than owner occupiers. You might not think that we would ever look back fondly at the yuppies, but we could.

Landlords will emerge who will make Rachman seem benign. As services are overwhelmed and councils infiltrated by crooks, every kind of corruption associated with housing will increase (backhanders in return for building permission, overlooking illegal structures and sanitary or safety issues). Some landlords will enforce their will by violence and intimidation of a kind that will shock the natives, or would if they heard about it. The law – already not keen to intrude into ethnic ghettoes – will be reluctant to touch the offenders, and the more bribes are offered to turn a blind eye, the more corrupt the police will become. In areas beyond the effective control of the council, the health authorities and the taxman, overcrowding and exploitation involving immigrant gangs and migrant workers are already happening. As the density intensifies in many places this will become the norm.

There's a few years to go yet, but on current form that's where we're heading. If you're thinking of leaving, I suppose it's another reason to get out while the going's good.

*

We didn't look at the television news last night, so the first we heard of the Heathrow bomb plot was in the French press. But it wasn't given much coverage – so much for European solidarity – and it was only when we saw the English papers that we understood its scale and seriousness.

The point of terrorism is to contaminate the mind with fear, and it's certainly succeeding. Like thousands of others we had our taste of it when the 7/7 bombings happened. Your sister had been going to work by Tube through one of the target stations at almost exactly the time the bombs exploded, and we couldn't reach her on her mobile for two hours because the lines were clogged. Meanwhile your brother was also on a Tube. Him we got hold of more quickly. A false alarm, but in your sister's case, not by much. A few coaches, perhaps, a few minutes. It being the middle of August this time we immediately thought, stupidly, about which of you was travelling where by plane that day, even though the plot was aborted.

I've been putting off talking about terrorism because like everyone else I try not to think about it. I need hardly say that in deciding whether to go or stay it's not something you can ignore. In small ways it's already influencing your behaviour. When we talked about it on the phone after the bombing last year, I remember you saying that you and Catherine had stopped going on the Underground. Afterwards Catherine told me she'd started using it again herself, where there was no alternative, but that she never takes the children. The implication is that whereas we must be ready to sacrifice ourselves, we must do our best to protect future generations. A wartime way of thinking.

The do's and don'ts of your life are mounting up. Keep away from the

Sunni triangle. Stay on the right side of the road, because over there it's not kicks, it's knives. Don't send them to the local schools, because the best they can hope to learn is street cred. And don't use the Underground if you can help it, certainly not with the kids. And now you'll think twice about taking them to Heathrow airport.

The wonder is that they've caught the alleged plotters at all. I had a certain amount to do with MI5 during my years in the Foreign Office, and have a smell for when the Government are in control and when they're not. At that time there was a swarm of Soviet agents about, we had almost no idea what they were up to, and the Home Secretary of the moment was in the habit of fending off awkward questions from colleagues by saying don't worry, the security services are keeping an eye on them. This used to make the MI5 people, who knew they were hopelessly overwhelmed, spitting mad. It took nine people, they told me, to keep tabs on a single intelligence agent, and till we summoned up the nerve to throw the whole lot out the Russians alone had over a hundred based here.

Think how many security men it would take to keep track of our terrorist suspects, who unlike the spies can go to ground in a community unsympathetic to the police. Then ask yourself how successful the security services are likely to be in the long term, and whether it's surprising that they make mistakes. Mistakes that are described by the communities that decline to assist the authorities as proof that we live in an Islamophobic police state. I know we should be glad we caught the suspects, but I'm afraid we're just at the beginning, and the scale of what they planned tells us what we can expect next time. The thing about Britain, I mentioned D.H. Lawrence as saying, was that it was mildly warm and safe. Not any more it isn't: it's getting hot, and it's dangerous. Not so long ago, when you and the family were on holiday abroad we tried (and normally succeeded) not to worry. Now we worry about you when we're abroad and you're at home.

*

After they caught the second lot of bombers last July I remembered something that happened when I was still in Parliament. My constituents were a level-headed lot, though some of the older ones could be a little out of it. One day an elderly lady sidled up to me at a function. 'I saw one of them in Aylesbury the other week' she said, in that tone people use when they're telling you something that should be passed on to the authorities. 'At this rate they'll be getting into the villages soon, Mr Walden.' Daft old bat, I remember thinking. All I saw happening in Aylesbury, besides some hideous new developments, was the creeping infestation of home-grown, hard-drinking, bovine-featured English louts. She was wrong about the villages too: there were 120 of them in my patch and in over fourteen years as an MP I do not recall seeing a black face in one.

When 7/7 happened I had reason to think back to the old lady. Since she'd spotted 'one of them' in Aylesbury, there've been many more black people in the town, most of them causing no worse problems than their native equivalents. With a single exception. It turned out that one of the 7 July suicide bombers was a Caribbean Muslim convert who'd come to live there with his British wife, also a convert. I know, I know, it's absurd, and I'm not saying that the old lady has been proved right. What I'm saying is that you'll never be able to convince her, or others like her, that she wasn't.

One of the things that worried you about Muslims, I remember you saying, was that so many of the representatives they put up in TV or radio debates seem unable to talk about politics in a rational way. In a sense there's no reason why they should. Islamic doctrine embraces the whole of life – the religious and the administrative, the spiritual and the everyday, the emotional and the factual. There's no separate sphere in which politics can be discussed, so there's a limit to how much sense you can expect from uncompromising believers. The hope that we're winning hearts and minds through education, and that strange-sounding process 'acculturation', is illusory if the hearts are hardened by atavistic resentments and the minds are addled by fanatical religion.

I remember you telling me years ago how you felt sickened when IRA or Protestant apologists came on the air (in those days you were an avid listener to the Today programme), with their double-talk about violence and their ghetto-thinking. It got to the point that when you heard an Irish accent on the radio you turned it off. And that's the danger apologists for Muslim extremism are running.

Every poll about Islamic attitudes brings its little ray of depression. After 7/7 40% said they understood the terrorists' actions, 13% thought they should be seen as martyrs, and 6% that they were right. A year later, nothing has changed. Depending on your estimation of the Muslim population, six percent means that between 90,000 and 160,000 British citizens rejoiced in the indiscriminate slaughter of their countrymen, Muslims included, and would have rejoiced even more to see the death of a thousand in the Heathrow plot.

Experts tell us that until Muslim grievances around the world are addressed, for the indefinite future this is the way it's going to be. Hardly reassuring for you and your generation. What it means is that unless the grouses of about a quarter of the world's population are rectified – unlikely given that they most often spring from failings in their own cultures – the possibility is that whatever we do, and whether we're in or out of Iraq, we face the prospect of decades of racial and religious tensions. And if this is Islamophobic then I am Salman Rushdie, who has voiced similar apprehensions.

Should you fear for yourself and your family, if you stay? Officially the answer is no. Not because there's nothing to fear, but because the British are never afraid. Fear is a national weakness of the Americans, the French and that class of person, but not the Brits. Remember how the media and the government behaved in the aftermath of the Tube bombings? Fifty-two people slaughtered in the most heinous way imaginable and the whole thing was turned into a proud national moment.

What were they celebrating? The fact that no one was afraid. The organizers of the attack would probably do it again (they tried), and we'd probably never find out who directed the operation (we haven't), but never mind: we were the victors because we were not afraid. Had they succeeded in slaughtering a thousand on board those planes, the logic of our position would have been that we were less afraid that before, because the more the deaths the greater our moral victory over the killers. Blessed with the spirit of the Blitz, there's no limit to how much we can take.

The problem with a stiff upper lip is that, by freezing your expression in an uncomprehending rictus, it makes you look bloody stupid: 'I have no idea what the hell's going on or how to prevent it, but by Jove I shall stand here and take it.' After the first attack some idiot in the City was quoted as saying 'is that all they've got to throw at us?' – an approach that obviously reflected City sentiment, since the stock market scarcely budged. Even for the dealing room mentality the crudity of that remark is pitiable. The answer is no, you ape, they've got a lot more. The tabloids and the qualities were full of this kind of heroics. Listening to all that crap about how nothing could frighten a people who'd been through the war and the IRA campaign made you sick for the country, sick for you and your generation.

It made me think of something else Arthur Koestler wrote about the English, this time about the Second World War: 'The people carried on business-as-usual, except that the routine of this business included killing and being killed. Matter-of-fact unimaginativeness has become a kind of cult with Anglo-Saxon nations. It is usually contrasted with Latin hysterics and praised for its high value in an emergency. But they tend to forget what happens between emergencies; and that the same unimaginativeness is responsible for the failure to prevent their recurrence...'

Do the British lack the imagination to see the situation they're in? From the Abu Hamza affair it certainly seems that way. The public saw him as a sort of Muslim Long John Silver, good for a laugh. We dismiss characters like him as jokers because we have no understanding of evil, and because of our patrician sensibility. That clown a threat to Britain? Nonsense old son. Foreigners can be nasty, but people who've chosen to live amongst us must surely be secretly won over by our kindliness, our irony, our sense of humour. How could they resist? And if the 7/7 people didn't do irony, never mind, the next generation will. To a certain type of English mind, all foreigners are pining to be Brits, however much they go on pretending to be foreign.

Our lack of imagination would help explain why we're always groping for precedents to explain what's going on. It's not only generals who have a tendency to fight the last war. Everyone blathers away about the spirit of the Blitz and how we stood up to the IRA campaign, but there isn't the remotest connection. Hitler's war aims were perfectly rational: to crush Europe and force it to accept his rule. Islamic terrorists aim to re-establish the Caliphate and take humanity back to a system that existed in the sands of the Arabian desert in the seventh century.

Comparisons with the IRA are just as barmy. It's enough to ask the question: can we be sure that the IRA would never have exploded a dirty nuclear weapon in England, assuming they had the means to procure one? The answer is yes. In the case of Muslim fundamentalists it's not just no, we cannot be sure: it's yes, they'd do it. The threat from the IRA was ultimately political. That from Islamic terrorism is civilisational.

'Well you say that' you once objected when we discussed it all after the bombing. 'But what would you say if you were still in Government?' A fair question, to which the answer is: none of the above. I'd be so alarmed by the situation I'd do everything possible to suggest it was under control. It's up to politicians to play mood music in a crisis, and up to the people to understand that there's little else governments can do. The last thing they can say is that we face a threat to which we can see no end because it's based on a fundamental clash of cultures. On the IRA we told the truth; on the Islamic problem, we lie. That itself is a terrorist victory.

'The vast majority of Muslims are moderate...' In government I'd be saying that too, though I'd have trouble convincing myself. Many Muslims – the kind of level-headed people you meet in daily life – certainly are. But 'the vast majority'? Look at the polls showing that half do not believe Muslims had anything to do with the Twin Towers. How moderate an attitude is that? And even amongst the remainder, there are moderates and 'moderates.' One reason we have to concentrate on winning over moderate opinion is that a lot of it is not all that moderate. If it were, we wouldn't have to win it over. And if it weren't for the tacit understanding of many a 'moderate', there'd be fewer extremists.

People who say to militant Muslims 'If you don't like it here why don't you go back to where you came from?' are missing the point. They stay *because* they don't like it. Technically it's wrong for a Muslim to live in an infidel country except if he's there with the aim of converting it. So we know where the fundamentalists stand, where the genuine moderates stand, and where we stand. Where the 'moderates' stand we can never be sure. Which in an odd way makes the 'moderates' the greater menace, especially amongst the Muslim new elites.

By this I mean the sons and daughters of wealthy immigrants who use their social and ethnic advantages to get themselves over-promoted, then take a fashionably indulgent view of terrorism. Did you notice what the BBC's Rageh Omaar said about Ayaan Hirsi Ali? (She's the Dutch/Somali MP, rather more courageous than Omaar, who opposes Muslim oppression of women.) He compared her to the London bombers, on the grounds that both are fundamentalists. There's 'moderation' for you.

The 'moderates' are tardy and ambiguous in any condemnations of terrorism that are wrung from them, though quick enough on the draw when it comes to playing the moral equivalence card, whereby a British soldier trying to bring civilised, democratic life to Basra is put on the same level as a religious extremist murdering 52 people on the Tube. Sometimes you get the impression that 'moderates' are only moderately in favour of democracy, freedom of speech, or women's rights. So whereas the wild men have every reason to live here – for them it's the front line – it's less easy to see why a 'moderate' should want to spend his life in a country whose way of life is only moderately satisfactory to him. Unless of course he's a pretty-looking rich kid playing radical chic games who gets taken up by the Establishment, like Rageh Omaar.

Another question is: moderate compared to what? Applied to a system of thought which can include the conversion of all mankind, by force if necessary, the word moderate loses some of its charm. And if it means a kind of halfway house between twenty-first century Western democracy and seventh century Islam, that places the 'moderates' somewhere in the late Middle Ages, when Christians were behaving towards heretics rather as the Iranians did towards Rushdie. An unconsoling thought.

If I were still in government I'd also be saying how much the Koran talks about peace, though this seems to me a curious line of argument. I'm not saying it doesn't: I'm saying, whence this sudden reverence for holy scriptures, especially on the Left? In recommending him for our attention TV announcers tell us gravely that such and such an imam is a revered student of the Koran. I don't hear anyone speaking deferentially about Bible scholars, though I suppose that's natural, since scarcely anybody reads it.

It's a strange world where British politicians and commentators incline themselves before the word of Mohammed but would never dream of invoking the words of Jesus Christ. Because that would make them Bible literalists, wouldn't it? Citing the scriptures to prove that Christians were peaceful folk would get you a horse laugh, and when the blimps say we must hold to the biblical line on homosexuals everyone falls over one another to show that all that stuff about the abomination of man lying with man is outdated, superstitious rubbish.

Muslims, on the other hand, are entitled to their point of view.

*

Disaster on the beach. An invasion of globally-warmed jellyfish is making it difficult to swim. They're the vicious little five-inch types the French call *pelagia*. Corpses are washed up on the shore each morning, hundreds of them, sparkling in the sun with a ghastly glitter. Exasperated by the sight of the clear, warm water I go in for a bit just the same, and have got myself bitten. A lifeguard warns me that if you swim into a shoal of them, it could be curtains. If jellyfish are here to stay, this is seriously bad news. Between them terrorism and climate change seem set to foul up holidays, along with everything else. Either you'll get blown up on the plane on the way out, or stung to death when you get there.

You have to be flip because the whole thing's so serious. Economically we live on borrowed money, and environmentally on borrowed time. It wouldn't be so bad if there were some certainty about which way things are going, but as usual it could go either way. Will the upheavals we are promised give us an Arctic or Mediterranean climate? Will we be swimming in warm, clear, jellyfish-infested waters or battling icy waves? Sprawled on pavement cafes like Italians, or huddled in ear-flaps, like Russians? Something else no one knows.

Do not assume that our only problem will be heat. If the Gulf Stream seriously weakens, our climate could be like Alaska's, I gather, with temperatures reaching −30, as in Russia. And to think we have a drink problem now. But that's only one informed opinion. Another, equally informed opinion has it that July this year was only the beginning, and that we are doomed to fry. So what's it to be? Warmer, rainier, frozen? The South of France? The tundra? In any event, that is presumably the end of the British personality, since climates have a fundamental influence on character. It'll be fascinating to see the kind of national type the chilled or fried Brit produces.

The biggest joke would be if there were huge swings of temperature throughout the world while in Britain, nothing changes. Somehow that would be appropriate, and apparently, it's on the cards. James Lovelock has suggested that North Western Europe may escape major disruption, because the 8% lost if the Gulf Stream fails is just about equal to the anticipated rise in temperature from global warming. So everyone else could be left gasping or shivering while the Brits, phlegmatic as ever, swan about much as before.

*

Reading a book about the psychology of famous pictures, Sarah remarked how little the pair of you resembled the couple in Ford Madox Brown's *The Last of England*. You know, the one with the nineteenth century couple staring back at the homeland from the stern of a boatload of emigrants, with the husband holding an umbrella to shield his wife from the spray. They're a morose-looking pair, but then it's a very Victorian picture, full of pathos. Where were they going, and why? The story (Sarah tells me) is revealing. Like all our most ardent patriots Ford Madox Brown was born abroad, in Belgium. His picture records the great wave of emigration to the colonies in 1852. Explaining it in the laborious Pre-Raphaelite manner, he said he'd deliberately put different social types in the background, including 'an honest family of the greengrocer kind'.

The choice bit comes when he describes why he gave prominence to the young couple. 'I have, therefore, in order to present the parting scene in its fullest tragic development, singled out a couple from the middle classes, high enough, through education and refinement, to appreciate all they are now giving up.' The educated middle class, he explains, are bound to their country by closer ties than the illiterate, whose chief consideration is food and physical comfort. I'm not so sure: today I suspect that it's the nobs and illiterates who feel most at home here.

*

We used to complain about the English newspapers arriving here in the afternoon rather than the morning, and assumed it was some Spanish practice at Heathrow that stopped someone throwing a bundle on the plane. Not my job son. Out of interest we made enquiries and it turned out the bloody-mindedness was French. Anyway now you get them early, and today I rather wished we hadn't. More Lebanese slaughter, and a public letter by Muslim 'moderates' about the Heathrow bomb plot of startling effrontery, more or less saying that if only we'd dispense with ballot boxes and let them run foreign policy we wouldn't have to worry about terrorism. The spirited reaction of the press and the government to this blatant piece of blackmail gives you courage. Meanwhile however, though the suspect murderers are British citizens, we are called upon to erase from our minds any connection between what is happening and immigration.

The reason immigration worries you, if I've got you right, is not only because of the security threat, or what happened to Billy. It's because you had a sneaking affection for the old place as it was, and are afraid that it will change in ways you will like less. Catherine, on the other hand, believes that the change could be for the better. But because she's a born traveller and the wide world beckons, she's disinclined to hang around long enough to see whether she's right. Have I got it straight? If so I don't agree with either of you.

My hunch is that immigration will not make the country worse, and it will not make it better. What it will do is leave the place as it was, only more so. Much, much more so. How? By magnifying our most salient characteristics, to the point where the whole place becomes a caricature of itself. We both know our beloved country well enough not to be taken in by the kind of guff about our pragmatism and moderation I used to churn out as a diplomat and politician. The fact is that in many ways Britain is a society of extremes, and immigration will stretch those extremes further.

The income gap, already vast, will increase. Social hierarchies will expand in parallel, as the distance between the bulging bottom (London, Northern and Midlands ghettoes) and the super-rich (unashamedly ambitious immigrants) yawns ever wider. You can see it already, and we've hardly started. Between the two extremes the native middle classes (which means you) will find themselves ever more pinched and squeezed. As numbers rocket and birth rates boom amongst the poor and undereducated, and the demand for public services soars, taxes to fund the swelling underclass will not come from the very rich, who have ways to minimise these things, they will come from you.

The solution would be for these middle earners to improve their qualifications and their incomes. But natives could find their aspirations for advancement thwarted as they are overtaken by incomers more energetic, more hard-working, more able and more ruthless than themselves. Talk about pushy parents: the English ain't seen nothing yet. Hungarians, Chinese, or Iraqis are not laid-back folk when it comes to their kids' education, and don't fret about over-stretching them, or about instilling egalitarian values in a niminy-piminy English way. Nor do they share our queasiness about elitism. They come from societies where social consciences are the reverse of tender, and many will bring their culture with them (what else are they to do with it?) Consequently many will use every opportunity we offer to go hell for leather for cash, self-improvement, and social position.

The result will be that the poorest Brits will be poorer (the Pakistanis or Bangladeshis of Birmingham or Leicester) and the rich richer than the plushiest natives (Mittal, the Indian steel magnate, Tchinguiz the property billionaire, Abramovich, the buyer of Chelsea.) Culturally the range will be just as vast. Large numbers of Pakistanis, Somalis and Caribbeans will fester in sink schools while many a Czech or Chinese will shoot to the top of the academic pile. The cultural gulf between the son of Islamic traditionalists at a Muslim school in Dewsbury and a Russian businessman's kid at Winchester will be colossal.

As for the cause of women, there too things will be just as they are today, only more so. On the one hand steely Chinese ladies will cut swathes through the City, on the other many a Muslim woman will waste her life in the shadow of her husband. (Seven out of ten Muslim women do not work; the national average is four.)

Catherine may ask how a mere 10% or so of the population (the official figure: treat with caution) can have that much effect on society? It's a question that's always intrigued me, and the answer I get from economists and suchlike is always the same: that everything important happens at the margin. Just as our marginal propensity to save or spend helps determine interest rates, which swing the entire economy this way and that, so immigration will affect society in crucial ways. Wage rates at the bottom are the obvious example: Albanian illegals working for £30 a day may be on the margins of society, but they help keep down the wages rates of millions more.

At the other end of the scale you can see the new Britons striding ahead of the old. Already a greater proportion of Indians from working class families have graduated to professional or managerial roles than white natives. To date a small percentage of minorities are represented on boards of the largest companies, but there'll soon be many, many more. The wealth of the richest 300 British Asians has almost doubled in the last year.

There's been a huge increase in ethnic people in business, academia, the police, the arts – virtually every walk of life you can think of except politics. Obviously there's discrimination: if Tory selection committees can't screw themselves up to choose indigenous women they're not going to fall over themselves to pick Asians. But then Westminster has a habit of overstating its own attractions. The dream of every up-and-coming immigrant is not necessarily to be allowed into the Commons club. The smartest of them are too canny for that, just as the cleverest women realise that Parliament is not where wealth and power lie. Who wants to sweat it out re-heating old arguments over an antique stove when you could be out in the world doing something useful, enjoying yourself and making money?

So where does all this leave us natives? Rather than going forth and multiplying the English tribe seems destined to shrink back and make way for the new. As immigrants show a marginal tendency to equal or out-perform the rest of us at every level – as footballers, criminals, lawyers, civil servants, terrorists, writers and intellectuals, entrepreneurs and unholy snobs – in time the question could arise: what's the point of the native?

Let's not exaggerate: there'll always be a place for him, somewhere, though increasingly the indigenous English will appear, not as failures exactly, just not the way they've always thought of themselves: as some kind of effortlessly dominant race. They underwent a crisis of identity over the meaning of Englishness after the rise of Scottish and Welsh nationalism, but that rather contrived little bout of heart-searching will be as nothing compared with the cumulative impact of immigration. Over the next years alone the population is scheduled to rise by the size of Scotland, though unlike the Scottish/English stand-off no one will be cracking jokes about it.

For the richest and most successful immigrants a hearty welcome awaits them at the top. On that high plateau of income and social status discrimination ceases to operate. The will for integration that may be somewhat lacking in Barking and Dagenham will here be all too apparent. It's amazing how smoothly the most snobbish of Brits can integrate with money, and the jingle of cash can turn even the most fretful Little Englander into a positive enthusiast for immigration – so long as it's not from Europe. Gold-plated Middle Easterners and new-rich Russians are already thronging the race meetings and grouse moors and polo matches (all that expensive leather), and it'll be fun to watch as cash-toting Indians, Iraqis, Chinese, Iranians and Pakistanis out-British the British in their social habits.

Aching for an occasion to climb into white ties or morning suits, their lives will not be complete until they're invited to a Buckingham Palace garden party with a thousand others. Amongst them will be many of the country's outstanding talents, together with some of the most abjectly ambitious, people whose social alpinism and moneyed vulgarity will out-class even the natives, who know a thing or two about such matters.

A few of course will head for the Commons. In fact within a decade or two I would guess we'll have an immigrant Prime Minister, possibly Indian, probably Conservative. We even have a good idea what he or she will be like. Though well-to-do they'll be flamboyantly One Nation people, whose patriotism will outclass that of Margaret Thatcher, who'll have a weakness for slightly archaic modes of dress (if it's an Indian woman she'll wear a sari), and whose most treasured moments will be the ones Tony Blair dreads – audiences with the Queen.

*

People like you and me see positives and negatives to the whole migration business, but for two groups of people – one on the Left, the other on the Right – mass immigration is an unmitigated plus. The first are the lawyers, activists, moralists, politicos and other tradesmen in mankind's grievances, real or imagined. The second are businessmen. The English entrepreneur may read the *Spectator* and the right-wing press, vote Tory and proclaim himself a patriot, but sound him out on immigration and you'll find him ostentatiously liberal-minded. I know, I've done it, several times. Like the Left he too favours freedom of movement, even if his motives are not so uplifting: less a question of cultural enrichment and the brotherhood of man than of keeping cash flows up and wages down.

You get the usual qualms about the changing nature of Britain, but his loyalty is ultimately to his way of life and to his caste, rather than to his country, and to the shorter rather than to the longer term. What do social tensions or public service bottlenecks matter to a man faced with the prospect of an endless stream of unskilled or semi-skilled labour ready to work for thirty or forty forty pounds a day? Personal benefits will be equally alluring: chauffeurs, gardeners and nannies will be in plentiful and more economic supply, and unlike the modern Brit (our entrepreneur will chunter) these people understand what it means to be in service.

You too gain, in a small way, if only through the number of immigrants employed in the health service and so on, though in your case the benefits in one area can easily be cancelled out by the drawbacks in another: the Caribbean nurses who took good care of Billy were a plus, but the same cannot be said for the Somali (?) who put him in hospital in the first place. Our businessman, on the other hand, will not live in perilous proximity to a council estate. The fellow who gives it to you hot and strong on the virtues of racial tolerance ('Look at the range of guys we're getting in the City') will stay well out of diversity's way in his private life, walled up in his gated or secure community.

In support of his claim to moral superiority over the doubting and the apprehensive he won't flinch from the phrase that *some of his closest friends are immigrants*. This may well be the case, though they won't be impoverished Bangladeshis from Tower Hamlets, fearsomely devout Pakistanis from Handsworth, or radically inclined Moroccans studying aviation. Ethically as well as ethnically they'll be a heterogeneous bunch. Some will be sophisticated, hard-working business folk from five continents who – fortunately for us and still more for themselves – have made England their home. Others will be mafia-minded Russians, or entrepreneurs from South Asia running chains of homes for the elderly where an unusual number do not remain elderly long.

Money sticks to money, and when high-rolling in night clubs our broad-minded businessman may even have come across the infamous casino-loving Chinese gangmaster who allowed twenty-one of his employees to drown in the North Sea while cockle-picking. On the other hand he is unlikely to have rubbed shoulders with the boss of the gang of Vietnamese illegals who, until the police brutally interfered, were peacefully cultivating their garden, in the form of a huge skunk factory in Woolwich.

The thing about the English is that they can't leave the world alone. Once they ran a third of it from their minuscule island, now they're importing a chunk of it here. What our business folk are really after, you sometimes think, is a return to the colonial era, the difference being that this time Britain would be a colony inverted. Why go to the trouble of travelling vast distances to exploit people, in the heat and the dust, when we can import them in their millions and exploit them here? What a lot of our profiteers are really after is a new generation of home-grown coolies and punkah-wallahs, preferably on a touch less than the minimum wage, no questions asked.

If mass immigration is bad news for the native poor, the answer is, don't be poor. It's they who live alongside newcomers, and must adjust their lives accordingly, they whose wages are likely to be shaved, they who may wait longer in surgeries, whose kids are more likely to be taught alongside children for whom English is a second language, they whose rehousing prospects fade into infinite recession. So far we've got away with a couple of riots and an increased showing in local elections by the BNP, simply because we've had a decade or more of stable economic conditions. If there's a downturn, all bets are off.

So there you are. In the country Billy and Sandra will grow up in, and you will grow old in, social and economic conditions are likely to become more extreme. The chances are that there'll be integration at the top and a stand-off at the bottom, with you and your family hovering nervily in between. Meanwhile you'll be called upon to listen respectfully to some Tory shadow minister, liberal judge or media toff who've never lived a minute of their lives in a racially difficult area, telling you there's no problem. All you have to do is brisk up, muck in, and behave as if it's Notting Hill Carnival every day of the week.

*

There's been a hiatus in the jellyfish invasion, so I'm swimming more, and people are coming back to the beach. Mostly they're French, and almost painfully well-behaved. No screaming children, no yobs, no bad language, no beer-swilling, no ice-cream vendors, in fact no eating or drinking at all, and so no litter. And no radios. It's the contrast with Britain that's so painful – though yesterday a discovery I made right at the end of the beach cheered me up.

There they were, four of them, and a feast for English expatriate eyes. A couple of French lads and their girls had driven their car onto the sand – *mal vu* in itself – and set up camp on the beach. When the French do something they do it properly, and externally at least this pair had everything: tattooed torsos, ghetto-blaster blaring British pop from the top of the car, beer cans in hand, pallid-faced, druggy-looking girlfriends. Everything seemed perfect, yet somehow none of it was right, as if their hearts weren't in it. What was missing was the animality. If you'd gone up and remonstrated with them for their ugliness and oafishness, instead of tearing your head off, you felt they'd have said awfully sorry (*désolés monsieur*), packed up their gear and sloped off. As it was the sight of them gave me a warped sense of pride. Here were the French doing their best to imitate our yobs, and they couldn't pull it off.

You'd have loved it. In many ways you've always been a better patriot than me – the opposite of the usual position between child and father. I first noticed it in the way you took to cricket: with a sort of fierce traditionalism. As you know it isn't my game (I prefer football), but having watched you and the team you run at fixtures I can see what it means to you. What impressed me was your determination to keep the game going against the fads and fashions of the times. Everything about cricket goes against the grain of city life. (Football has taken over so completely that when I went to get you some cricket gear as a birthday present I had trouble finding a shop). The dowdiness of those London Transport sports clubs, or wherever it is you play, is poignant, with their disused industrial sites or marshalling yards or overgrown allotments. And there you all are, got up in whites against this scabrous background.

And the wonderful amateurism of the matches, with their appealing English mixture of tension and casualness, rules and relaxation. Here is a sport where no one has to be fit, and a large part of the enjoyment comes in the drinking or scoffing that accompanies it. The waddling runs, the bulging jerseys, children wandering onto the pitch, someone's wife keeping the score. The unevenness of the Sunday teams and the expertise of the commentaries. The generosity to opponents, so rare at this time of triumphalist air-punching and aggressive yelling that's all but taken over the professional game. And the way you solemnly arrange fixtures against Caribbean or Pakistani elevens, even when your own team is half-ethnic already, and no one seems to notice, or to care.

*

I thought of this traditionalism of yours when you told me that you'd mentioned to an Indian cricketing friend that you were thinking of living abroad, and he'd said: 'What's happened to your patriotism?' You didn't say how you answered, but if he hadn't been Indian and a friend I can think of a number of comebacks. Such as how can it be wrong to abandon the land of your birth if you live in a city full of people who've abandoned theirs? And if the future is racially diverse, and all cultures are equal, what can it matter where you live? You wouldn't be forsaking your homeland by moving out, you'd be leaving one multicultural society for another.

It's strange how everyone goes on insisting we must be patriotic in a country whose biggest firms are multi-national, whose most popular films and TV programmes are American, whose best workers are Eastern European, and whose criminals are amateurs compared to our more resourceful imports (half of the inmates in Wormwood Scrubs Prison are foreign). And when we're cheering our favourite foreign players from the sofa our national TV dish is chicken korma.

The other odd thing about our modern-day patriots is that they can't wait to get out of the country, just as soon as they have the money and the leisure (fourteen million to Spain and eleven to France, annually). Not

that there's much reason why they should holiday here. They've no interest in the country's history, except that they're keen on the monarchy so
long as it models itself on celebrity culture, so as to make it relevant, give
it a bit of context. They're keen on the Church of England too, always
provided the subjects under discussion are homosexuality or the conjoi-
ning in holy matrimony of adulterous royal couples. Where all this leaves
patriotism I'm not sure, unless by that we mean affection for the familiar,
the way a dog feels patriotic towards its warm, hairy cushion.

The death of patriotism in the old sense is best demonstrated by the
politicians' tawdry attempts to keep it alive. The latest is Gordon Brown's
dumb-assed notion (somehow only the American expression suffices)
that the way to manifest our love of country is to display Union Jacks –
an idea that betrays a complete misunderstanding of what British patriotism is about. The whole point used to be that we didn't have to bang on
about it. The reason we could afford to be undemonstrative and ironic
was because it was so evident that, given the choice, everyone would be
born British.

Sticking the national flag in people's faces would be a sign of failure:
a recognition that the old game of effortless superiority was finally up,
and that in the end we're much like the others. Meanwhile we go on being
ironic and undemonstrative, mainly because we've no idea what else to be
while our national culture is altered radically, often for the worse (identity cards, the end of freedom of speech on race and religion, the institu-
tionalization of fear). Watching an entire culture ironise itself out of existence can be fascinating, if a little sad.

The best hope for patriotism is that we get something new to be
patriotic about. A coalescing of cultures around a British norm, achieved
gradually and voluntarily, would be a true extension of our best traditions.
In the past we've been a model for the world politically. If we could turn
ourselves into a model of race relations that would be something to boast
about. If we're lucky we may get a bit of that. If we're not I'm afraid that
the patriotism of the future will apply less to the collectivity and more to
an individual or to a caste. People will not be inspired by the idea of a

country: they'll stay attached to it because it works for them.

A banker in Belgravia may once have felt a distant kinship with the far-mers of Northumbria, but is unlikely to feel an umbilical attachment to the Sikhs or Muslims of Birmingham or Bolton. He certainly won't feel that in some mystic way they share a common destiny. He'll say that they're as British as he is, but he won't believe it, if only because he finds it hard to see how you can be British and have no more than a minimal command of the English language, or minimal respect for British cus-toms. And however much their presence in the country helps fill his pocket, it will dilute his patriotism.

Countries – or at any rate Britain – are becoming more like football teams than nations. To keep on top you import players, and the suppor-ters cheer on their team against all-comers, even if they're three-quarters French or Caribbean or Italian or Asian. But it's all a little fragile. Some players will develop an allegiance to the country, others will be out of here just as soon as the next transfer cheque arrives. Why shouldn't they? The same thing goes on in City boardrooms, and our national stock index is increasingly made up of non-British firms.

The Brits are becoming little more than groundsmen rolling the pitch the foreigners play on. The biggest banks in the City are foreign, and foreigners run many a British bank too. They just love our country, on account of how regulation is light, so they make huge amounts of cash which they invest in prestigious Georgian houses. Ultimately however their dedication to the national team is as great as a striker on the lookout for a nice fat transfer fee.

So why should you feel guilty about contemplating a life abroad? (I sensed from your tone that you did a bit). If old-fashioned patriotism is no longer *de rigueur* at the top of society, or at the bottom, why should people in the middle struggle to keep it alive? You're showing your patrio-tism by paying most of the taxes, and if your country is now primarily a business venture you have to take a businesslike view of it: ask yourself what are the benefits of investing your life here, or might you get better returns somewhere else? Sentiment doesn't enter into it – unless of course your heart glows at the sound of those uplifting words UK PLC.

When people emigrate from Britain today they don't gaze from the back of a boat humming *Jerusalem* (we're the least religious country in the Western world). As they stare at the receding cliffs they won't think of the villages and meadows beyond (we have the least amount of countryside per inhabitant in Europe), or murmur verses from John Donne or John Betjeman, because they won't know a line (English schools don't approve of rote learning.) They'll probably go by plane, and as they rise over London they'll look down at the towers of finance owned overwhelmingly by temporary residents, reflect that the whole place will soon be half-ethnic, and think what they think. Which 'in our increasingly globalised economy' may be nothing much.

How can the words 'sense of national purpose' retain their meaning in a country increasingly composed of cohabiting tribes, whose only point of agreement seems to be the urgency of abandoning indigenous habits and institutions? This is not a lament – you know my views on some of those sacred institutions – but a matter of fact. If you follow these strands of thinking to their conclusions it becomes more and more difficult to see why, except as a kind of giant floating souk, and a source of marketable produce such as tours of Buckingham Palace, mementos of Diana or of ready-made sets for inane films, there's any reason for the United Kingdom (in the old sense) to continue to exist. There's certainly less and less to bind people to the country. So why should you feel any obligation to stay, rather than try your luck elsewhere? If anyone can be British, a Brit can be anyone too.

As well as attachment to the soil and to the past, patriotism is based on pride in a national type. Personally I never gave a thought to what it meant to be English till everyone started talking about it a few years back. It was only then that I realised that, my parents being Scottish and Irish, I didn't have a drop of English blood in me. Which might account for the way I tend to admire the race from a distance: their sanity, their poetry, that certain sweetness I spoke about earlier. It could also explain my impatience with some of their attitudes and habits, from a dozy philistinism to unmerited self-satisfaction to an excess of social self-conscious-ness to looking terrible in shorts. Say this to an Englishman and he will retort, rubbish, I once knew a totally classless girl sharp as a button who looked stunning in shorts. Literal-mindedness, come to think of it, is the Englishman's most maddening characteristic.

But that's an old story. I've remembered another English fault, brand new this one. Ours is an un-flamboyant sort of place: gentle landscapes, subtle tones, a talent for water-colours and miniatures, understatement and the rest. For many that was part of its charm. Now everything's gari-shly over-blown, or farcically inflated. Think of our Prime Minister's attempts to puff himself into a president, then of the endless efforts to find something big enough to fill the Turbine Hall at Tate Modern, and you get the picture. Or of Gordon Brown saying he's going to educate the children of the world before we've managed to teach kids in this country to read and count. Or how we're going to lick world poverty single-handed by Prince Harry wearing a wristband. Or of our surreal house prices and pumped-up population, and of laughably swollen repu-tations in literature and the arts. Anthony Gormley's got the spirit. His gruesome angel of the North has wings large enough to ground a dodo, and the religious afflatus in our godless land is an embarrassing joke. And all that blown-up art-speak he goes in for, Turner and Constable never indulged in that (Whistler did, but then he was American.)

What's it covering up, this big sculpture, these bloated claims, the lugu-brious jollity and forced hilarity, this Beastie Burger culture? Could it be that not knowing who we are makes us throw reticence to the winds and strive to be something we're not? A surrogate America, for example? And might it be that that's why we fall on any excuse to hate them – because we secretly want to be them, and never can?

Not that the pinched, fusty, censorious old England of the Fifties holds many attractions. I suppose I'm arguing for something in between: a Britain that's more like it's supposed to be – decent, tolerant, mature. Now I write it down that sounds a bit like Switzerland, and you wouldn't want that either. Death by neatness. So I'm not sure what I want, except that it's not what we had and not what we've got.

Of course we can deconstruct pretty much any country in the way you and I do Britain, when we're in the mood (sometimes I'm not, but I do it anyway, to get a rise out of Catherine, who has her own deft ways of provoking me. I always know when she's doing it: she puts on what I call her Emma Thompson face). Where I do get a flush of patriotism is at the suggestion that the only people with faulty genes are Anglo-Saxon Protestants. Invariably they're portrayed as congenitally flawed: aggressive, imperialistic and generally obnoxious, while the characters of less developed countries are seen as a blank slate on which something rather beautiful is waiting to be written.

Having encountered at close quarters many an overbearing Russian and corrupt African and vengeful Chinese and duplicitous Arab and insolent Frenchman I've developed at least one prejudice in favour of the British: I can no longer be made to suspect that, in aggregate, we're demonstrably inferior to the rest. If it weren't for the English constantly telling me how wicked their behaviour has been historically, and how appalling its legacy in a world of otherwise guiltless folk, I might be rather more patriotic than I am. Not so much because of our glorious past, but because of the element of spiritual pride inherent in our self-abasement.

You see it most glaringly in the Archbishop of Canterbury apologizing for everything. If he doesn't believe that the Church of England has much to be proud of, it's not much of an incentive to people like me to reconsider their agnostic views. I used to be quite moved by English hymns, with their combination of tunefulness, cheeriness and solemnity, but now the Archbishop has started apologizing for them too I must try not to be. Think of it: all those wicked hymns.

Did you see that Dr Jonathan Sacks has now joined Dr John Sentamu, the Archbishop's number two, in saying we should be proud of the national identity the Archbishop thinks we're guilty of foisting on the world? You couldn't make it up: the Archbishop of Canterbury turning the other cheek, and his black number two and the Chief Rabbi declining to slap it.

*

As a parent you can accuse me of many things – over-protection, under-protection, over-frequent absences, inopportune presence – but one thing you cannot hold against me is filling your head with politics. My lack of attempt to interest you in the governance of the country appears to have borne fruit. I've scarcely ever heard you raise a political subject in conversation, and have no idea who you vote for, or whether you vote at all. I assume Catherine votes Liberal-Democrat, but I'm not asking to be told, and am prepared to be contradicted.

As you know I approve of young people taking less notice of politics, now that politicians are going out of their way to smarm themselves into their affections. The idea that they might capture your interest by grinning, shedding their ties with a flourish or enthusing about pop would be a dismal portent for the future. Indifference to politics also suggests that the young see through the pretence that there are distinct policies on offer. Everyone says how terrible it all is, but to me it seems that a refusal to play the game on Parliament's terms is a sign of maturity; it's the middle-aged who are suckers for youth, not the young. Still, it would be sensible to ask yourself where British politics are taking us before making up your mind whether to stay or go. Since Parliament is playing a decreasing role in running the country, it won't take long,

That said, it's possible to overdo the cynicism. Whatever you think of politicians remember that things are a lot better than they were. And don't forget that on all sides of Parliament there are people doing a worthy job with bugger-all public recognition. Think of Alastair Darling, of the two-toned hair and eyebrows. Here is a qualified lawyer who could be grossing hundreds of thousands. Instead he's become a Cabinet minister, whose ninety-five hour week dealing with insoluble problems like health or transport will gain him no status or recognition whatever, and not much cash. And when people say 'there's nothing to choose between them' they forget that the reason for that is that we now have a bi-partisan economic policy: a great leap forward when you think back to the days of those titanic, heroic and mostly phoney wars between Left and Right, capital and labour just a few decades back.

'It's the rule of the runts, dwarves and pigmies running the show' is another thing people say. Maybe so, but the runts seem to be making a better fist of things than the so-called giants of yesteryear: I don't recall Michael Foot, Tony Benn or Enoch Powell doing much for the country. It's true that our so-called 'senior statesmen' – Kaufman, Hattersley, Patten, that class of person – are smirking nonentities, and that no one can remember what it is they're supposed to have achieved, beyond grandstanding. All anyone knows about Kaufman is that he's a film-buff who's spent half his life alone in a cinema watching *Singing In The Rain*. No one knows why any normal person would do that, though everyone understands why Kaufman would be alone.

I don't suppose either you or Catherine could tell me anything about Alderman Hattersley's contribution to the nation, but then nor could anyone else, so we'll let him pass. As for Patten, a number of smarm-proof Frenchmen and Americans who've met him have told me he must be the least impressive Chancellor of Oxford University in modern times. Foreigners notice, you see, even if we don't.

Never mind. At a time when the political function is shrinking it's natural that the politicos should shrink with it. People who are nostalgic for the old days say they remember the time when it was all such won-derful theatre. As if government was a kind of amateur dramatics and you could run a country with a bunch of prancing actors. So one way and another there's much less reason for people like you to trouble yourself about what goes on in Parliament, or for anyone of any talent to trouble themselves to get elected. We should be thankful we get enough compe-tent, public-spirited people to do these jobs at all.

I know this is not Catherine's view, but then the charm of our rela-tionship is that we scarcely agree about anything, while continuing to like each other. She said she thought Cameron would wake up British politics, but he won't: he clinches the anti-politics argument. Should anyone rebuke you for taking an insufficient interest in the way the country is governed, you now have the perfect comeback. If we have reached the stage where someone whose experience of life consists of six years as a

PR merchant and three on the Opposition benches, and is bereft of any ideas, can breeze to the fore of his party and say 'you want a new Prime Minister, how's about me?', and the media and the polls cry yes, we just adore your image, then you have every reason to say that politics is less deserving of your attention than it was before. We're adults, for Christ's sake!

Assuming it's of any interest to you to know who the Prime Minister will be after the next election, it seems to me beyond doubt that Cameron will triumph, if only by a few seats. How can I be so sure? Because the economy's not brilliant and Brown is boring and Cameron is young and frightfully caring and he's as good-looking as Blair was and the women like him and he's got a disabled son and anyway it's time for a change. On top of that there is the Brits' grubby little secret: providing it comes from a good class of person they love nothing so much as a bit of populist ingratiation, and that's something Cameron and his boys are giving them in spades.

Dickie asked me not long ago whether I regretted leaving the Tory Party now that it's coming good. My answer was that if there's one type of Conservative I'm less comfortable with than right-wing ideologues, it's left-wing patricians. (Not very sensitive of me, Dickie being Chairman of his local party, but there it is.) He of course buys the whole Cameron modernization thing, but the idea that the Conservatives are diving head-first into the twenty-first century is a fallacy. What they're doing is reverting to their roots, which are tribal rather than intellectual. That means turning away from ideology (frightfully earnest) towards old-time pragmatism and a top-down approach.

I caricature a little, but basically Dickie's line was that Willie Whitelaw had it right all along. Which is not to say that Thatcher and her kind weren't necessary at the time. The place was a mess and the servants had to be called in to clear up, but when the job's done servants can be dispensed with. The lower middle classes have their uses, like Norman Tebbit, but they can be so pushy, so alienating, don't you find? To really hit it off with the man in the street you need a good breed of fellow, blessed with an instinctive feel for the national mood. The two understand each other, always have. The best people to take charge are those who know when it's time for a bit of masterly inactivity, and with the charm and confidence to keep people sweet. Character they used to call it, people skills they call it now. You can't keep banging on at the country about its failings like Thatcher did, nag nag nag, because you don't want to make people feel low, you want them to feel – well, jolly.

I don't agree with any of this, but in one sense Dickie is right. Cameron's a moderniser in the sense of being an updated, one-man distillation of Thatcher's wets. Willie Whitelaw with an iPod, Chris Patten in unctuous mode, St John Stevas in a stylish shirt. As a self-confessed political innocent you may ask why anyone should want to go back to that kind of patronizing, problem-dodging bullshit. So do I, but my hunch is that with a contemporary gloss people will buy it. In fact I was going to put money on the next election till I discovered that for Cameron you only got 6-4.

All I know about him is that he rides a bike and was educated at Eton. Not his fault, mind you, merely his good fortune, but the socially fortunate owe us something in return: which is not to exploit their privilege by pretending to be like the rest of us, when they're not. I have children. You have children. Can we imagine ourselves playing on a son's disability to show we're in touch with the health needs of the masses? Nauseating, isn't it? You can't imagine Churchill or Macmillan saying I'm one of you really, because I've got a disabled son and he's treated on the national health. Did you know de Gaulle had a disabled child? The only thing he said publicly was when she died: 'Now she is like everyone else.'

The healthy British reaction to Cameron would be: 'Balls. Unlike us you have the option of using private medical care, except where the NHS has the best expertise and facilities. With your money and social advantages I would do the same. What I would never do is exploit my son's illness to suck up to people.' The trouble is I don't see a lot of healthy Britishness around. People seem to swallow this kind of top-down sentimentalism with a contented ahh. If your only criteria of whether to go or stay were how far your countrymen are suckers for a bit of condescension, you'd pack your bags smartly.

*

Since you're so resistant to talking about the governance of the country, I've thought up a short-cut to understanding how it works: the bicycling theory of British politics. The force of Norman Tebbit's remark that the unemployed should get on their bikes came from its nostalgic, old-world image: anything that harks back strikes a chord. Working class people today do not have bicycles, of course, they have cars. Tories, on the other hand, can frequently be seen on bikes – but not any old Tory. And if a Tory MP rides a bike you can be sure that it's not for exercise, or to get anywhere quicker, or a plea for environmental sainthood. It's because he went to Eton.

The public instantly conclude that he's not a toff at all, but a sportingly classless fellow communing with the masses. The truth, of course, is the opposite. Our high-born knights of the saddle are slumming it with a purpose. By poncing about on bikes when any sensible person would walk, get a bus or drive a car, they're scoring three points in the national game of one-upmanship at a go: being 'original', a prerogative of the upper classes, drawing attention to themselves, handy for politicos, and underlining their superior status by behaving in a way that the public will find charmingly incongruous. It's cheap and it's tacky but invariably, it works. Boris Johnson does it, David Cameron does it, but to date the most successful at the Eton bicycle game was the least conspicuous of the genre: Sir George Young, Bart. And his is the most instructive case in the bicycle theory of politics.

Young, you will not recall, was the man who pushed through the disastrous privatization of the railways as a minister of transport. (I have no complaint against him on personal grounds. I was one of a handful who refused to vote for the Bill, but he was always courteous.) Even the Tories are beginning to realise that privatization was an historic blunder, so why has it never occurred to anyone to blame Young? Because he's an agreeable fellow whom it pleased the press to call 'the bicycling baronet.'

Ask anyone you like who Young was and what he did and one in a thousand will be able to tell you that he was Minister for railway wrecking. The rest will give you a knowing smirk and say 'wasn't that the bicycling baronet?' If the non-bicycle-riding and not especially agreeable David Davis had fouled up the entire railway system the way Young did he'd never have been allowed to forget it, and those terrible crashes would have been laid at his door forever. Nor could he make up for it by vaulting into the nearest saddle: if he were seen anywhere near a bike people would groan and say, we know you were born on a council estate, give us a break.

The revelation that Cameron is not actually bicycling at all, in the normal sense, but has a Lexus in tow bringing his shoes and a clean shirt, is conclusive proof of my theory. Which is that in British politics as in British society it's not so much what you do that matters, it's the social perception of it. Never forget this, oh my son. Think Tebbit, Cameron and bicycles, and in matters political you won't go wrong.

In this weird, Wodehousian atmosphere you see things that would be inconceivable in any other modern democracy. *Warriors, Statesmen, Prelates. Can Young David Live up to his Ancestors?* was the headline over a priceless piece in *The Times* by Lord Rees-Mogg. His chief concern, as ever, was genealogy. Recalling the fact that an ancestor of Cameron became First Minister in the late seventeenth century, Rees-Mogg asks: 'How did he do it? Exactly as David Cameron proposes to do it. By charm and moderation.' The fact that Rees-Mogg's previous pash was for John Redwood, whose charm and moderation were never the most striking things about him, is a reminder his notoriously flaky judgment. And to think this guy used to be an editor of *The Times*, not in the eighteenth century, but at the end of the twentieth.

There's something comical about the Tory party's uncertainty about who the country they think they personify actually is. In the space of a decade their image of England has gone from a 1920s fantasy of little old ladies bicycling to Church, to a raffish, laid-back place in which drugs and homosexuality are pretty much the norm. When people who by and large lead blameless, humdrum existences start championing 'lifestyles', something is up. The Tories think it's part of their rejuvenation. Normally it's a sign of middle age.

*

But all that's the froth of politics, which interests you not at all. The point at hand is whether there's the remotest chance any government will deliver the three things you and Catherine need most: a health service that works, schools that teach, and transport that gets you somewhere promptly and at reasonable cost. The answer's simple: I don't know any objective person who believes that in the foreseeable future they will. For you certain consequences follow. In Britain today we still have our two nations, but they're no longer defined simply by class or accent: they're about whether or not you're reliant on public services. If you stay, to have a decent life for yourself or your children you'll need the means to contract out. The trouble is that I cannot see how you can afford to be amongst the chosen.

Let me do the arithmetic for you. Tired of waiting a week for a GP appointment, months for a consultation, and a year for action? BUPA for a family of four would be about £4,000 a year. Private day schools I have covered: the cheapest would be about £15,000 for two. And allow another £10,000 if you're going to forget public transport and make free with taxis, cars, parking and congestion charges. Total so far: £29,000. And while we're about it let's sort out your accommodation. To live in an area where they don't piss in the street or kick your kid's head in you can throw another £200,000 onto the mortgage, say £10,000 extra interest. So the price of contracting out of society as you have regrettably come to know it into a comfortable (though not luxurious) middle-class existence would be another £38,000 earnings, say £50,000 pre-tax. Which as I understand it is not far short what you earn between you now, so we're talking about doubling your income.

Sordid, these calculations, aren't they? And to those who've never had to think about these things, frightfully lower-middle-class. But you have to face up to them, and think ahead. The fact is that at your current rate of income you are condemned, not to poverty or anything like it, but to a hassle-full existence. It's when you think about your peace of mind, your privacy and your leisure, and how your thirties and forties could disappear in an unending series of cares and anxieties and dramas about schools and doctors and transport and mortgage payments, that you begin to see what you're missing. Wear on the soul is what we're talking. We were lucky to avoid it. The way things are going I don't see how you can.

*

So much for politics. Though if you stay conventional politics could become increasingly overshadowed by race and religion, and this time you wouldn't be able to ignore them. My worry is not that you'll be caught up in racist violence (though in a small way you already have been), it's that racial and religious consciousness will deform the country. That is a more prevalent thing than racism itself. (By the way, I loved your story about how everyone turned glassy-eyed with horror when someone said at a party that a girl you all knew had married an Arab. Not horror at the idea of marrying someone from the Middle East, but because they were terrified that calling an Arab an Arab might have something offensive about it, like calling a black a 'Nigger'. The psychology behind it has something deliciously nineteen-fifties lower-middle class about it – and would infuriate Arabs.)

Believe it or not I'm an optimist about all this. But a long-term optimist. It depends on how long you're prepared to wait till a growing section of your fellow-countrymen acquire twenty-first century mindsets. In the case of Christianity the reformation took some four hundred years, and it isn't complete: think of America's nutty evangelists, or of Northern Ireland Protestants marching about banging drums in celebration of the battle of the Boyne. Then think of Muslims cursing the Crusaders and the siege of Jerusalem a thousand years ago. The message is that when it comes to modernizing religious attitudes, long haul isn't in it. We're talking decades, at the very least.

In other words, your lifetime. Next to the security risks the worst thing is the boredom factor. The physical dangers might not be sufficient reason to emigrate, but the tedium would. It comes from the predictability of the discussion. We know for an absolute certainty the form the soul-curdling debate about Islamic extremism will take, and how it will invade our lives. Think of the parliamentary time, the broadcasting time, the police time, the Home Office time, the Security Service time, the commissions and reports and books and leading articles that will be devoted for decades to come to containing the repercussions of a virtually uncontrolled influx of people we have no room to accommodate and little cultural ability to absorb. Think of the tensions, the misguided passions, the evasions, the poisoned feelings, the hatreds and bitterness and hypocrisy and mendacity all this will occasion.

In all this one factor will predominate: fear. Fear by politicians, fear by natives of speaking the truth as they see it, fear amongst sophisticated Muslims about what might be said or done in their names. Sarah heard an item on the radio the other day that made her sit up. A reporter had been interviewing local people about this and that – education, the NHS, the environment – and was replaying her tapes when she discovered there were no replies to any questions touching on race. It turned out that the interviewees had answered her questions all right, but in such low voices the tape was useless.

But it's the groaning predictability that's the killer. Within a year or two I'm ready to bet that the following scenario will happen. A shop will be selling Islamic publications in Nottingham or Dewsbury, with a back room for inflammatory material about jihad. A newspaper will get hold of some of the more bloodthirsty stuff, and call for the ban on it to be enforced. A *Times* leader ('One Country, Two Laws?') will ask why it is forbidden for British citizens to publish and sell books inciting murder, but not Muslims, and call for action. After nervous consultations between the Home Office and the police it will be decided that the bookshop must be raided.

When the police move in gangs of youths will appear from nowhere, stone the cops and burn their cars. Newsnight will show pictures of a blood-spattered Asian, and none of injured police. An MP with a growing Muslim minority will argue that the police were 'heavy-handed.' A gentleman described as a distinguished Muslim scholar will point out that many British bookshops sell things to which Muslims object. Out of respect for his venerable aspect, or fear of his tongue, the interviewer will forbear from pointing out that sexually salacious material is in a different category to incitement to murder.

As the programme winds up the interviewer will go back for a round-up to a Newsnight journalist standing by a wrecked police car, whose opinion it will be that 'whatever the aim of the police action, all it will have achieved will be to create martyrs.' And when the subject crops up in an edition of *Have I Got News For You,* Boris Johnson will say that he has no idea what the fuss is about: the comics he read at school were ferocious, and if we're talking about violence, you should have seen the Eton Wall Game. The audience will laugh, and the sale of the murderous material will continue.

Plays, films, and TV shows on the subject are equally easy to predict. Remembering the murdered Dutchman, dramatists and filmmakers will tiptoe round the Muslim issue. (After writing this I heard that a film of Monica Ali's innocuous novel *Brick Lane,* due to be made in the area, has been abandoned after threats from the Bangladeshi community. Germaine Greer, a clever/silly woman, backed the ethnic censors). On the other hand there'll be no lack of films and plays about Muslims being driven to violence out of a sense of exclusion, or from disapproval of British or American behaviour somewhere in the world. The writers and directors, atheists all, will nevertheless be respectful of Islam, and the image of fundamentalist-inclined characters will be sympathetic ('Given their convictions, what choice did they have?' – an argument that could be used to exculpate Hitler.)

In media interviews Muslim starlets will insist on the right of women to wear the veil, in which they themselves look cutely mysterious, though no one – not even Jack Straw – has ever suggested they should be forced not to. They will add with a charming giggle that, although their parents are rather old-fashioned, they respect their views and traditions, and have made it plain to producers that nude scenes are out. They too will have a lot to say about exclusion, while confirming with a simper that last year's earnings topped a million, and that there's been interest in Hollywood.

Meanwhile in down-at-heel Midland towns skirmishes between Muslim and native yobs will tail away, not through diminishing hostility, but because of diminishing points of contact, as the Muslim population expands and the natives move off God knows where. Instead of no-go areas there will be no-go towns, a solution of sorts. Meanwhile non-drinking and non-fornicating Muslims with high career aspirations will excel in their University studies, to the private grief of work-shy, boozy native students, but what can they say? (According to a report issued at Cambridge University, what you say is that the natives should drink less because of the risk of Muslims feeling excluded. I'm not making this up.) Fundamentalist-inclined students, frequently from rich families, will champion Osama Bin Laden (another rich boy) or his successors in campus meetings. Calls for them to be expelled will be resisted by Vice-Chancellors twitchy about retaliation.

Amidst all this perturbation one thing will remain constant: as today anyone attempting to take a sober and realistic view about these matters will be condemned as Islamophobic, reactionary, racist or defeatist. Alternatively they'll be given the 'grouchy old fart' treatment. Anything to avoid intelligent discussion. So no change – and not much future – there.

*

Not that the Brits have much to learn from others, and when there is we never seem to learn the right lesson. Take our reaction to the French race riots last November. We ought to have been looking on in appalled silence, thinking there but for the grace of God…. In fact we watched our TV screens with undisguised satisfaction. Rarely can so many British hearts have lifted at the sight of so many burnt-out cars. The froggies were getting it in the neck and everyone loved it. A wondrous example of how antique animosities can override self-interest.

Well before the French riots people on the Left in Britain had begun saying that multiculturalism was a mistake, and that we should take a leaf from the French integrationist book and instill Britishness. *'Multiculturalism Feeds Radicalism'* is the kind of headline this attitude had begun to attract. And what did the British press say after glorying in the French riots? *'Colour-blind policy has fed Muslim Radicalism'* was an example. The joke is that as soon as things had quietened down in France the Minister of the Interior, Sarkozy, began suggesting that the answer lay in the Anglo-Saxon multicultural approach. So each of us thinks the other has got the answer. Ironic, or what?

France tells us something highly sobering that we do not want to hear: that you can insist that Muslims are as French as yourselves, oil your way into the affections of odious regimes like Saddam's or Syria and exploit anti-American feeling till you are blue in the face, but whatever you do there'll be a tendency for Muslims to end up in sour, alienated, crime-ridden ghettoes. The fact that French methods have worked no better than our own is scarcely a cause of rejoicing, however, because it suggests that both countries are in a blind alley. Treat Muslims as Frenchmen and you get ghettoes, unemployment and riots. Treat them as British Muslims with rights to diversity and you get ghettoes, unemployment, and bombings.

Every European country is reserving the right to make a cock-up of immigration in its own way, but the end results are remarkably similar: however you go about it, assimilation looks like a no-hoper.

*

There was a report on French TV last night, *Terreur à Londres,* a follow-up to the attempted Heathrow bombings. Just the job for holiday viewing. We were going to give it a miss but ended up watching, to see what angle it would take. It turned out to be the usual: a not especially sympathetic piece in which Britain, as always in France, was portrayed as the centre of terrorist operations in Europe, which there is every reason to suspect it is. It certainly made you feel at home, in the worst sense, and it made you think.

When you're walking in the street and you see a woman in an all-over veil, how do you feel? Your first reaction is probably the same as mine: to censure your thoughts. Tell yourself it would be wrong to feel anything. The sight may not warm your heart, but then that's their way of life, and who are we to find it primitive and oppressive? The woman obscured from head to toe in black, as if condemned to a lifetime of mourning, is driven by the dictates of her religion, her husband, or her own preferences, insofar as they count, and she has every right to dress as she wants. After all she's as British as yourself, is she not?

But it's all self-deception, isn't it? The truth is that the sight of the woman spooks you. Don't feel ashamed: it has nothing to do with racial prejudice, because when you see an Ibo woman in her glory you feel exactly the reverse: she's giving drab Britain a touch of colour, which women who cover themselves in shrouds do not exactly do.

And if the veiled woman makes for the Tube, and you find yourself sitting opposite, it might cross your mind that in parts of Belgium they've banned all-over burqas for security reasons. You may even reflect that the largish lady opposite could conceivably be a man. Or maybe a woman, who in her natural state might not be all that large…. A female martyr in the making…. You smile to yourself, uneasily. Well they've certainly made us paranoid, to the point where here you are thinking that every burqa hides a bomb. On the other hand how can you judge what kind of woman she might or might not be, if you can only see the eyes? On the third hand the very fact of the veil tells you something about where her ultimate allegiance lies, and it may not be to Britain.

You might even dart a quick look into the letter-box eyes, where you would discover – what? The ecstatically dilated irises of someone about to bring about her (and your) final moment? Or the pathetically anxious eyes of a poor ground-down woman and peaceable mother of four, obliged to walk about a civilised city in medieval clothes, and frightened of being mistaken for a human explosive whenever she takes the Tube? Irrational fears on all sides? No, in present circumstances rational in both cases. Fears that can be dissipated with a little more trust and contact? Perhaps, but not yet, and never quite.

*

Will there be another attack? Is terrorism now endemic – a risk you and Catherine and the children have to live with for the foreseeable future? Probably. If we come out of Iraq will we be safe, as Catherine seems to believe? I don't know, but I doubt it. Nobody knows any of this, it's new territory, so never let anyone fool you into thinking they do. All we can say is that not being in Iraq (because remember they weren't at the time) didn't help the Americans on 9/11. Or the Balinese, or the Dutch film producer, or the Germans, who've just had a near-miss when some Lebanese students put bombs in two trains.

The only advice I can give, if you stay, is to be sensibly afraid and scep- tical about authority. Which in this case means not just the government but the judiciary. Until recently I'd have said that one of the reasons for living in Britain was the primacy of the rule of law. Now that terrorism is going to be part of our future I'm not so sure. If you were to make up your mind whether to stay or go according to the pronouncements of senior judges, you'd be out of the country in days. Not because of the threat that you and your family might be blown apart, but on account of authority's plot to rob you of your civil liberties.

That, at least, was the view of the appeal court judge Lord Justice Hoffmann, when he let a bunch of terrorist suspects out of detention. He didn't just say that there has to be a balance between liberty and secu- rity, or that in seeking to counter one threat we should be careful not to lose sight of the other. He said that the threat to human rights in Britain from anti-terrorist legislation was greater than that from terrorists them- selves. Six months afterwards the terrorist attack on the Tube took place.

His Lordship was not alone in his grandiose fatuity. There seemed to be something of a competition: one of his distinguished colleagues, Lord Justice Scott, bathed in glory for his report on the arms for Iraq affair a decade ago and no doubt looking forward to another dip, said something in similar vein. His contribution to the safety of the realm was to com- pare the temporary and preventive incarceration of eleven terrorist sus- pects to the Soviet gulag. In Russia millions of innocent men, women and children were tortured, starved or worked to death in the service of a vicious totalitarian regime, and Lord Justice Scott informs us from his eminence that locking up a handful of suspects under emergency legislation is an equivalent outrage.

He got his headlines, but it's not much of a recommendation for the profession, is it? Confucius he say (and he really did) that the point about a judge is that he's judicious; otherwise he's not a judge. Which fits the case exactly. When the Law Lords' utterances on terrorism are shown to be grossly injudicious they go on being judges because no one can boot them out, but they forfeit the respect we owe them. Asses and the law we know about, but it's troubling when senior figures bray so loudly and so inanely.

Normally the reason is because they're out of touch. In the days when the law's un-worldliness took innocent forms – enquiring whether *Lady Chatterley's Lover* was a book you'd want your servants to read, asking what is karaoke? and so on – this mattered less. Now they make out-of-touch pronouncements on matters of national security while posing as the defenders of our rights, though not it seems the right to life and limb.

Judges, of whom I met a fair number as an MP, are a case. Suddenly they've stopped behaving like old buffers and turned as a man into liberal patricians, with an eye on their media image. Not long ago I sat next to a judge at dinner. This one was complaining about his workload, though he declined to say whence it came. A suggestion that there'd been a rise in crime evoked that pitying smirk that must have been centuries in the making and that the contemporary English man of law has perfected. Well, if it wasn't that, what was the reason? The smirk was non-committal. Had immigration put up the crime rate? The smirk grew positively disdainful. Well, had it? His Honour wouldn't say. So maybe it had brought it down? No view either. Good to think our judges are so impartial on these matters.

When it was remarked that appointing more judges might help to lessen the burden, the smirk faded, and we got a trenchant view. His self-interest was engaged now, and he was flat against. Said it would destroy their collegiate nature. Judge-speak for old boy's club I suppose. Who are the college members? Who you would expect, only more so. I saw an analysis of judges not long ago. They turn out by and large to be what the French call *fils à papa* – their fathers' children – complete with hereditary mentality. In Britain it's not just the law that's based on precedent, it's the judges.

Three quarters of the Law Lords and judges in the Appeal and High Courts hail from astonishingly similar backgrounds. Half went to boarding school (the national average is 1%), virtually all to private schools, and 81% are Oxbridge men. And they're not too good on their ethnic quota either. So when you next hear them prating on about our increasingly diverse society you know what they mean: that diversity is for others, not for them. How can this possibly affect you? Because it means you live in the sort of country where, whatever their talents, it would be statistically almost impossible, on education alone, for Sandra or Billy to end up as judges, or similar. Can't have jumped-up outsiders in our college.

The point about precedent is that you go by what happened in the past, on the assumption that, essentially, nothing changes. The Islamic terrorist threat has no precedent whatever, but the men of precedent are dealing with it on the basis that everything is as it was, and that no infringement of our liberties is called for in the preservation of our lives. Emergencies have a tendency to throw up things that were half-hidden before, so that people are revealed in their true colours, and the judiciary are an example. What it's brought out is how much they see themselves as a morally as well as a socially superior caste, and the first interest of any caste is self-preservation.

They're detached from normal folk not simply because of their background (not their fault), but in their seeming indifference to the way most people have to live their lives (which is). People most at risk from terrorism do not live in country houses or, when in London, secure premises. (Note the contrast between the appeal court's unanimous conclusion that the terror-suspects must be freed, pronto, whatever the consequences, and the equally unanimous vote to give gypsies occupying council land the heave-ho: for judges, snug in their rural retreats, gypsies are the greater menace.) The average Law Lord and his wife are likely to spend little of their lives on Tubes and buses, and their children are probably safely ensconced in boarding schools. Gotta stick to precedent.

*

Something happens to people who enter the Lords, even those from modest backgrounds. The dressing up gets to them. They become enchanted by their surroundings, literally transported to another realm. The echo of their words in the mostly empty Chamber gives their most banal sentiments a mystic resonance. In the House of Commons people put each other down. In the Lords they talk each other up, as if they constituted some fantasy government legislating for humankind. 'The Noble Lord, if I may say so, has made a most sagacious speech...' It's like actors who follow the Stanislavski method: by dint of addressing one another as lordly fellows they actually believe they are. The Noble Lord Black, the Noble Lord Archer?

Calling them senators rather than Lords, Sarah believes, would help bring them to earth. I think she's right. It comes as a shock when you meet some perfectly ordinary woman you've known over the years who's done a bit for charity or been in business or used to be an undistinguished MP, and discover you're talking to a real live Baroness. You'd have thought they'd never use their title, from sheer embarrassment, but they do, they do! And the British are supposed to have a sense of the ridiculous.

It's as if I were to go around with my Order of the Dannebrog round my neck, a Danish decoration which I've never shown you but which I assure you exists, of which I am the undeserving recipient simply for having been the most junior member of the household on a Royal Tour of Hamlet's country. (It was when I was Private Secretary to Lord Carrington). Desolating to think that some meritorious Dane may have spent his entire career earning that decoration, or worse, that an equally meritorious Dane slaved away and never got it.

The lack of self-awareness of these Lord fellows is amazing. Some fat fool called Strathclyde who's the Tory leader in the Upper Chamber talked the other day about Tony Blair having a 'coterie of cronies.' As if he and his fur-lined friends were anything else. I love the idea of all those peers who owe their powers over us to the fat purses of their forefathers getting indignant about the selling of honours, even if all you get for your money nowadays is a lifetime seat. 'Brings the House into disrepute' they chunter. Beyond comedy.

Of course everyone makes a joke of the flummery (such nonsense, what?) in that phonily self-deprecating way the English have perfected. But it doesn't stop them dressing up for their games of Lords and Baronesses: suggest that it's time to bring down the curtain on the whole Gilbert and Sullivan show and the self-deprecators are liable to lose their rag. The Mother of Parliaments and we can't even devise a sensible, up-to-date second chamber. Ten years our constitutional experts have been at it. The Founding Fathers set up the USA in less time. And on and on it will go. Think of the years of debate to come, with the rearguard still arguing that people from good bloodstock should continue to have a legislative say in Billy and Sandra's future, by virtue of their birth. More tedious predictability. Something more to look forward to if you stay.

I knew someone once who was elevated to the Lords and who changed overnight. To him it was the making of him; to me it was his ruin. Suddenly the amiable fellow who'd previously contented himself with dealing with humdrum matters of public policy became a high-toned arbiter of world affairs. You could see the change, physically: his shoulders, under the burden of his non-responsibilities, gained a lordly stoop. Instead of being concerned with the mechanics of daily life the formerly sensible fellow was overcome with a conviction that humanity was pining for him to play a role in the governance of the planet.

That's enough about Lords and Baronesses. It's one of those subjects where merely to have a view is a sop to the system, since it helps keep the whole ding-dong going. So I'll shut up about it.

*

Remember Thérèse? You met her when you came here to stay with Catherine before you were married. She's still cooking and cleaning for our hosts, and still about twice the size she should be. Last week she told us she'd been getting a bit breathless and had gone to see her doctor. Nothing to worry about, he'd said, but she should see a consultant, just in case. So she did. A couple of days later. And two days after that she was given a scan. (It turned out she was OK, though now she moves in a kind of jog-waddle, as if exercising as she works). So all fixed in a week. Imagine getting that treatment in Britain. Of course the French health service is broke – broker than ours – but at least they deliver.

I tried that line with Thatcher once, at some brain-storming lunch at Number Ten. The storming was coming from her and poor Geoffrey Howe was getting the braining. As far as I recall he was being accused of being a Euro-fanatic because of some mildly positive remark he'd made about German finances, and that set her off about public ownership. I told her there were two sorts of nationalised industries: those that soaked up public money and were grossly overmanned, but who produced the goods, and those that were overmanned, soaked up money and didn't. The French railways, health service etc fell into the first category, and our own public services into the second.

I could see it was a new thought for her, but as usual she wasn't going to admit it. Nonsense she said, publicly run services never work. Which wouldn't prevent her from using the point with the next poor devil of a transport Minister she saw: 'At least the French railways work, even if they swallow even more taxpayers' money than ours.'

One of the reasons you gave when you broke the news about emigrating was the prospect that in five, ten or twenty years time we'd all still be sitting round discussing the bloody NHS. A safe prediction, I guess. As you know I persist in using it, not from loyalty, but stubbornness. It's as if I were cashing in a government cheque: *I promise to fix the bearer's health free of charge, rich or poor, young or old, no matter how senile the population and without regard to the expense of the treatment in a world where the cost of new techniques is escalating out of sight.* Well here I am, not all that old, not all that poor and not all that ill, so you'll have no problem fixing me, will you? And of course they can't, in any reasonable time. So I tear up my dishonoured cheque and stump up again for private treatment, which luckily I can afford and that thank God has been minimal to date. A couple more years and I'll be in there with the BUPA brigade, though please don't regard it as a privilege. Think of it as a sacrifice, to you and your generation, so you can all move up one more place in the queue.

But what if I were a sixty year old with a low income and a heart condition, and no option of going private? Could I be blamed for reflecting as I wait and worry in a crammed surgery that, having paid my taxes and national insurance for forty odd years, it seems unfair that I must take my turn for treatment with people who've contributed nothing, and insofar as a fair number will be illegals working on the black market, or visitors milking the system, are contributing nothing now?

Why should it be wrong for him to think like that? For the simplest of human reasons, Catherine said when I tried it out on her: because it's an attitude that lacks charity. I see what she means, of course. But then try that on the old fellow and he might retort that it's a funny world where it's poor devils like him who provide the charity. It's easy to label people like him closet racists and lay about the old boy in Parliament and the media – though remember his heart condition. Also that it's unlikely he'll be persuaded by columnists or politicians on salaries twenty times higher than his pension, who haven't used the NHS in years.

*

Remember the scene when we came to see you when you were waiting in A and E with Billy? It was a Saturday night, you live close to a war zone, this was the field hospital, and there were some lethal-looking types around. The sort of people who'd put Billy there in the first place. Druggies and drunks queuing up to be fixed after they'd knocked hell out of one another, or got so pissed or stoned they'd fallen on their faces, or crashed the car.

For obvious reasons I didn't tell you at the time that I'd collared the doctor who was on the case when you weren't looking. Is his brain OK,

I said? Stupid of me to ask, but I was thinking of those sharp eyes Billy has, and the horror of seeing them decline into a dull placidity. *We get a bit overloaded on Saturdays, but don't worry, we'll let you know. These things can go either way.* Everyone in the country, it's since occurred to me, seems to have taken to speaking to you while looking past you. I don't think he was being arrogant: he was glancing about to see how many more patients had come in. *These things can go either way* was hardly comforting, though what could the fellow say? An Indian or Pakistani, he seemed competent and sympathetic, he just didn't have time to put his words in a reassuring order.

Not that I wanted reassuring: I wanted the truth, which in a way is what he gave me. What he was saying was, *look around you. With that number of casualties and this number of staff how can you expect me to give an informed reply to your question? Or for your grandson to be given the priority treatment it may turn out that he needs? The fact is I haven't had time to examine him properly. With this lot waiting, how can I?* In retrospect I suppose we should be grateful. Billy waited a mere two and a half hours for attention, when the average (a health minister proudly told us recently) is four.

Open to all and free at the point of delivery. Warms your heart, doesn't it? There's equality for you. And in case of non-delivery all will suffer equally too. It was one of those middle-class moments when you wished there was an A and E where people who hadn't smashed themselves or other people up could get priority treatment, and let the violent buggers wait. But of course that cannot be: in this war enemy combatants must be treated on a strictly equal basis with their victims. The message for people like you is clear: keep as far as you can from the battle.

The experience made me think back to the time of Sandra's birth. Another anxiety-inducing moment. Twenty odd years ago, when I first went into Parliament, the scandal about the NHS was that it was so badly managed no one had any idea how many people worked for it. In that respect things have improved. Now we know how many people they employ: what we don't know is how many patients they've got, because no one has any idea who's in the country. However much cash you invest in a business you can't expect much in the way of performance if no one is in any position to match the number of employees to the number of customers.

The moment we entered the maternity unit it was evident that they were completely submerged – a particular worry for Catherine because of the complication she had. Lucky neither of you witnessed a nasty scene in the corridor. A group of mothers whose deliveries (we later learned) had been postponed several times lost their cool and were shrieking for attention. It was a strange sight – a mini-demo by fat ladies. The ugliness of the situation was that, in a hospital where the patients and staff seemed 80% ethnic, the revolting mothers were white.

It was a leading hospital, the same place you and your brother were born, though since then it had moved premises. It used to have a great reputation, but there'd obviously been a decline in service, and compared to Sarah's time it was jammed to the gills. Catherine is one of the most unfussy women I've met, but even she felt she was being given minimal attention. It wasn't because the nurses and doctors were taking it easy – they were scurrying about. The delivery was postponed twice, the monitoring of Catherine's condition was incomplete, and as a consequence you and Sarah and I had a few days' serious anxiety we could have done without.

Just after Sandra was delivered Sarah noticed a report in the papers about a hospital not far away that had been placed under investigation because of a sudden rise in deaths in birth. At the end of the article, as a kind of afterthought, it said that the number of deliveries at the place had gone up by nearly a hundred percent in three years. I don't suppose the hospital was built for that. The fact that the immigration thing works both ways – about a third of NHS doctors were trained abroad – somehow doesn't help. Of course you're glad to have them here, though it's the kind of statistic that prompts impious thoughts. While they're helping us out over here who's coping with the poor in their own countries? And if the doctors worked there rather then here, with people who are in greater need than we are, perhaps their countrymen would feel less need to emigrate?

The lesson for the future, so far as you are concerned, is clear. Remember what we said: that if ever you decide on another one, and Catherine still has her problem, do us a favour and don't use the NHS. By steering clear of a failing service you'll be helping yourself and others. Feel free to send us the bill. Keeping the child out of over-crowded and under-cleaned hospitals will be its first birthday present.

*

Meanwhile everyone goes on swelling with pride at our free, our unique, our irreplaceable NHS. Alan Bennett would no doubt think that a wry comment on the quirky English character, but then he's never had a baby in an over-crowded hospital. Here is a centrally run, grossly inefficient Soviet-type service. On the other hand it's one whose promise to treat everyone free of charge brings tears of compassion to the nation's eyes, just to think of it. The NHS is not so much about health as social sentiment. Which is where it all gets a little weird. People are emotionally attached to a service which is the least effective in Europe, but because of their sentimentalism the Stalinist system of delivery can never be changed.

Everything about the NHS is drenched in feeling. Redundant, old-fashioned hospitals must on no account be closed and replaced by sparkling new ones, because of local sentiment. And (my screaming mothers excepted) people who've paid through the nose for years for the service can be astonishingly meek and humble when it comes to using it. They sit for hours in serried ranks in surgeries and hospitals, uncomplaining, as if it were part of some patriotic endeavour. There's even a perverse sort of pride in doctors' overworking and nurses being exhausted, as though the whole thing were some kind of wartime effort.

Even doctors can succumb to the mawkish mood. Some friends of ours told us a terrifying story about a doctor they called when their daughter had a bad fall. There was the familiar delay, and when the fellow eventually came, he took one look at the pitiful condition the child was in, and cried. Her parents were appalled. Crying they could do themselves.

Crying gets in the way of cool treatment. Crying you don't need to be trained for. It's partly because the French are such tough-minded bastards that their system works. Think of my optician.

The fact that the NHS is as close to a religion as most British get encourages an atmosphere of sanctimony that makes it impossible for politicians to tell the public the truth, even if they wanted: *we're sorry to have to break it to you like this, but the reason the NHS is free, darlings, is because its founding fathers, blessed be their names, got everything wrong. They calculated – hilariously, in retrospect – that the improvement it would bring to the health of the nation would be so great that the cost of treating the sick would steadily diminish, and the Chancellor would be quids in as a result.* Of course the improvement has been great, but public expectations have been greater.

Instead of coming clean politicians use the NHS to play on heart-strings, and prevent thinking. Gordon Brown tells us that our creaking, unreliable, broke and unhygienic service is the national institution we should be most proud of, and Cameron plays on the same cheap emotions. It's bad enough to speculate on people's credulity about his private arrangements, worse when he shuts off debate about reforming an NHS which informed people know can never work. Not that it's surprising. I think I know what his chief policy criterion is: *would Diana have done it?* I can see her in Greenland with Dave and the huskies, or out there with our lads in Afghanistan in a becoming camouflage jacket, but I don't see her carrying the NHS reform banner. So no, he'll dodge it.

What the public can never understand is that one day they're going to have to take a little responsibility for themselves, probably through some kind of insurance system, and that their NHS problems are by no means all about money. If the government were to stack gold bars on street corners with a sign saying 'help yourself', three things would happen in swift succession. The first is that people would collect as much as their cars could carry. The second would be a public outcry when the bars were gone. The government would be obliged to come up with more, but by now the four-by-four merchants would be onto it and shift more than the rest, in the way the middle classes are wont to do with any form of public provision. The result? Another outcry, as the press complained that a two-tier gold distribution system was in operation, one for the Landroving classes and another for the rest. So more gold bars, more outcries, and so on till the Treasury ran dry. That, pretty much, in where our NHS, envy of the world, is heading.

The comprehensives were going to succeed so well in raising standards that no one would go private, and the NHS was going to make such a great job of looking after us that the costs to the nation would fall. The result in both cases is that the costs have spiralled and quality has declined, to the point where everyone who can afford it uses private medicine and independent schools. As national failures go, that's pretty comprehensive.

*

On a pleasanter aspect of our homeland, I don't think I ever told you about the afternoon we spent with friends at the celebration of the bicentenary of the Battle of Trafalgar near Nelson's home village on the Norfolk coast. It was one of those events so typical of the country that the only parallels you can think of are in France. By that I mean that it was a moving local occasion enlivened by Clochmerle overtones.

The place was on an inlet, Burnham Overy, a fine-looking village whose pebble houses have a defiant solidity to them. It is much used by weekend boaters, of the kind who seem more at home in the Range Rovers lining the shore than in their boats. As you might expect everything about the occasion seemed designed for maximum discomfort: damp grass, spitting rain, lunch in an open field. The big event was the review of the fleet (a huddled armada of yachts and motorboats) by an admiral, no less, a ceremony that proved charming in its improvisation. Everything and everyone was exactly as they should be: wet dogs and children, wellies and Barbour coats, the vicar and the MP. A brave little band played away while we awaited the Admiral, one of those groups where you could easily pick out the musicians' professions: the face behind the trombone was undoubtedly that of a schoolmaster, and the trumpeter was clearly a bank clerk.

A row of sea cadets, alternately plump and gawky, one with tragic Ken Dodd teeth and all of them unsuited to any form of exertion, stood in line, First World War rifles at the slope. The Admiral turned up late and conversed with each at length, whether out of duty or because of the difficulty of getting the awestruck and inarticulate kids to say anything at all was impossible to be sure.

At the moment everyone had been waiting for, they piped him aboard a small row-boat, manned for some reason by women. The admiral stood gallantly as they rowed him out to sea. As the boats set off ahead of him against the incoming tide one capsised and another ran aground. The admiral remained upright as he passed. There was a lot of wading in the chilly water. A biplane looped fitfully overhead.

What struck me about the event was the absolute separation between one England and another. It's now nine years since I gave up my rural constituency, and it was a shock to see a crowd composed entirely of native faces. With their winter pallor they seemed indecently white. Deploying her conservator's eye, Sarah claimed you could see a line of continuity in these features with those she'd seen in many a painting of Nelson and his officers and men. I suppose you'd expect that, though somehow the idea comes as a surprise.

I found myself thinking that these were exactly the kind of people who would listen to the BBC's morning medley of English music, recently abolished. It's of no consequence to me, I'm not up that early, and some of the melodies drive me mad. But these things symbolise something to people that is not disgraceful. It makes you understand what Cyril Connolly meant when he said there was only one thing that annoyed him more than old colonels, and that was the kind of people who made fun of them.

Watching this very English ceremony in a remote spot on the Norfolk coast was suggestive. It was as if these too were refugees, internal exiles driven to a wilderness from where they were defiantly preserving their culture, in this case the right to stand in a field in the rain eating lunch off paper plates and drinking beer that was warmer than the lunch (though the suckling pig was delicious). In France the equivalent occasion would have been funnier, because of the pompous provincialism: the Mayor in his ribbon, the band all got up, the swankier naval uniforms. Here the humour came from the DIY nature of the event, though in an odd way that lent a greater authenticity to the memory of a very professional victory. If you want to emigrate from the capital maybe you should live in Norfolk? It doesn't get more English than here, because in an easterly direction it's as far as you can get from England as it has become without falling off.

Coincidentally a few days later Sarah heard *Farming Today* on the radio (too early for me) trying to push the thesis that ethnics were under-represented in the countryside. To do this they took a black man to a farm, showed him the sheep and the granary and so on and asked whether he felt excluded? Nope, the black guy said. But didn't he have as much right to our countryside as anyone else? Yup, he said, and it's interesting to see. But I couldn't live here, no way man. You see what I really like is the action in the town. Collapse of BBC prig.

*

But you don't live in peaceful, escapist Norfolk, you live in the metropolis, and what we've been seeing and hearing about the Lebanon brings me again to the security problem. Sorry to keep coming back to terrorism, but it keeps coming back to us, doesn't it? Not long ago I suggested to one of those statesman-manqué journalists that the nuclear terrorist threat could become worrying – a notion he shot down instantly, from a great height. The whole thing was nonsense, inconceivable, part of the government's scare tactics. Did that mean that if he were Prime Minister he'd instruct the Home Office and the security services not to waste time seeking out people who might be preparing an attack? No reply. Like many a high-placed commentator he'd never held any responsibility for public affairs in his life.

As it happened I'd discussed the same issue with one of the Government's chief scientific security advisers, a cool-minded civil servant I'd known in my Foreign Office days, who'd spent years studying the nuclear and biological threat. One of the people, in other words, who the journalist was convinced was wasting his time. His conclusion was simple: for obvious reasons – Al Qaeda and its money, the spread of technology, the break-up of the Soviet Union and the pauperization of many of its atomic scientists, and the nuclearisation of Iran – the level of both the atomic and biological threats had increased sharply.

But we've faced down the nuclear threat before, haven't we? Always the search for precedents. In Cold War times the risk of a 'suitcase' attack was far lower than today: the Russians were not stupid enough to do anything that might trigger an all-out exchange. Theirs was a heavy-footed bureaucracy, and behind the intransigence and aggressiveness were rational minds. We know for example that schemes by the KGB for psychological warfare on the West, including wild ideas to de-stabilise Britain by attacks on Royalty, were turned down by the Politburo.

What is there to restrain Islamic terrorists? Where is the disincentive that would prevent them attacking? And if Al Qaeda struck, what would we strike back at? In the Cold War disarmament talks were permanent and failsafe procedures were in place. How do you negotiate with Al Qaeda? Where is the hot line to Osama bin Laden, and what exactly would the British Prime Minister or the American President say if they got through? And how would Osama, speaking from the Dark Ages, respond? Looking at where we stand today deterrence based on Mutually Assured Destruction (MAD) begins to seem rather less crazy than once it did. Who would have thought we might one day be nostalgic for the Soviet Politburo, with their homburgs and their granite faces?

It would take more than a lordly dismissal from a journalist to persuade me that these things can never happen. And if ever it did a statement by Lord Justice Hoffmann (retired) from his country house, that looking back over his long and eminent career he had only one regret, which was that in retrospect perhaps there ought to have been more rather than fewer preventive detentions in Belmarsh prison, would do little to improve things.

Should such a remote eventuality be a factor in your decision? It depends what we mean by remote: in the sense of highly improbable, or remote from our thoughts? If you'd asked me thirty years ago whether you should stay in Britain, it would never have occurred to me to say that in reaching a decision you should weigh up the possibility of a nuclear attack. With Islamic terrorism it is a factor. Try thinking it through: the deaths, the contamination, the chaos. Then the repercussions: the collapse of the stock market, of the central London property market, the closure of businesses and the rise in unemployment.

This is not America, where a city the size of New Orleans can be virtually wiped off the map and the country continues largely as before. It is a small, highly centralised nation. However 'miniature' or 'dirty' or locally concentrated the blast the effects on the country's future would be appalling. And once they had the technology for a first strike, there'd be nothing to prevent it happening again. The repercussions on race relations are scarcely thinkable. After July 7 there were insults and aggressions against innocent individual Muslims. The absence of large scale civil disturbance is a tribute to genuine moderates on all sides, and to the tolerance of the British (a tolerance that, some would argue, had helped facilitate the attack in the first place.) Though remember the ostrich and the lion.

I'm not trying to frighten you, or myself. Why should I? I'm not saying that the risk of nuclear terrorism is such that you would do well to get out: I'm saying you have to include it in the balance. The idea of Britain as an island of tranquillity is so entrenched that it's hard to shake off history, and look reality in the eye. If Catherine thinks I'm being alarmist, I'd suggest that she think of the face of Richard Reid, the shoe bomber, and imagine what was going through his mind when he tried to light his bomb. What does it matter to that sort of person whether he dies in a plane crash or in a dirty nuclear explosion? The only difference is that the more deaths he causes the better his afterlife will be. On second thoughts don't think of the face of Richard Reid, it's terminally depressing.

*

Remember the story about Disraeli being served a poor dinner? When the champagne arrived with the dessert he took one sip and sighed: 'Thank God for something warm at last.' Passing from nuclear terrorism to education is a little like that. It would be going too far to say it's impossible to decide where the prospects are bleaker, on the other hand I'm not going to pretend that the quality of our schools is something that should detain you in the country.

Billy and Sandra haven't exactly got off to a flying start, have they? Your local primary has gone down several notches since our BBC friend used it as a surrogate prep school. For the first year after you moved in it wasn't so bad. A growing percentage of children came from the estates, but it kept its balance, and there were bright and well-behaved kids from both sides of the frontier. They were the pivot on which the whole thing swung, and you built your hopes on them. As the immigrant quota climbed abruptly the children went on making friends across the widening divide – I remember an Iranian girl with an uncannily serene face, and the Nigerian boy in glasses – but it was a small and shrinking circle.

Everything, in fact, was shrinking. The number of kids with English as their first language. The number who could tie their shoelaces when they first came in. The number who hadn't spent their lives parked in front of a screen, and could consequently talk. The number with two parents (down from 70% to 40% in four years, Catherine said). The number who showed any inclination to learn. The number of staff who behaved like teachers rather than social carers, though if the caring is essential, what do you do? It was poignant for us, coming to the open days and the childrens' plays. One moment you rejoiced to see Billy and Sandra, members of a diminishing minority now, mixing with their friends. The next you caught the wariness in Sandra's eyes when some tough-looking or clearly disturbed child approached her. And how quickly she turned away because she didn't want us to see.

Knowing how keen Catherine was to make a go of the school I was careful to avoid saying anything that might rile her, but I must have let slip some remark about one of the teachers we'd met during a school play. You know the one? A surly bitch with one of those soft/defiant faces the most ideologically immovable teachers have. A single hint of criticism and they react like the Soviet Politburo. You have to remember what a challenging job they're doing teaching English to children with nine different languages, Catherine rebuked me at the time. Think of the courage it takes to do a job in a school like this at all.

And the courage to send your kids here, I remember thinking. All this talk of bravery makes me uneasy. Bravery about crime, bravery about terror, bravery about schools. Just how brave are you going to have to be to live in this city of ours? And how right is it to be brave with your children's education? Every time I asked how things were going you both said fine, lovely to see them making friends with kids of different races and so on. But there was an earnestness about the way you said it, and the tension began showing on your faces whenever we talked about school. That's when we stopped asking.

Things came to a bit of a head at Sandra's birthday party, didn't they? We're not much good at children's parties, but this time it was just as well we came. Because apart from the Iranian girl and the Nigerian boy and their mothers, and a couple of native kids, there was no one there. She'd moved up a year, and this was to be the big occasion that was going to bond her with her class. Catherine sent out thirty-one invitations, and the take-up rate was two.

We told each other that something must have gone wrong with the invitations. With little Ms Kommissar in mind, I suggested that it looked as if someone had failed to distribute them, but the Nigerian woman (child psychologist, wasn't she?) put me right: she'd seen her handing them to the parents after school. So things were worse than we'd thought. It was a straightforward, racial thing. The kids will come into your territory to go to the school or make trouble, but to socialise with you, no way. Middle-class white kids from the other side of the tracks was not where it was at.

From that day on I saw Catherine's attitude evolving. The big change came when she began sharing her anxieties with Sarah and me. She was worried about Billy's reading and had asked Ms Kommissar why they didn't encourage him to take home books. Instantly the ideological lash descended: if they made everyone read books, she said, it would disadvantage children whose parents had no books at home. Funny how these ethnic warriors have such low expectations of black people. I don't have to remind you of where things went from there: Catherine trying to find time to get more involved in the school, the resentment, the racial overtones, the whole ghastly urban middle-class multicultural English thing. It ended with Mrs Nigeria and Catherine pitched against the rest. And losing.

The government is talking about ethnic quotas for schools, to be implemented by local councils. You can argue this one way or the other – and personally I don't like the idea of draconian social controls in the hands of politicised local bureaucracies – but it'll certainly solve the problem, if not in the way intended. White flight will get a massive boost as the natives move out faster, and so will segregation.

Which reminds me of something you told me that Catherine said when you'd discussed looking for a house near better schools: that moving out would be a cowardly and despairing thing to do. I know what she means, but I don't think that's the way to look at it. Staying on would be heroic, but I'm afraid I don't see education as a charitable enterprise, in which middle class natives are required to set an example by donating their children to the state's immigration policies. A little too Maoist for me. If we could be sure that the results of sticking it out would be to raise the general standard, you might think about it, but there's little reason to suppose that would be the case. One by one, you tell me, other white parents have been pulling their kids out, which leaves you in an ever contracting minority. Majorities tend to overwhelm minorities, not the other way round. The forces against you are too great.

You could argue that staying on would do more than help the others, it would enrich your children's lives by making them aware how the other three-quarters live. There's something in that, though it's a bit too close to the street-smart argument. Socially it might enrich them, culturally and academically they'd be impoverished. Our black Minister of Culture

David Lammy has just said, I see, that too many Africans and Caribbeans suffer from a poverty of aspiration and a laissez-faire attitude to education. If he says it, can we not think it, and reflect on the consequences for our children?

*

I think I'm right in saying that you've never knowingly read anything I ever wrote about education. I'm not blaming you – there are millions in your position – but given that your life for the next ten years is going to be dominated by the claims of schools and universities for your attention, not to speak of your cash, I feel I should say something now, even if it breaks my resolution never to write another word on the subject.

Why did I make it? Two reasons. Having thrown my rock into the pool as an MP and watched it sink, I find it hard to see a way forward. Secondly, the dishonesty of the British education debate makes it unattractive to be associated with the discussion. Whether it's Cameron pretending his kids will go local, the head of the London Oratory (the Catholic school where Blair's kids went) claiming that his rather select establishment is a comprehensive like any other, or a celebrated newspaper columnist prating on against elitism and selection while his son goes to Winchester, the hypocrisy on education is worse than nauseous: it corrupts the English public culture. (The canting columnist has now been knighted for services to journalism.) Blair and Cameron tell us how profoundly concerned they are about it, and as an earnest of their sincerity Blair made Estelle Morris schools minister, and Cameron has made Boris Johnson minister of higher education. By their appointments ye shall know them.

It's the predictability again, the great British boredom factor. You know exactly who's going to say what and when on anything connected with schools, and they never let you down. There are many ways a man can waste his life, but one of the worst is to become in any way involved in the sterile, fetid, cant-ridden, caste-ridden English educational game.

Yet schools will be a key element in your decision, so let me say this: that the fundamental reason we're in trouble is that in most countries schools are about education, whereas in Britain they are mainly about social class. The best solution is probably Germany's, which the British set up during the occupation. They had a tripartite system – technical, secondary and grammar – the key being the high quality of the technical schools. People didn't think it was the end of the world if their children didn't get into the local grammar; they could always settle for being doctors or engineers, or high quality technicians. So unlike here you weren't written off. The system has evolved since then (they select at fourteen now, which seems sensible) but it seems to have done them well.

If only we'd managed to do here what we did in Germany, the trouble we could have avoided. The top of the state sector would be better than the independents, as it is in France and Germany, and we wouldn't have our Berlin Wall between state and private. The half-arsed experiments in reading and the rest that have done wonders in boosting our underclass of semi-literates would never have happened: with their own children in the system influential, well-to-do parents would have stopped them in their tracks.

From top to bottom society would be a different place. The careers of Blair and Cameron would have been rather less effortless than they were: with a bit more competition from the bottom they might never have made it to Oxford. We wouldn't have a working class waxwork as Deputy Prime Minister, who owes his place to the fact that he can't string two words together, and a leader of the Opposition who uses his glib articulacy to tell us how frightfully keen he is on the latest rapper. The Poet Laureate, Andrew Motion, would not feel moved to write poetry glorifying the TUC as well as Princess Diana, and Mr Madonna, another penitent of his background, would have been spared the trouble of removing the silver spoon and getting his tongue round mockney.

Think of it: an England where the whole debilitating charade of inverted snobbery and populist insinuation that dominates and debases our culture, our media and our politics did not exist. (I seem to remember you contesting this when we last took the subject for a walk, on the grounds that if you took away the class element, the English would end up with no bloody culture at all.)

*

Whatever you decide I don't see how you can stay where you are. In London everything is moving to extremes. Either education is free, or it costs a fortune (there are twice as many children – 13% – in private schools as in the rest of the country). Either the schools have classes of fifteen, or thirty. Either children walk a couple of minutes to school for a lousy education, or their mothers sacrifice their careers to bus them to a more favoured location. Either the kids are scarcely taught English, or they buy themselves a head-start in French and Latin. And they tell us that the English are moderate, pragmatic folk, much given to compromise.

Billy is a bright boy who is a year behind with his reading. It was when you told us that we began thinking about offering to pay for prep schools. As you may have noticed, we never did. You would have been in favour, we decided, but we were unsure how Catherine would react: I've heard her say she would never consider going private, and however we covered it up it would look as if we were telling her that her experiment had failed, and that by way of compensation we'd bail her out. In the end we gave up the idea altogether, for a simpler reason: money. Since there are no decent secondary schools in your area it would have meant paying for them too, which would mean doing the same for your brother and sister when their children came along.

We did the sums. It's just as well Catherine has a problem about private education, because I can't see how you'd be able to afford it, now or in the future, and neither would we. The cost comes out – you have to believe this – at something approaching a million. *A million?* Yes a million, just about. You have two children, to date. We have three. On the assumption that we end up with eight or nine grandchildren, from prep to eighteen for nine kids at modestly-priced schools, a million would be the ballpark figure.

All of which tells us another great truth about the times in which we live. There are three classes of parent in Britain: one that is well enough off to help their children with housing and education, a far larger group who are in no position to do either, and a third that can do one but not the other. That is where we are. We stand ready to do what we can, with tutors and so on, but after helping the three of you with housing we're not in that league, I'm afraid. We thought about seeing if we could come to some agreement with Dickie, but then I gather from something Catherine said that he lost a bundle on privatised railway shares.

In any case we decided against. It wasn't just the money. There's another factor. Although in the right independent schools they'd be better taught, no doubt about it, there's something distasteful about being caught up in the English public-private business. However much you try to avoid it, from the earliest age all those little evasions and affectations and snobberies and anti-snobberies and pretences and counter-pretensions that plague English schools get bred in the bone, and it's not a pretty sight, even in your own family.

*

There's nothing like education to bring out the truth about people. Think of Blair. I knew him a bit in Parliament, talked to him about education across party lines and felt fairly positive about him – till he was asked what he was doing bussing his kids half way across the capital to avoid the schools in Islington. If only he'd said he was doing his best for his children like everyone else and stuck at that, there would have been a grudging understanding, especially since in an average inner city school the Prime Minister's kids would in all probability have got done over daily. Instead he said he was not going to impose political correctness on his children. Turn that phrase round your tongue and savour it. The cant is fathomless.

And now Cameron is playing a similar game. When a journalist asked whether he would send his children to a state school, like Blair he had his suavely duplicitous response at the ready: 'Yes, absolutely. I've got my eye on a particular one. I'll make my decision for my daughter based on my views as a parent and not as a politician. That's the right thing to do. But I would like them to go to a local state school.'

'Based on my views as a parent and not as a politician' comes to the same thing as 'I'm not going to impose political correctness on my children.' And of course we're talking about primary schools. Come the moment I have a feeling that Cameron might find his local secondary less than adequate for his daughter, for reasons that might be entirely valid.

And there's a racial sub-text, in both cases. Islington, where Blair lived, and North Kensington, where Cameron has his house, are ethnically mixed areas. Which in plain English means that our top politicians are finding themselves in the same boat as you, except that they have the means of getting out, and you haven't. It's hardly an encouraging sign for the future to think that, when it comes to education, the Prime Minister and the Leader of the Opposition are a couple of condescending phonies.

*

Having failed in education for half a century doesn't mean (I feel obliged to add) that we'll fail for all time. It just means it may take another half to put things right, time that Billy and Sandra have not got. What are their talents? Billy seems good at music and Sandra is breaking the mould by being promising at maths. Will they get the teaching, the encouragement, the universities they merit? Possible, but unlikely. Music is patchily taught and maths teachers are in short supply. In any case 'merit' has become a suspect word.

It's a pretty screwed up country where every political party bangs on about how each child must achieve its potential, and yet none of them believes in advancement by merit, but it's the one you live in. Anything resembling a meritocracy suits neither the philosophy of the Left nor the interests of the Right. That's why we don't have one. Labour have a rooted aversion to selection, and you can't have promotion by merit without it. The Tories make positive noises, but their heart isn't in it, because whatever ethnic effigies they recruit essentially they remain a social caste, especially in their upper echelons, and selection means opening up to all the talents. To date the only thing the Tory new elite have opened up are their shirt collars and their iPods.

Everyone says they're going to make state schools so good that no one will want to go private, but it can't happen. Why? For chicken and egg reasons: you cannot upgrade our educational culture without the whole of society participating, and the most powerful people in the country will have nothing to do with state schools till they're upgraded. Which they can never be without their participation. So round and round she goes.

When pondering whether or not to educate your children in Britain I advise you to keep three facts in mind. One: the OECD say that the gap between the state and private sectors in Britain is the biggest in the Western world. Two: the London School of Economics has shown that we are the only country where social mobility has actually gone backwards over the past thirty years, and that it is mostly for educational reasons. And three – the most dismal fact of all – one reason why the poor in Britain get nowhere and the better-off cream it is the new economy. What they call 'soft skills', ie knowing how to talk and dress and behave and be persuasive and present yourself with confidence, are vastly more important in a service than in an industrial economy. In other words slickness gets you everywhere, whether or not you have a brain. Obvious when you think of it. For examples, look around you.

*

Assuming you stay and aspire to a university education for the children, you should start thinking now. My fear is that they could face a double whammy: low standards at primary level will hold them back, but at the top of the tree they could face the opposite danger: that able and ambitious immigrants will provide them with tougher competition. I have every confidence in Sandra and Billy's ability, but already we're seeing some of the sons and daughters of newcomers out-smarting our children, and by the time yours are eighteen the competition will have hotted up.

Alongside the low achievers from backward cultures are people for whom education has miracle-working status. We borrowed the idea of competitive examinations for the Civil Service from the Chinese, who established it thirteen hundred years ago, and you will have noted that their instincts for self-improvement through study have not diminished. The Indians have similar beliefs, and the less well-off will make extraordinary sacrifices to get the best for their children. Meanwhile the Russians are buying up places at boarding schools as fast as their (frequently ill-gotten) incomes allow. Sensitive to the idea that they were the barbarians of Europe, ever since Peter the Great they've made a fetish of education. And when it's not stymied by dogma and passivity Muslims can approach their children's schooling with a seriousness that has long been out of fashion here.

So what I'm saying is that whether it's Asian or Eastern European, future generations of native children will face a wall of competition they've been spared before. A couple of figures I saw recently give the flavour: in the 2004 GCSEs 75% of Chinese got from five or more A to C grades, 65% of Indians, 51 of whites, and 33% of black Caribbeans. 16% of all students are ethnic, and it was you who told me that the library at the London School of Economics, where about half the students are foreign, lends out four times more books than the average university.

The bright ones, a scientist explained to me, literally can't help wanting to put the natives in the shade. The reason is that the spirit of risk-taking that can go together with migration can wind up in the genes (the D4-7 allele, if you want to know). The earliest migrants who left the African savannah to populate the earth turn out to have a particular genetic profile, believe it or not, which gives them a bias towards entrepreneurial behaviour. One of the reasons that America is as vibrant as it is. Good news for us, it would seem, except for the Brits who are crowded out. Those who've coasted for years on the English tradition of effortlessness ('Didn't do a stroke for the exams') could be in for a shock.

The message for you, meanwhile, is to avoid getting into the position where Billy and Sandra are held back at primary and secondary level because of one group of migrants, only to face tougher competition from another at university level. Sod's law of immigration, you could call it.

*

As she may have told you, I had another chat with Catherine about Cameron, when she rang to assure us you were all safe and well in the follow-up to the Heathrow alert. She asked if I thought he was a cynic, and I told her I thought it was worse than that. He's probably persuaded himself that because everyone wears chinos and has done a bit of clubbing and taken drugs (and everyone has, haven't they?) and goes about saying *yeah, right,* class is history. He's got it into his head that people can be frightfully nice if you take the trouble to pal up with them, and that the way to get the best out of them is to be frightfully nice back.

All this is the reverse of Mrs Thatcher, who more than once told me of her scorn for her indolent, evasive, consensus-loving countrymen. It's an attitude she shared with de Gaulle, whose patriotism went along with a mighty disdain for the fractious, frivolous, and hopelessly egotistical French. And in rather an extreme form I suppose with Chairman Mao, whose contempt for the Chinese peasant was such that he killed seventy million of them.

On Cameron I suspect there's nothing to be done: the nation is stuck with him because in a perverse way he represents the nation. Such is the unbearable lightness of British politics that he's now routinely described as the future of those politics. He may be less superficial than he seems, and do an adequate job. On the other hand a bit of genuine competition might have thrown up someone better (by which I don't mean David Davis). What's happened is that the Tory new elite are being touted as the natural party of government.

Dear old Max Hastings told me he'd thought that a toff could never again lead the Tory Party, and seemed agreeably surprised to discover that he could. The reason, in his view, was that people had lost their hang-ups about their social betters, and that in our egalitarian times we were open-minded enough to recognise that an elite had something to give the country. Max's problem is that coupling of toffs and elites. Elites have certainly got a lot to give, providing they're open, which ours is not. And if it's closed how can you be sure that you're getting the best available – which is to say a true elite? Whether toffs have something to give the country is a simple matter to decide: if they've proved their superior capabilities, then there can be nothing against an entire government of toffs.

Which in Cameron's case appears to be pretty much what we're promised, though we've still to be convinced about the superiority. Of the thirty-five members of Cameron's first shadow cabinet, six attended comprehensive schools, and if you throw in his closest advisers like Zac Goldsmith he has as many Etonians as state educated people. Perhaps his old school pals are the best available. Maybe the 93% non-privately educated rump of the population who scarcely feature in the Tory party line-up are bone-headed Untermenschen, rightly condemned to exclusion from affairs of state. It just seems statistically improbable that over 90% of the country should have so little to offer.

So Cameron and his mates are not an elite in any twenty-first century sense. I'm not saying they're stupid. They seem to me to be a bunch of savvy upper class operators, the kind of people you've always found in the City and can now find pretty much everywhere. You see them in the media, selling posh-tosh magazines or populist bilge on the box (Peter Bazalgette, who does *Big Brother*, is a high-born former President of the Cambridge Union). You find them in the pop industry (Will Young atones for his background by masquerading as a Marxist, which doesn't prevent him coining it on the pop scene. Maybe he's not homosexual either, and sneaks home after his gigs to some expensive piece of skirt?) And you find them running PR operations, fashion houses, butler boutiques, or hilariously over-priced restaurants.

Cameron himself was communications director of Carlton TV. The programmes Carlton promised to get its franchise were ambitious, which didn't prevent Cameron, who already enjoyed a reputation for a total absence of principle, touting some of the scummiest stuff broadcast at the time (*Hollywood Women, A Woman's Guide to Adultery.*) A fact worth remembering now that he's giving us the sweet talk about decency and moral values. 'Glib and superficial' was the judgment of the Independent Television Commission – of the programmes that is. When one of society's favoured sons uses his position to foist on people with an education less fortunate than his own programmes that coarsen and cheapen their lives, that is bad enough. When in pursuit of his political ambitions the same man expresses wrinkled-brow concern about the state of our

schools, says it's wrong to encourage young girls to wear padded bras, or
that life is not all about money, what matters is the quality of our culture,
it seems reasonable to regard him as a Janus-faced, lightweight, upper
crust political spiv. And when the man who says he wants each of us to
fulfil our potential looks back with a smirk on how he used a lady-in-wai-
ting he knew to pip someone to a job at Conservative Central Office, as
if it was all a bit of a jape, you wonder how funny it seemed to the poor
sod who was done down by Cameron's connections?

The old question: what does any of this have to do with you? Because
if we're in for a Cameron era the values he projects will be symbolic of
the kind of society your children can expect to grow up in. The TV executive who sold pap to the nation is selling them pap now, and as Prime
Minister he'll sell them pap again. And convince himself he isn't. Soon
after he won the leadership race he said something that illustrated his
world view perfectly: 'I like this country as it is.' This is adman's politics:
the slogan of Channel Four TV – 'We like stuff' – is on the same slick,
ultra-democratic level. The obvious response to him is: *Why shouldn't you
like your country as it is? Seen you all right, hasn't it? Just one thing, sunshine: if you
like it so much why have you come into politics to change it? Or perhaps you haven't?*

In a Cameron government none of our root problems will be tackled.
The man who really, really likes his country will tell us there's nothing
wrong with things like health or education that a little benign attention
from well-intentioned folk like himself won't put right. This is the
mouldy apple syndrome. You toss them to the peasants, ever so charmingly, who cry as one man 'you're a toff, squire!' Then sink their teeth
into the apples and discover they're full of worms.

Being a politician is no longer a serious vocation, it's a celebrity choice,
another way of dancing in the beam of public attention. For all his affected earnestness Cameron is a kind of political playboy, a little in the Boris
Johnson mould. I'm not sure I ever told you that before deciding to look
for a seat, Johnson, a journalist at the time, asked me whether it would be
the right thing for him to do. I told him it depended how interested he
was in the minutiae of the social security budget. Not enormously, I got

the impression, or in anything else except knocking the French so far as I could see (*Can't beat a bit of frog-bashing to keep the spirits up. What? Eh? Ha!*), but he got himself a seat and has prospered mightily outside Parliament, if not in.

It's only six in the evening but I feel suddenly weary. Must be the effect of writing about politics. I haven't done it for some time, and somehow it makes you feel unwell, as if your brain is being smothered in garish, squeaking balloons. Time for a drink.

*

I know you're not much of a money man, any more than you're a fan of politics, but it's one of those things it's advisable to keep an eye on, and before waving goodbye to Britain it might be sensible to ask yourself what are the long-term economic prospects if you stay? The fact that everyone from City gent to gloating homeowner is locked into short-term considerations makes this hard to say. For the moment at least the government can go one better than Harold Macmillan, put its hand on its heart and tell the country that most people have never had it so good *for so long.* One measure: in the nineteen seventies GNP per head in France was about 10% higher than in Britain. Now it's the other way round, and we've just overtaken Germany.

Why aren't we dancing in the streets? We are. And on bar-tops, and on the heads of people our yobs beat to a pulp on the pavement. You need cash for the 'good life' and it's because people have got it that so many of them spend their leisure clubbing, puking and fighting from Newcastle to Marbella. At the other end of society the effrontery of money can be just as vulgar. Name your toff, or your celeb.

These of course are the extremes. For those like you and Catherine, with no annual bonuses or housing costs subsidised by the state, it would be nice to have a little cash to be vulgar with. I've just read a new survey about taxation, according to which a fifth of the country (i.e. a chunk of the middle classes) might one day think about emigration if taxes don't come down. It was you who told me that whatever the figures said about us being richer than the French, for anyone who knows France and who lives in Britain, and who lives on incomes like yours, it doesn't feel that way.

French take-home pay is lower than ours, but there are compensations. Not too many people in Paris have to pay half a million pounds for decent accommodation, with mortgage to match. Nor do they have to hoard money for school fees, because the state schools are fine. A metro journey does not cost £4, the average restaurant is better and cheaper whatever our foodie nationalists pretend, and there's no need to pay for private medicine. Plus you can walk about central Paris at midnight without being cut to ribbons.

So our prosperity is relative, and like everything else increasingly insecure. How long might it last? No idea. All I know is that everywhere you look there's a feeling of flimsiness and precariousness. I say 'feeling' because the new economy is impossible to calculate in concrete terms. Not long ago you could count up how many cars and ships we were making and selling, compare it to the Germans or the French, tot up exports against imports, throw in the value of the pound, and get some idea of how we were doing. Which was usually disastrously. Now the rules of the game have shifted drastically, though not to worry. Four fifths of our economy in services rather than manufactures? Absolutely no importance my dear fellow. Balance of payments deficit? Irrelevant old chap. And you are a touchingly antique creature if you take the slightest notice of the level of the pound. These were the old, earth-creeping ways of looking at economics. Today we are told that none of it matters.

Never mind how many British cars foreigners are driving, or vice versa. The main question is how many Chinese-made jeans/shoes/brassieres we can afford to buy with the notional increase in value of our semi-detacheds, so as to keep the high street humming and the whole thing turning over. The next question is how we can fiddle the interest rates so as to keep the house price rises down and the shoe-buying up. Such is our unreal, post-modern economy, in the venture capital company that is Britain. I saw something the other day about how hedge-fund bosses are amongst the biggest buyers of contemporary art. If so it's no surprise: in today's economics, as in the art market, everything's what anyone says it is, so long as in the end there's someone willing to come up with the cash. Just don't get caught holding the parcel.

The very last thing that matters (everyone tells you) is whether we own our companies. I remember Catherine saying a couple of years back that one of these days they'd sell off the stock exchange itself. Well as a matter of fact they are, to a foreign buyer it looks like. I can't see anyone else doing that. The others pay lip-service to the global market, but the Brits are the only ones who not only obey the rules, but take them to extremes. Other countries do not open up their economies or their frontiers as widely as we do, not even the market-worshipping Americans, let alone the French or the Japanese.

You might say it's admirable of us to be out there on the edge, leading the way. Perhaps it is. To me it seems another case of literal-mindedness, plus a touch of patrician insouciance. International bankers apparently regard the UK as a single huge hedge-fund with a one-way bet on growth in financial services. Risky? Don't you worry your head, dear boy, everything will be fine. Always has been in the past. Just sit back and watch our multi-cultural open market model become the envy of the world.

And close your eyes to the social implications. I was struck on our grand tour of the North by how much our provincial towns have lost their character because they've lost their most characteristic businesses. These had local roots, local personnel, local loyalties. First their HQs went to London or the South East, then abroad. And if the Chinese knock the bottom out of the market the owners have no reason to feel obliged to find ways of holding on. Nothing binds them to one place more than another. Though if the populations of these towns are becoming as cosmopolitan as the businesses, why worry? From now on it's all one big floating, international thing. Thinking about this deracination of everyone and everything, I suppose it's less surprising that people like you and Catherine are considering uprooting yourselves too.

It's so hard to know what's solid and what's flaky. One minute we're told it all looks a bit fragile, the next that everything's fine. True, no one's got a penny to lay out any more on consumer goods and unemployment is snaking up, but relax. The City's doing well, and the conjuncture remains favourable. The City meaning the square mile rather than the country ordinary people inhabit, and the conjuncture meaning today, maybe tomorrow. As for the future, no one knows.

Ask people better informed than yourself how things are likely to shape up and they shrug and rock their heads. Too many variables. Could go one way, could go the other. The national lottery again. No wonder Tessa Jowell wants to open casinos in every town and village: dicing with the future seems to be in our blood. Our attitude to borrowing is more evidence of this curious insouciance about where we're going. In the most sober-minded of nations this year the level of consumer debt overtook the size of the economy.

And thereby hangs a tale about interest rates that's always puzzled me. Since they're destined to rule your economic life in one form or another, even you might find it interesting. In one of your rare displays of concern about these matters, you asked me why it is that British interest rates are almost invariably the highest in the Western world. I put the same question to a former Chancellor of the Exchequer, expecting a sophisticated reply, but he just shrugged and said it was a cultural thing: 'The British live for the day.' Meaning we don't save enough and have a tendency to splurge. I asked a deputy director of the Bank of England: are we really so irresponsible we can't be relied on to make sensible decisions in our personal finances? Again the answer, broadly speaking, was yes. If interest rates were halved overnight most of us would respond in catastrophic ways.

First we'd fall on the offers of cheap loans and finance that pour through our letterboxes and run amok with our plastic cards. Next we'd binge on new kitchens or bathrooms imported from Germany, or electronic gear made in the Far East, because our industrial capacity is not big or adaptable enough to meet new demand, or because we never made the goods here in the first place. And finally there'd be queues outside house agents as we vied with one another to take on colossal mortgages, the better to jump another rung on the housing ladder. The result of our collective idiocy would be a steep rise in inflation and a giant step back to boom and bust. Giving the British cheap credit, it seems, is like giving too much pocket money to children, while telling them not to spend it on anything silly.

Whether immigration will prove an upper or a downer economically is another of the Great Unknowns. You may have seen the Government's claim that we're getting so old we have to import youth, like a commodity, and that immigrants will pay our pensions. The obvious answer is, well that's decent of them, but who will pay theirs? And their housing benefit, NHS costs etc? The other line of argument is that we need people to do the work the Brits don't want to do. Which doesn't speak too highly of our motives, does it? I thought they said we were doing it for cultural enrichment. So which is it? Importing unskilled labour to do rotten, low-paid jobs that are beneath us, or making our lives richer by diluting the Anglo-Saxon component of the national blood? Personally I'd be happier with the blood dilution, but it's the cheap labour that drives the system.

Though it's all speculation. There's no evidence that importing labour on this scale actually works, once you measure costs against benefits, not to speak of the burden of economically inactive women and high birth rates. And you can't make even that calculation properly. How can you compute the economic effects of immigration if many work in the black market and don't pay income tax or national insurance or council tax or car tax or buy TV licences? Leaving aside the question of how many there are in the country. So it's all statistical hooey.

The general feeling seems to be that, though immigrants do contribute, the net effect is small. So it doesn't sound as if there's much in it economically one way or the other. Looks as if we may just have to live on the cultural enrichment.

*

Speaking of which my opinion of Salman Rushdie is improving. You may have seen his article not long ago. He's one of the few who address the menace of radical Islam squarely, by insisting that the faith is due for some radical modernization. What got his goat was that when Muslims were calling for his murder in 1989 Iqbal Sacranie, till recently the head of the Muslim Council of Britain, had said that 'Death, perhaps, is a bit too easy for him.' Since then Sacranie has been knighted to keep the Government sweet with the community, something which can't have improved Rushdie's mood. I suppose you would feel narked if you were him, seeing Her Majesty tapping Sacranie on the shoulder, rather than running him through as punishment for threatening her subjects. It must be the first time the monarch has ennobled a man who speaks in this manner – an illustration of the way the Muslim question is deforming the way we think and live.

Rushdie impressed me further when he signed an international manifesto earlier this year: 'After having overcome Fascism, Nazism and Stalinism, the world now faces a new global threat: Islamism. We writers, journalists and intellectuals call for resistance to religious totalitarianism and for the promotion of freedom, equal opportunity and secular values for all.' It went on to pledge that they would never give up their right to criticise Islam for fear of being accused of Islamophobia.

I waited to hear how many other writers and intellectuals had the guts to adhere to its statement of values, in a show of solidarity. Our literary critics, perhaps? You're joking. Our Poet Laureate? Tell me another. To date the score is zilch. Everyone wants to steer clear of the whole business. Depressing to think that the only commentators likely to tackle the issue honestly tend to be of Jewish extraction, like David Aaronovitch, Nick Cohen or Melanie Phillips.

Everywhere a pattern of mute mendacity is developing. Recently I was reading an extract from a book by a philosopher, Simon Blackburn, lamenting how far gone we were in credulity and superstition. Feng shui, homoeopathy, flying saucers, conspiracy theories – all were vigorously denounced. And of course Bush was accused of pandering to creationism and the like. Everything was there – except clear and specific criticism of fundamentalist Islam, the most irrational, most powerful and most dangerous creed of our times. I don't feel too threatened by feng shui, or flying saucers. What makes me apprehensive are the cowardice and evasions of intellectuals about terrorism, and there's a lot of it around.

Richard Dawkins is another. Read his writings against religion, or watch him on TV. What you get are fiery denunciations of creationism in the United States, and nothing about the kind of madrassas where children's minds are filled with hatred of godless materialism, and of infidels like Professor Dawkins who preach it. Give me a bit of old-time creationism in exchange for old-time Islam any day, and I'll be happy. If we can't rely on scientists and intellectuals to tell the truth, even when the threat is directed at everything they assure us they believe in, God help us all. All this is appeasement on a grand scale, but because it's silent, no one seems to notice.

You even see it in art. We've been to a couple of Islamic shows in the last year, both of which were so-so; enlightening if you didn't know much about it, with moments of brilliance, but seen over a long historical period, by any international measure not outstanding. How could they be, when religion has so often fettered the Muslim artistic imagination by forbidding depictions of the natural, sensual world? I see the attractions of calligraphy and abstract geometrical forms in carpets, pottery, architecture and so on, but have difficulty with the notion pushed at me by race-conscious critics that this is the equivalent of the Renaissance, the neoclassical school, the Romantics and Impressionists and modernists and the rest, and that far from being in any sort of decline over the last centuries, Islamic creativity has continued in full flood.

Of course we have to show respect for Islamic culture, and I can see the point of making that respect doubly clear today. But when you start exaggerating the value of art forms in the hope of lessening the chances of getting yourself blown up, it's not a great day for intellectual freedom, is it?

*

One of the reasons I love it down here is the lack of aircraft noise. (As I finished that sentence some rich idiot's helicopter started revving over the hill, but he's getting to be an elderly rich idiot, so he only does it once or twice a week). In our shrinking island you can scarcely take a step without some vast airliner thundering and screaming over your head. There's an immense, blundering stupidity about low-flying planes and the noise they make, as if they were intent on drowning out debate about where the endless expansion of airport traffic is taking us. It's one of those things from which there's no escape, not even for the rich: wherever and whoever you are the mass society will get you. The Western flight path goes over some of the plushest places. You can barricade yourself in a ten million pound Chelsea house with a half acre of lawn, but try opening the windows or sitting out there and three hundred and fifty economy passengers will buzz you every three minutes, defecating noise.

To general amazement (ie yours and mine) the British Airports Authority wants to allow flights from 4.30 a.m. The insolence of the airport industry is amazing. Think of it: hundreds of thousands of people jolted from their womb-like sleep at four-thirty in the morning and lying there semi-comatose for three hours till it's time to spring from their beds and get on with their busy day. Try objecting to the BAA (not that I have – I know the response) and you'll get the same one-word reply you do when you question our over-reliance on the arms trade: jobs. Heathrow must expand, they tell us, otherwise French airports will attract our customers. I hope they do. Let's have a bit of environmental competition. Charles de Gaulle airport was purpose-built on a plain outside Paris to minimise pollution. Heathrow is where it is because… well for the same reason we still have hereditaries in the House of Lords: because they've always been there, and it's too much trouble to shift them.

Shunting people in and out of the country seems to be the one big industry we have left. The numbers using Heathrow doubled in the fifteen years to 1998, and have been soaring since. A growing population with roots in the four corners of the world means more air travelers, which means airport expansion, for which more immigrants to build and man the new facilities will be needed. Which means a bigger London, which means…. A growing number of the jobs the BAA says are vital to us all are done by ethnic folk who live in the Southall/ Ealing/ Hanwell/

Hounslow area. Being so close means it's they who suffer most from noise and other pollution.

So let's see if I've got this right: we are importing workers to expand an industry so as to provide jobs for immigrants, whose presence will entail more expansion as they become part of the flying public. And we do this irrespective of environmental damage, not least to the incoming workers themselves. I don't see the Greenpeace boys getting to grips with this aspect of the matter, but it seems to me a strange logic. I see a similar situation developing on the other side of London, where they're building the Olympics.

An advantage of getting the games, we're told, is the regeneration of a deprived, largely immigrant area. That I understand. But to complete the construction on time it turns out we need to import a lot more. When the few weeks that the games will last are over, where, it seems reasonable to ask, will these new immigrants be accommodated? The thinking appears to be a little circular.

*

If I go on about Heathrow it's because it's a neat symbol of where the country seems to be heading. Like the airport, the sole purpose of our national existence is expansion where there's patently no room for it. Maybe our future is not as a nation at all, but as one huge terminal, an international facility with no customs or characteristics to call its own, and with every religion and none. I once heard Mrs Thatcher getting carried away in a private speech about the productive capacities of places like Hong Kong and Singapore, making dubious comparisons with the Italian city states of old, and finishing by saying that the future lay with that sort of compact, agile state. (Tough luck on the Americans, the Chinese and the Russians). In some hazy way she was obviously thinking of Britain as a kind of offshore economic engine, the Hong Kong powerhouse of Europe. Is that what we're aiming for? If so I have seen the future and it is dense.

For years we were told that the thing about modern economies was that more can be produced with less. The idea was that Asia would make cheap shoes and sweat shirts, whereas we would make cars and airliners. Of course Asians would get smarter, but the better-trained they became the higher-skilled we would become, so their manpower advantage would be endlessly negated. Now it turns out that, far from being too smart for menial tasks, we're amongst the least skilled people in Europe. That's why we need the better-educated immigrant, like Indian IT specialists. But we need their manual labourers too, and their entrepreneurs. In other words, to keep up with the Chinese, the Indians and Brazilians etc, we need more of everyone. A hopeless race, you might have thought. We're like a frog who imagines that if it ingests enough tadpoles it will grow into a bull. But there's no room for a bull in our shrinking English pastures. There's little enough space for the bloody frog.

In any case I'm not sure I recognise this division of the world into Western technological Wunderkinder and Eastern helots. I don't recall the Chinese being slow to pick up Western tricks when I lived there. They managed the H-bomb alright. Instead of importing more skilled and manual labour maybe we'd do better to educate our own workforce to a higher standard, and ensure that the unskilled ones are at work. Otherwise we'll find that in a couple of decades we've lost our technological edge and gained a bigger underclass than we had before.

What it all comes down to is economism. We no longer live in a country, we live in an economy. A country has a way of life and a culture and a history and traditions and dreams and aspirations. An economy is composed of factories, roads or offices, and people's skills. A country needs an economy, but if the economy swallows up its life it ceases to be a nation in the accepted sense. If we're doomed to become one vast international airport, why should anyone care about its past or future? Who gets attached to airports?

*

So what are the prospects for you, money-wise? If taxes have to be raised and services cut back, you will be the first to suffer. And if the ship holds steady, or even surges ahead, I'm afraid it won't be dutiful, tax and insurance-paying citizens like yourself who benefit. So tails you lose, and heads you don't win either.

It takes time but people cotton on, and it's when the middle classes start coming out of their shells that things get ugly. The danger comes when the feeling gets about (and I sense it in some of the things you say) that those who play by the rules get nowhere. Unlike those poorer or better-off than themselves they have no means of dodging taxes or fiddling benefits, even if their tender middle-class conscience allowed. Meanwhile the rich scoop in their bonuses and the poor have all expenses paid: in one East London borough, of the 190,000 inhabitants 90,000 are on benefits. I know you and Catherine don't think in these rancid terms, but I can assure you there are millions who do, and an entire civil society is at stake.

With so much uncertainty about, people will have to get used to living on their nerves, and to keeping an eye on the main chance. Already an undercurrent of *sauve qui peut* is developing, not because things are going through the floor, but against the day when they might. Short-termism isn't just a City disease, it's the national culture. In the grab for education, the snatch for space, the search for privacy and security (all those gated squares and armoured apartments they're building), more than ever it's each man for himself.

As you know I'm not normally sentimental about Britain, but I've seen how our government and society work compared to others, and the idea that beneath the surface decorum we've always been as venal and corrupt as the next nation is a lie. Notions of fairness and decency and civility, and the stability and security of benign tradition have not been entirely hollow. They still mean something, but the balance is fragile, and when it goes, it's gone.

Believe me, this is about to become a much, much wilder country. I'm not just talking about violence on the streets. More and more people you meet behave like well-bred wolves – and these are the natives! More and bigger fortunes will be made, some legally, and financial crime will soar, from mysterious movements in your current account as the banking system is targeted by crooks of all nations, to major frauds in the City. At the same time confidence in institutions, from local government to the police, traditionally high in Britain, will decline.

Ask the average native how the country's going and he or she will make the obligatory noises about vibrancy and creativity and the rest, and in a material sense, that can be true. But put a stethoscope to their chest, and what do you hear? The sound of a dickey heart, because the English are a worried race. Beneath the patriotic bombast (a lot of it in the arts) there's a sense of things slipping through our fingers. America has taken the culture. Foreigners have taken the City. The Chinese are taking what's left of manufacturing. Immigrants will soon be running major cities. And if the environmental doomsayers are right the North Sea is going to take slices of territory we can ill afford to lose.

*

I've just got it about David Cameron, and who he really is. Everyone says he hasn't said or done enough for us to say, that he's still finding himself and so on, but suddenly it's obvious. All you have to do is to look at his new official picture, taken to adorn Conservative offices up and down the land. It was in the paper. Did you see it? It's a beauty. Naturally he's casually dressed and grinning, 'cos you know – yeah, gotcha, right – but what strikes the eye (at least Sarah's eye) is an almost feminine softness. It was when I began looking at him in that light that I understood exactly who Cameron is: a transexualised Diana.

The lips are hers. The smile is hers, as is the winsome tilt of the head. Of course Blair does his Diana impersonations, but he's less persuasive. Cameron actually looks a bit like her. All you need is a touch of kohl round the eyes and a blond wig to bring out the whole cross-sexual thing. And the extraordinary fact is that they are in fact (at least so I've read) distantly related. I hope it's true, it would explain so much. If so I don't know why he doesn't make more of it, I would have thought it was worth a million votes.

From this august kinship everything flows. She spooned with the masses, and so does he. She played the from-my-heart-to-your-heart sincerity game (the opium of our era) and he's doing it too. And as with Diana the whole barrel of tricks will work. The country will go for Dave-the-new-Diana because their minds read increasingly like the pages of OK magazine, where royalty, the stars, the toffs and the celebs are confounded, and in Cameron you can find trace elements of them all.

*

As I scribble away about what you and Catherine can expect in the future, the generation thing keeps coming back to me. My life began unpromisingly, but everything's always got better. Decade by decade I've had more money, lived in pleasanter houses, eaten better food, drunk better wines, travelled more freely and easily, met a wider variety of people and had increasingly satisfying work. In other words, in personal terms I've absolutely no complaints.

Once you assumed that the same progress would hold good for your children and grandchildren. You had some idea of the kind of country they'd live in, and reason to suppose that their lives would be an improvement on your own. Now you have no idea what to think. Assuming life expectancy goes on increasing, you and Catherine could have some three score years to go, and Billy and Sandra might be around for not much short of a century. The trouble is that neither Sarah nor I have any inkling of what England will be like by that time, and I suspect we are the first generation to feel that. It's bad enough to begin losing faith in one's country, worse to have no image whatever of what it may become.

As a result the feeling of belonging is weakening. When you kept saying you felt you had to get away more often, but it was too expensive, I asked why you didn't make more use of the cross-channel ferry for cheap vacations with the children? You said it was because you couldn't bear the journey home. Coming back to Britain by ferry after a continental holiday, you said, was like a blow to the brain. The English herd lowing towards the bar to slurp down as much as they can before entering territorial waters. The red tops with their grinning headlines about some new idiocy involving Charles or Camilla, each of them shown grinning too. And the boatload of pissed-off faces.

I remember you telling me how you once paid £20 to escape to the club lounge with your two babies, whose presence there offended the poncy types. (I'm with the ponces on that one.) You described how you had the stifling feeling of being trapped between the proles and the bourgeoisie, that you couldn't decide which was worse, and felt you had to get away from both. Everyone has these moments. On the other hand staying at home because if you leave you can't bear the thought of the journey back is an unhealthy psychological position. I know what you meant, but I think you were being unfair. You can't compare home with abroad. One place you live in, the other you don't. At home you're painfully aware of every grating detail; abroad the language and the novelty act as a shield, a distancing factor.

*

We went down to the little museum on the port today, to see a new exhibition. The place is a gem: Matisses, Monets, Gauguins, Signacs, Braques, many of them things you've never seen, since a lot are from private collections. Price of entry, 5 Euros. And as always no one there except ourselves. Outside, within a stone's throw of these splendours, hundreds of Brits/Dutch/Germans gawp at the efforts of local artists – slick, laughably overpriced pictures of Hyde Park railings quality.

It reminds me of the time some years ago when Sarah was restoring a battered fifteenth century religious painting in a country house. The radiators weren't working, she was freezing, and eventually a plumber was called. A chatty fellow, he took an interest in what your mother was doing. Are you an artist, he enquired? Well, in a way I suppose, she replied. And are you famous? Not at all said your mother. Well you will be, said the genial plumber encouragingly, indicating the six hundred year old picture, because you're very good.

Not that the culturally deprived classes get much encouragement from above. When there was a major Caravaggio exhibition at the Royal Academy a little while back Tony Blair turned up. We were surprised to see him there, and by the looks of it so was he, and he stayed as briefly as he could. The choice moment came when his minders took elaborate care to ensure he wasn't photographed against a background of boring, elitist Old Masters when he dashed off his speech. It isn't the philistinism that appalls you – you get used to that – it's the absoluteness. The idea that the merest contact with Old Masters, far from broadening your image with the voters will actually contaminate you in their eyes, is something else.

The thought of Alastair Campbell and the lads being on the watch for cultural mantraps is funny. Can't be too careful. A poem here, a Rubens there, a bit of the Bard, and before you know it they've got you down as a fucking elitist. (Did you know by the way that for all his four-letter swagger and tabloid spirit Campbell went to Cambridge? Shows what a top-notch education can do for a man.)

Tony's all-time cultural favourites are the Foo Fighters, and Dave's is a track from the album *The Queen is Dead*. Not that she'd be seen dead at concerts or art galleries if she can help it, any more than her Prime Minister or Leader of the Opposition. If there's one thing you can rely on government and royalty for it's that they'll do what they can to ensure there's no danger of the plumber or his mate being able to tell the difference between a twenty-first century canvas and fifteenth century angels on a rotting lump of wood, or of going to an exhibition by Caravaggio.

End of cultural lamentation. I'm not saying the country is on its way to becoming a wasteland, and so far as it is, migrants may help. This is a field where they could have the most positive impact, because they'll have spent less of their lives marinating in English class resentments, working up their anti-elitist juices. Look at literature. Today you're beginning to get a lot of successful ethnic writers (for want of a better term), a few of them over–promoted for the usual reasons, some of them good. In ten years' time I'd expect to see a Booker Prize list largely composed of the sons and daughters of immigrants. The same we must hope will happen across the arts, from dance and music to cinema and the theatre, and by then people may be recognised not just for their skins, their politics or their 'ethnic story', but for their talents. If I'm wrong and immigrant talent goes native, then we are in trouble.

*

Hearing you talk about England, sometimes it strikes me that you're in danger of being nostalgic for a homeland that never existed. (And by the way the word nostalgia, I recently learned, began as a mental illness: nostos=homeland and algia=pain. No offence.) The trouble in your case is that you *are* at home, but it doesn't feel like it, so you want to leave. You have a sense of being a foreigner in Britain because it doesn't live up to an idea you have of it.

This is where I'm inclined to slouch (I don't feel like springing) to the country's defence. I suspect your image of England has something to do with Rupert Brooke and Alan Bennett taking tea together on a lawn, an image that for some reason gives me the heebie-jeebies. Never forget Jimmy Porter's lines in *Look Back in Anger* when he's remembering a forgotten England: '… high summer, the long days in the sun, slim volumes of verse, crisp linen, the smell of starch. Phoney too, of course.' Now I'm home and have had a chance to check the quote I see he went on to add: 'Still, even I regret it somehow, phoney or not.' Which rather undermines my point, but never mind, it's not a bad description of yours.

You know those people who keep turning up in foreign countries because they've had a blackout and forgotten who they are? I sometimes think England is a bit like that. It's broken free of its past, and has little or no idea of what it is, or of what it used to be. Instead you get a sort of flaccid acquiescence. The British used to have an art of making compromises to keep things on course; now they make what they think are tactical concessions, but it isn't done through wisdom and maturity, it's done because they have no idea where they're going, except with the flow. An entire nation liquidizing and melting and dissolving into what it mistakenly sees as the warm sea of humanity.

But there's something else happening. Beneath it all one gets a sense of suppressed anger, which has been growing for some time. After a trip around Britain a few years ago Jonathan Raban (like all the best British writers, since departed, for America in his case) described the typical expression of the average Brit as 'insulted.' A.A. Gill was talking about the same thing when he recently wrote that 'A simmering, unfocused lurking anger is the collective cross the English bear with ill grace.' It adds up to a kind of mute indignation. What Gill and Raban and I are saying is that the attitude of the Englishman in the street is 'we deserve better than this.' Look around and you'll see it everywhere. In the bitter resignation on the faces on the railway platform. Or at the airport. Or the Post Office queue. Or the NHS waiting room. Even the expression of the barman in the pub (my Manchester man was an exception). 'I deserve better than this'.

Not an encouraging thought for a man who's losing faith in the future of his country. Though I'd advise you against making a habit of despair. If you feel there's nothing to be done in the community or in politics your only course of action is to look to yourself and your family, and in doing that you'll be helping the community, and in a way politics. The thing to avoid is the horrified fascination to be had from seeing the people or institutions you dislike – politicians and the media, celebrities or royalty – behaving in exactly the way you abhor. It's a satisfying but perverse pleasure. The danger is of being trapped in a cycle of deprecation. At that point everything you touch becomes a sad reflection of the times we live in, and there are better things to do with your life than to spend it reflecting sadly.

*

Reading over what I've written, Sarah wonders whether I may have overstated the dangers of staying put, and looking back I see what she means. Nuclear terrorism, natural disasters, the risk of economic instability and the certainty of David Cameron wearing a flowery shirt at the next Notting Hill Carnival err a bit on the Armageddon side. But I'm not keen on watering it down. When it comes to handing out advice to their children parents have to cover themselves, like house surveyors. So look at it as a brief survey of the country's future from a buyer's perspective, rather than a seller's. And remember that surveyors never get lyrical about the charms of the place – the way the sun falls on the living room windows, the ancient creeper on the back wall, the cosiness of the kitchen. They note down every creaking floorboard, assure you the creeper's roots are getting into the foundations and that it's a miracle the place is standing, because that's their job. And remember, too, that surveyors can get things wrong.

If I played up the positives too much you'd suspect us of wanting to keep you in the country for our own purposes. But believe me when I say that there are cons as well as pros to getting out. And there *is* an optimistic scenario in Britain which you have a duty to imagine before you take the leap. It's this.

The political parties settle down to mainstream politics, with less of the posturing and point-scoring of the past. A less adversarial approach opens the way to tackling the NHS and education, with gradual but significant improvements in both. The tide of immigration tails off, as controls start biting and immigrants themselves begin saying (some already have) that enough is enough. Those already here adapt over time to the British way of life, as British traditions of tolerance prevail. They not only contribute to the economy, they give a huge boost to science, intellectual life, the arts. After a bad start the Muslim community turns its face against violence and throws up educated, modern-minded and moderate imams. The efforts of black leaders and social programmes gradually bear fruit in turning black youth away from guns and drugs. Meanwhile the country continues to get richer, even if a regrettable percentage is due to a black economy, Italian-style, and we hold off Far Eastern competition. And in the arts we tire of our bouncy castle culture, become bored to death with the non-shock of the not-all-that-new, and grow up.

If this reads like a wish-list it's because that is what it is. Which doesn't mean that some bits won't come true. The one thing no one has ever questioned about the British is their resilience; it may be foolish of them to endure so long and so much, but in the end something could be done.

*

Assuming you're not convinced (I tried this line on you before, and you weren't) where will you make off to? If you're serious about leaving the country it has to be for somewhere else. It worried me a little that you seemed to proceed from the negative rather than the positive, keener to get out than to think about where you wanted to go. Isn't that the wrong way round? In one of her private fits of frustration with the British,

Margaret Thatcher said that if it weren't for being Prime Minister she'd emigrate (she didn't say where she'd go, or whether they'd let her in.) I think your instincts are a bit like hers. The point is that you don't have to be an anti-patriot to feel that sometimes you just have to get away.

When it comes down to it I suspect there are few places you could happily and conveniently live. For me it would be three: Britain, America and France. There aren't even any runners-up. Wherever it is for you, I take it you're without illusions about life elsewhere, and remember what Dorothy Parker meant when she said that there's no *there* there. Though today it might be truer to say that there is here, because there's no arguing about where the grass is greener when it's Astroturf on either side.

I also take it you realise that there's more to Britain than city centres. Do not overlook the option of internal emigration, which a lot of people are choosing. To begin with you have the suburbs. Personally I'd go crazy, but if you're in the self-sacrifice business, which parents are, they can be good places to bring up children. Between where you are now and the Continent or North America lie places like Barnes and Wimbledon. Then there are the smaller towns. You both seem to have a yen for space, without illusions about country idylls, and you could buy a nice place somewhere pretty with your London money. You are a mellow fellow and, short of going out there and ruminating with the cows, there are mellow lives to be lived.

*

As you see I'm still havering around the central question. Let me broaden it out as a first step to narrowing it down. Who are the kind of people who'd be wise to consider emigration, and who would be wise to stay? For one group it's easy. Anyone who is well-born, anyone with money, and anyone with a promising career in politics, the media, the City or the law would be mad to leave. For them the rewards of life in Britain are disproportionate to the penalties. People like this don't live in Britain at all, but in a separate realm: a genuinely green and pleasant land of attractive town and country houses, with schools and hospitals that work, and the wealth to enjoy the livelier side of the metropolis.

Those at the top of the tree have it easier in Britain than in comparable countries. There people have to fight their way up; here the run-off for top positions takes place amongst the upper ten percent, and it shows. In forty years in diplomacy and politics and the media I met many a smart and able offspring of the upper classes, and a rather larger contingent of over-promoted mediocrity. Lower down I've seen no end of under-promoted talent, especially women.

So much for the non-incentives to emigration at the top. As for the bottom, for them there's little choice but to stay. In the past the poor were driven abroad in search of work, but social security has put paid to that. In the EEC they have a right of abode, but with the lowest educational and cultural levels in Europe, and nil linguistic skills, the English would find it even harder than the nationals of those countries to get work. Emigration demands a certain dynamism and such people are inexpert at planning their lives. In short, you can't take them anywhere and in any case they wouldn't want to go. Like their *frères enemis* at the other end of society, they're happier where they are.

So emigration doesn't arise for the underclass, or for the elite. It's the in-between folk, the middling sort of person, who will be increasingly inclined to consider their position. And who would be an enormous loss. In a normal country it would be open to them to aspire to rise by their talents to become leaders in their field. By dint of exceptional effort, luck and ability some do, but as social mobility in Britain slips into reverse (even our pop singers come from the wealthier classes now – and what a frightfully rebellious bunch they are!) it's less and less the norm. And should things go badly in the next few years it'll be people in this intermediate band – teachers, scientists, civil servants, middle managers, academics, shopkeepers, small businesspeople – who for the reasons I've given will be exposed to the highest risks. A category, I'm sorry to say, that includes you.

Would you be able to lead safer, more roomy, more prosperous and aspiring lives elsewhere? You lean towards France. Apart from your memories of your early years there, when I was in the Embassy, the reason for your fondness for the place seems to be that it's a country that has modernised without trampling its past. For you that makes it a kind of substitute England.

Catherine favours Canada. I don't know Canada well. After Britain the space would be terrific, but something about the country makes me hesitate: its goody-two-shoes side makes it an Englishman's America. If you're going to go all that way, why not America itself? It has the best of everything, pretty much: the best scientists, universities, orchestras, films, popular television, literature, geography. I know it's a steep drop from the best to the bottom, but then that's the deal. And it's better than having a bottom and a middle, and no best.

I can see you both in Boston, rather than New York or Los Angeles, New England being in a strange way still more English than the English. The children would have better chances, though America being America you'd have to fight for them. Then there's the politics, but never mind: Catherine would have a great time hating Bush or his successor. For what it's worth I think the country is fated to swing in a European direction, though not just yet, and not to the extent that it won't be worth going. Australia and New Zealand I have little opinion about, except that they have a habit of producing brilliant people like Barry Humphries who tell us they're terrible places. In any case they'd be a hell of a way for us to come and see the children.

France would be a cosier choice for all. There you could sink back and be engulfed in the perfumed bosom of the welfare state. For the moment. The children would be safer and better educated, though not at university level unless they cram themselves into the *grandes écoles*. You speak excellent French, and would probably get a job more easily than Catherine, though with her education degree she might get one teaching English.

Emigrating to a country that sees itself as being in an historical cul de sac would be an original move, but then the English are famed for their eccentricity. The words you'd hear most often would be *morosité* and *la crise*. There's an element of self-dramatization in all this breast-beating, but then that's the French. For them distinction is everything, and as Alain said to me yesterday, if they can't be the best in the world at something they'll insist on being the worst. When I ask French friends what French film I should be seeing the answer is a shrug. With novels the shrug becomes emphatic, and with art a veritable explosion of nihilism. Historical writing, they tell you, is the only genre that's flourishing, because in a country with no future burying yourself in the past is the only option. Economically I have no idea how they'll get out of the impasse they're in. On the other hand it's a kind of blocked society in which, when they're not on strike, everything sort of functions. Maybe they'll surprise us.

I don't have to tell you that the only way to live in France is by wholesale surrender to French norms, French values, French ways of thinking. Unless you're going to live in an English community, which defeats the exercise, you have to become French. Not a bit French but totally. A bit will not be acceptable. You can't be French with an English dimension: that would not be *cohérent*. And allowances will not be made for you being foreign, because it's not in their nature to make allowances.

So impermeable is the membrane that separates the two cultures that few English are capable of the effort of conversion. That's why the majority of the half million Brits who have a house here are ghettoised. I'm not sure this total surrender would be easy for Catherine, whose spirit is independent and whose French is patchy. If she wants to work – and I'm sure she would – a huge cultural and linguistic investment would be necessary.

Then there's the legendary cheek of the French, which I've mentioned, and which their lack of self-esteem is doing nothing to improve. Personally I find it hard not to hit back. To thrive in France you have to develop a hide as tough as theirs, especially in dealings with the state, of which there would be many. When Sarah was restoring her Titians and Correggios for the Louvre, dealing with the bureaucracy, she discovered, could demand as much intricate attention as the paintings. There was a suggestion that she should be grateful they'd allowed her to work on some of their greatest masterpieces, which in a way she was. If you went there you too would be treated as if you should be thankful to be allowed to live and work in what remains, whatever else is said of it, the most beautiful country in Europe.

*

I've still not come up with a recommendation. Seeing too many sides of a question, including some that aren't there, is one reason I was a lousy politician (people have suggested there were others). Anyway, it's getting on for drinks time, so now I have decided.

Forget emigration. Don't give it a thought. The whole thing is a false dilemma. But that doesn't mean you shouldn't leave England for a while, and live abroad. As a father I would like you to stay, but in your shoes I would go. Between you, you combine the two best reasons for getting away: you are terminally frustrated with the country, and Catherine has a yen to see new worlds. The one thing you must never do is become spiritual émigrés pining for release, but never daring. Don't let the national fungus get you. The world is a big place and there's no reason to spend your life on a single scrap of land. And don't for a second think you're being in any way disloyal by going: scattering the national seed to the corners of the earth was once seen as a patriotic act.

I suspect that Sarah would prefer you to sit things out for a few years in an English country town, and see how we go. That would obviously suit us better, but it's your decision, and I can see you have the itch to go. If you end up somewhere that turns out to be a chimera, nothing will be lost. Look at it as a tour of duty abroad in the business of living. And don't feel any pressure of age. You may think you're over the hill in your mid-thirties, but your generation has time on its side, and plenty for mistakes.

So just go where you want. I doubt if you'll ever regret it. And if ever you hear the sound of an ostrich wrenching its head from the sand, and of a lion roaring, you could always come back.

Love to all, Dad.

August 2007
South of France

Dear Guy,

Thanks for your last letter, whose contents more than made up for its brevity. We must be amongst the last people in the Western world to be informed by mail that they're about to have their third grandchild. I'm not complaining – the birth of a baby is worth a line of ink, and somehow the news is more pleasurable coming by post than by email or telephone.

It was of course a surprise, since we were led to believe that you'd stopped at two. Maybe it was that sprawling new house of yours and its large garden that persuaded you there was room for more? Neither your mother nor I is given to bouts of patriotic mawkishness, but the fact that the third one will be a Canadian rather than a Brit is a little poignant. Sarah says to tell you that you can look forward to a second visit from us around the time, assuming that might be useful, rather than an encumbrance.

It's getting on for nine months now since you and Catherine left. I need hardly tell you how we miss our weekly moments with the children. In all the glib talk about international migration no one spares a word for the effect on families. In the vacuum your departure has created your brother and sister have been getting more parental attention, which we must assume they welcome, though they tell me they are beginning to feel under psychological pressure to produce replacements for Billy and Sandra.

*

I don't know what the emigration equivalent is to the house-buying-justi-fication period, where couples spend their time one another that they went for the right place, but whatever it is I imagine you're past that phase; we certainly got that impression during our visit. Still, I'd better avoid saying anything excessively encouraging about the state of the nation you've left behind. Not difficult, as it happens. Let's just say that the news from home is fine for us and only moderately disastrous for the country.

It has to be said that the horrors I felt it right to evoke in my first letter have yet to strike the country. To date we have not been bankrupted by a house price collapse, submerged in seawater, taken over by the BNP or terrorised into accepting Sharia law. We have, however, been forced into accepting Gordon Brown as Prime Minister. I saw a bit of him in the Commons and can confirm that he comes across better in private than in public. Hardly the best of recommendations, however, for a public man.

One piece of bad news for you and Catherine is that, officially, crime in London has fallen since you went, but don't be too depressed: nobody I know has felt any beneficial effects, and my hunch is that the figures will soar when people conclude that if the police have nothing much left to do, they might as well report the mugging, car theft or punch-up they didn't bother reporting before. On the positive side you may be grimly pleased to learn that, driving along the main road close to your old house the other day, I saw a police notice saying they would be grateful for information about a young man who brandished a gun at one of their officers in the vicinity. There were notices in the area like that before, but this one was on *your* side of the frontier. So on the personal security front, it seems like you got out just to time. The people who bought your house at a (let's face it) ludicrous price will be unlikely to share your pleasure. I don't suppose there's another city in the world outside London where people have to pay that kind of money for the privilege of living in an area where hoodlums go round flashing guns at the police.

More crime news for the recent emigrant: there has been a spate of black on black killings, and not too far away from you, in Hammersmith, a black teenager was stabbed to death in the street by a rival gang. Knife and gun troubles have so far been largely confined to South, East and North London, so the Western extension has the virtue of completeness, encircling the city in a ring of steel. To judge by what I saw Toronto sounds safer, though it seems a hell of a way to go for a little peace of mind.

*

Back from our visit, we did a sort of audit of your new life compared to London. Your Ontario existence is quite a contrast to the one you left behind. Having imagined you ending up in a modern apartment, we loved the old brick house with wooden trimmings in the Riverdale area – bigger than your London one and, at £220,000, less than half the cost. Not to speak of your country place at Muskoka: a healthily simple cottage, but with the swimming and boating and fishing on all those lakes, a cut above Ruislip Lido. Two houses instead of one, and enough cash left over to see you through till Catherine has had the baby and starts work, seems a fair rate of exchange for what you had.

It helped ease our loss a little to find you both so happy. Seeing Canada up close for a week or two also took some of the edge off my prejudices about its culture of non-alignment ("Why did the Canadian cross the street? To get to the middle of the road.") I can see why the children took a few months to settle into the new primary, and Billy and Sandra still seemed a bit timorous about it. Or perhaps it was seeing us that made them homesick. But after their first full summer at the cottage they'll shake off any nostalgia they feel for London.

School-wise their prospects are so much brighter than here. With nearly half of their classmates English-speaking Chinese, and some of the rest Indian, you'll get a good work ethic, and not so many linguistic problems. And it's good to hear that, when the time comes, they look set to get into the nearest state secondary. A city-centre school with no problem of drugs or knives – and that teaches Latin! – would have been off the radar here. Not having to worry any more about marauding gangs minutes from your home must be a huge relief. And despite what many a Canadian appears to think, to have America on your doorstep is a bonus. I don't know how easy it is for Canadians to get to the best universities over there, but perhaps that's looking too far ahead.

We were relieved you picked up an academic job so quickly, paying rather more than you got in the UK; it could hardly have been less. With taxes and the cost of living lower, financially you should feel more relaxed. And when Catherine comes to look for a job the English accent can still help, I gather.

The very fact of having less than half as many people as us (29 million) in a land many times bigger is good for the spirit, not to speak of car-parking. Even we felt the sense of self-expansion, in our brief stay. The ethnic population is about 14%, higher than here, but the Canadian mosaic (their US melting pot) works better, you tell me. Maybe that's because immigration is more selective. The points system they operate seems pretty rigorous, and it was only your chemistry qualifications, I suspect, that got you in so smartly. Also the ethnic pattern is quite different to here, with the Chinese the largest element, followed by Indians, and fewer ghettoes. As Catherine said, a strong secondary state system, such as we do not possess, is a key to integration.

We had a taste of the rigours of the climate, but that's part of the package, and they say it may get milder. And Toronto being 600 metres above sea level means that if the worst should happen it could be around longer than London.

*

It was good of you to agree to the idea of publishing my first letter to you as a book, with suitable adjustments to protect your privacy. Inevitably the main thing people picked up on was immigration, confirming that it remains a taboo subject, though my hopes of opening up adult debate have not been realised: the last thing most people wanted was a mature discussion. The way the TV and radio avoid it is the adversarial game. By structuring interviews to provoke a punch-up about race, rather than a cool examination of the facts, the BBC have perfected the art of non-debate.

My first opponent was a writer and broadcaster called Sarfraz Manzoor. A down-the-line political conformist of the kind you get in the arts, his basic position was that someone who had been a minister under Mrs Thatcher had no right to a view. The poor guy couldn't get over the fact that he was cheek by jowl with a political infidel who didn't share his artsworld views. These are very sheltered folk, who should meet more people. He put me in mind of a character in a Martin Amis novel who says he couldn't understand how Mrs Thatcher had become Prime Minister, because no one he knew had voted for her. It also recalled a moment during an election when I was canvassing on an estate in Milton Keynes, the roughest in my Buckingham patch. I knocked on one door and the woman who opened it took one look at me, blue rosette and all, opened her mouth in incredulity then bellowed to her husband: "'Come and look at this. It's a fuckin' Tory."

The political primitiveness of our intellectuals never ceases to astonish. In their work they are obliged to face up to opposing views on the basis of the evidence. On politics the majority rely on moral grandstanding, and decline to acquaint themselves with the facts. The results can be strange. I seem to recall Margaret Drabble coming up with the novel notion that everyone should be paid the same. Not even Stalin or Mao had thought of that, but then they'd never had their ears bent by an English lady novelist. Anyway I had a bit of fun with Manzoor. When he mentioned he was from a poor background I said something to the effect that we self-made folk should stick together. You should have seen his face.

Another non-discussion on BBC TV was with a young economist called Philippe Legrain. He's written a book advocating open frontiers, an idea so inane I was almost interested to meet him. He turned out to be a curiously distraught fellow, not unlike those weirdly intense ultra-Thatcherite right-wingers. When I asked how open frontiers would actually work he said everything would be fine provided we followed the Dutch example, by which I suppose he meant providing generous housing and social services for newcomers.

Flakier than this it does not come. Holland is a grossly overpopulated country where towns like Rotterdam are 50% ethnic. Its politics have been convulsed by an ugly backlash against immigration, a film-maker has been killed by crazed Islamic fundamentalists, and judges go about under armed guard. And here I am trying to have a rational discussion with someone arguing that we should see Holland as a model.

In short, the book had a wide exposure and no serious discussion. The BBC complains about the phoney adversarialism of the House of Commons, and does exactly the same itself. The difference in its eyes is that, whereas the MPs are indulging in yah-boo politics, the BBC are engaged in promoting "lively debate." The real purpose in both cases is problem-dodging, and immigration is top of the list of no-go subjects. A serious discussion would risk getting into the meat of the issue, and nobody wants that.

The whole business was a waste of time: heat-not-light, two-minutes-a-head exchanges where you just hoped no one you knew was listening. Doing them at all makes you feel a bit grubby, but publishers insist. While getting it in the neck from the modish left I was also receiving abusive emails from the BNP, accusing me of being what American racists used to call a "Nigger lover." Being attacked on both sides, by people who frequently deserve each other, has its comforts.

*

It's a poor augury for the BBC that the only place to go for an honest-to-God discussion is talk radio. The shows I did there were far more genuine, and a lot more fun. I'd done plenty of phone-in shows as an MP, but enjoyed these more, mainly because now I can now say what I think.

"You're drunk" James Whale, ebullient compère of TalkSport Radio, said to a burbling caller while I waited my turn. "Ring back when you've slept it off." I was me next. After James has made an introduction and I've had a say, it's Mark from Manchester making critical but balanced points against me, assisted by Whale, whose ability to vary the tone from narky to sober is impressive. While the ads were running James, the most British of blokes who tells me that he now lives half the time in France, because he finds life there more civilised.

Next up was an hour with Vanessa Felz. I'd never met her before and found her intellectual span as imposing as her physical girth, though she doesn't talk down to her customers or despise the lower middle classes.

Who that morning rang in in their hundreds. Vanessa told me later that they had enough calls to have gone on for another three hours. A tribute to her fearsome articulacy, certainly, but also to people's irritation at the queasy silence of politicians.

There's a lot of folk out there with plenty to say, though mostly it's not what you might think. In a total of nearly four hours at the talk-radio mike I don't recall a single racist remark, even crypto: a tribute not just to the efficiency of the loon-filterers they use, but to the sense of responsibility of the callers. Any of these people could have slipped in a poisoned comment, but none of them did. As someone who has heard a lot of vicious racial talk abroad, notably in Russia but also France and America, it was one of those moments when you regain your pride in being British.

The trouble is that responsibility about race is a form of English civility that is unlikely to survive if politicians and the media continue to disregard the difficulties mass immigration can create. For those living on the front line of race relations, as many callers clearly did, the problems can be stark. Like the melancholy-sounding Bolton man who was thinking of emigration but who couldn't sell his flat, because his neighbourhood had changed so drastically no one wanted to buy it. Or Joy from Nottingham, who said she was black and had a degree, but despaired of bringing up children in this country and was thinking of hopping it to Miami (having been there, I advised caution.)

Of course you come across people as daft as Legrain, such as the 5 Live compère who threw out the thought that frontiers were a thing of the past. Try running a health service when you don't know from one day to the next who's in the country, or for that matter M15, I felt obliged to respond. I hated hearing myself say it, on the other hand you're afraid that if you don't make these po-faced points, no one will. My fellow panellist that day was a comedian.

Some years ago Peter Lilly, a thoughtful fellow I've always rather liked, wrote a prescient pamphlet entitled *Too Much of a Good Thing*, and that was the tone of many a caller. Several factors, I would guess, contribute to this restraint. Living in closer proximity to migrants than the better-off, they see the human side, and their fears of "the other" can be allayed. Even if you're afraid your neighbourhood's hurtling downhill by the day it's hard to nurture a resentment of Poles or Pakistanis when you meet their kids along with your own every morning at the school gates. But it won't stop you worrying about your children's prospects when there's a Babel of languages in the playground, or Somalis dealing drugs round the corner.

At the posh end of the media scale, when you suggest that integration isn't going swimmingly, interviewers say you're being frightfully gloomy. Global warming isn't a heart-lifting topic either, I try not to reply, but that's hardly a reason for refusing to discuss it. Talk show callers are different. They don't say you're being pessimistic because they recognise the picture you're painting, and if they could think of the right place to go, a surprising number say they'd emigrate too.

The worst show I did was with a bishop. It was a Northern audience, people were ringing in saying they'd had their wages cut or lost their jobs due to immigration, yet my Man of God, brimful of spiritual conceit about being the immigrants' champion and protector, lacked the honesty to admit there might be some minuses amongst the pluses. In the circumstances I was quite restrained – a throwback to the days when you had a certain respect for bishops – till he said: "I don't suppose you've spent much time on council estates". It seemed a good moment to let him have it, so I did, my Dagenham lineage, the estates in my constituency, the lot. Normally I dislike doing this sort of thing, but this time I rather enjoyed it. I'm not sure His Grace did.

Why did I publish a book that was bound to cause me trouble in the first place? Partly I suspect because I spent years of my life in totalitarian countries, where simply to point to what you could see before your eyes was condemned as "a provocation", and I feared we were getting uncomfortably close to that state of mind here.

*

I'm glad you didn't hear my brush with the Bishop, it would have depressed you. Yet another institution dissolving before our eyes. Like me you're one of those agnostics who would like to see a Church of England they could respect, which is less and less the case. I remember being appalled at times as an MP by some of the people we are getting in vicarages, who increasingly look and sound like social workers, except that social workers can be of practical use. Listening to my bishop confirmed that the rot goes all the way up. I'm not surprised that church attendance has suffered a catastrophic slump, from 11% to 7% in a decade.

Rowan Williams looks set to get that figure down a couple of notches. He may be an accomplished scholar, but I see little evidence of his intellect where it counts – in practice. He was sold to us as a new force, yet all we hear from him is what we've heard from the Church for decades: that the Government should spend more and have a pacifist foreign policy. Pretty much every whiffly sermon and pronouncement you hear boils down to that. His predecessor, Carey, was not so erudite but more honest, and sounds increasingly good in retirement.

Williams has taken to bleating at politicians for being guided by expediency rather than ethics. This from the man who managed to go to Darfur without condemning the Sudanese government for its massacres. He's ready enough to put the boot into his own government for trying to build a democracy in Iraq and get rid of the Taliban, so Afghanistan isn't used as a terrorist base and its girls can go to school. But on genocide by Sudan – no comment. We know why, of course. He wasn't going to say anything critical of a Muslim state, even if it's Muslims who are doing the massacring, because he doesn't want to offend Islamic opinion in Britain. It wouldn't be expedient.

The man who wants to teach politicians how to do their jobs is himself making a historic hash of the politics of the Church of England, on the moral as well as the practical level. There's something equivocal about his position on homosexuality, which he has allowed to become the central issue of the Church. Whatever he says I don't actually believe he's a conservative on the issue, I think he's a closet liberal. Which he has every right to be – but why disguise it? Like you I take an open-minded view of the gay thing. In the end I simply don't understand how you can discriminate against practising homosexuals in the Church in the modern age.

I can see the sensitivities about holy writ, and people argue back and forth about what the Bible actually means. Yet the only question that matters is surely what the scriptures would have said if it had been known at the time that homosexuality is largely genetic? How Christian would it have been to deny them a sexuality that was God-given?

So why doesn't the Archbishop say what we all suspect he believes? Expediency. If he came clean the roof would fall in. First, there'd be an even bigger schism in the Church. Next (for reasons it would be inexpedient for me to discuss) the number of homosexuals in the Church – already not negligible – would grow way beyond the national average. This would impact on people's view of the Church, even amongst the young and modern-minded, and the pews would become emptier than ever.

The ethical course for the Archbishop would be to stand up for what we must assume he believes nevertheless. Or he could just resign, as ministers are constantly called upon to do. Instead he dodges and weaves like the politicians he so sanctimoniously condemns, though he gets away with it, because unlike them he's given an easy ride in the media.

I'm told he's writing a book on Dostoyevsky, no doubt about grand spiritual dilemmas. He might do better to concentrate on the hero of his most brilliant story, *The Man From Underground*. The opening line is the best of any book in the nineteenth century: "I'm a sick man, I'm an angry man, I'm not a pleasant man. I think there is something wrong with my liver." Imagine writing that in 1863. The hero is the mass man of the future, a narky little nobody who keeps raising awkward questions, to which no one can find an answer. It would do Williams good to get inside the head of this fellow. He's a sort of constituent from hell, the kind of person people involved in government, rather than just moralising about it, have to deal with.

*

I don't suppose you go out of your way to keep up with the political situation here. I can hardly summon the energy myself. First we're expected to get excited about Cameron, now we're supposed to be mesmerised by

Miliband. I suppose the media had to manufacture an artificial equivalent to the Tory boy, and more synthetic than Miliband they do not come. The bland aping the bland. It would be fun watching them going head to head, to convince us that, despite appearances to the contrary, their plans for a green and pleasant land are radically different. Whatever differences they are supposed to have I feel sure could be ironed out over a half of cider.

As well-brought up boys they could surely agree for example that the British should improve their manners and stop being so beastly to one another, as Cameron has taken to saying. Our television adman who till recently sold the lower orders pigswill for a living now expresses dismay at their porcine proclivities. Curious how nobody has picked up on this aspect of things.

Even socially the two Daves are convergent, because whatever his affectations of classlessness Miliband too is a child of privilege. Yes he went to a comprehensive, but Haverstock in London was rather a select one. Within handy reach of Hampstead, Primrose Hill and Belsize Park, it was patronised by the not noticeably impoverished sons and daughters of North London left-wing intellectuals, of which Miliband père, a distinguished Marxist professor at LSE, was one. Not that we should judge anyone by their fathers; let's just be grateful Miliband junior doesn't bang on about the dictatorship of the proletariat.

Haverstock was perfect for the kind of parents who were happy to send their children to comprehensives attended largely by the kids of people like themselves, then claim that this showed that the all-in system worked. No fault of their children of course, and I'm sure the school was very good. How else would Miliband have made it to Oxford? His social and political provenance can surely have played no part in his good fortune, any more than Cameron's.

Tony Benn's son Hilary, Minister for Overseas Development, who went to Holland Park Comprehensive, is a not dissimilar case. Curious how the Brits go on forming political dynasties, on the Left as well as the Right, in the twenty-first century. Sixty million people to choose from and it still comes down to a handful of parentally favoured folk. If this goes on we'll end up like the Americans, with the top job alternating between families, like the Clintons and the Bushes. With their royalist predilections, the Brits might like that.

Miliband's main problem, it seems to me, is his eerie normality. You sensed there must be something wrong with him, and sure enough there is. You know how it is when people are marked in your mind forever by one thing you hear about them? Well, whether he gets to be Prime Minister or not for me Miliband will always be the father of a surrogate child who nevertheless wanted to be present at the birth. That seems distinctly cooky, wouldn't you say?

Not that I'm against the principle – I was present for you and your brother, though not your sister, who was born in a hurry, in France, where they're less delicate about people's feelings. But whenever I see Miliband on the box all I can think of is that this is the man who insisted on watching a strange woman bringing his child into the world. No doubt the purpose was to establish a bond where none existed, though to me it sounds more like the action of an ambitious, and therefore robotically conformist, modern man. Catherine may say I'm betraying a lack of emotional intelligence. But whether it's Miliband with his surrogate pieties or Cameron playing on his poor child's disability, the words "cant" and "bullshit" are the first to come to mind.

So there you are. The Brown premiership has started under a cloud (no one much seems to want him in Number Ten outside his party, and the economy is beginning to look dickey), and the alternative leaders of the future give you little reason to hurry home. Catherine once accused me of being too ready to judge politicians by their personalities, but these two have given us precious little else to judge by. They don't shine very bright in the personality stakes either.

The distinguishing feature of the two most likely Prime Ministers after Brown is that they are both thought to be very nice, if somewhat lacking in character. But then so are their parties. To that extent our big political beasts of the future (the phrase doesn't quite work for them, does it?) seem a representative couple: which is to say people who would be more in place slugging it out for the premiership of Sweden, Norway or one of the German Länder.

*

Curious how the word "community", spoken in a sort of pietistic sigh, is becoming the mainstay of every discussion. Maybe it's because we sense it slipping away. Every day you come across evidence that our national and social cohesion are declining. The process of semi-detachment from their country and from society creeps up on people, stealthily. Wherever you look everything seems to be drifting apart from everything else. I'm not saying that things are falling apart – that would be over-doing it – just that there's a growing feeling of disconnection. The country is not disintegrating, but disaggregating: politically, socially and in people's private lives.

The Balkanisation of our existence is happening on a national scale. Scotland's falling off the top, self-sealing ethnic communities are proliferating in the Midlands, and London's got its own thing going at the bottom. It's London that's the truly awesome phenomenon. The prosperity we boast of is confined ever more to the capital and the South East – an island within our island. Maybe Margaret Thatcher was right about us being a bit like Hong Kong. The big city is where the big money and the overwhelming majority of people are, with more inflows of both promised, and the rest matters increasingly less by comparison. We should get used to thinking of the capital and its environs as a city state on the Hong Kong, or maybe Italian model. The way sea levels are rising we could end up as the Venice of the North.

Next to our crumbling sense of nationhood the most obvious disconnection – between the rich and the rest- is nothing new, though it seems to be growing. And unlike in the past the fate of those at the top is divorced from those lower down. When the housing ramp collapses, as we must assume it will, most of the falling masonry will hit the little guys in the middle and at the bottom. The top prices helped drive the entire market up but are less likely to fall when it comes down. At the multi-million end of the market they don't have mortgages, and with plenty more international entrepreneurs piling into London falling demand is not a risk.

One result of this insulation from other people's reality is that the rich will give an even smaller toss for the rest than before. There's no feeling that we're all in this together, and the fact that an increasing proportion of the seriously well-to-do come from abroad (see the latest rich list) is hardly likely to increase their sense of national community. I'm sure Roman Abramovitch is a kind-hearted, community-minded fellow, but how far does his sense of patriotism stretch beyond Chelsea stadium?

Financially and socially the divisions run from earliest youth to grim old age. The gap between the underclass and the sons and daughters of privilege has never been wider in modern times: more boys at Eton get five good GCSE, I've read, including maths and English, than in the entire borough of Hackney. And now there's another divide growing up: between those who have a decent pension to look forward to and those for whom longevity has become more a threat than a promise.

In our dislocated society everywhere you look new barriers are going up. The congestion charge is an example. It's hard for me to be against it because I'm lucky enough to live inside it, which means that for a couple of hundred a year I have the freedom of the city. The congestion charge is a kind of gated community on wheels: another way of sparing the comfortably off the pitfalls of modern life. What could be nicer than to have the hoi-polloi banned from driving into your territory on pain of an £8 fine, leaving you free to swan about your exclusive enclave undisturbed by the motoring masses?

It's ironic to see Livingstone clearing the roads of the Mondeos so as to free them up for the Jags to cruise. His anti-car vendetta has blinded him to this aspect of things. But to be fair to our depressingly low-grade mayor, which I am loathe to be, whoever was in his shoes would have had to do the same. In the end it's a matter of numbers, and in London the numbers are out of control. We used to laugh at the Japanese cramming people into the Tube in Tokyo, because it was undignified, inhuman behaviour, and as the psychologists will tell you we laugh when humans are robbed of their human attributes. But that's what you get in a crazily over-populated megalopolis: the individual becomes a thing rather than a person.

Then there's the widening gap between the married and unmarried, or rather those with children and those without. So much of our towns are now havens of hedonism for the money-flashing singles – clothes shops, cafes, cinemas, clubs and pubs – that they're pretty much out of bounds for the poor bloody infantry who keep procreation going. Everything is geared to the needs of the drinker and consumer and little to the couple with the buggy. Maybe it's one of the reasons married or cohabiting couples don't stay long together. Compared to the attractions of getting wasted every evening in clubs (for which they now have Royal sanction) or shopping the day away, bringing up kids can seem a drearily selfless way to spend one's life.

Not that I don't understand the instinct to prolong one's youth (I didn't marry till thirty), but the new tendency to delay having children as long as you can is part of the flight from responsibility. A French writer who has just died, Jean Baudrillard, put it wittily:

"People are almost astonished to have children. They are astonished to have to take charge of themselves. They haven't got the conviction for it, they are persuaded of nothing. They are even astonished to have a body."

(The last phrase is no joke. Discovering how many people felt no personal responsibility for their bodies, and wanted someone else to take charge of them – ie the government – was one of the many things I discovered as an MP.)

The coarsening of relationships between parents and children as the elderly insist on living on to an inconsiderate age is another aspect of our splintering society. Watching their inheritance dribble away year by year, when their parents have to pay for long-term institutional care while the children struggle with a mortgage, is not designed to promote family ties. The attitudes and emotions engendered can be ugly. Let's hope we never reach the position they have in the States, where "granny dumping" – leaving your aged grandmother anonymously at the hospital door – has become a problem.

Educationally we are disconnected as never before, as comprehensivisation has worked its magic. Instead of bringing children together it has divided them more than ever, as those who can escape the dead hand of institutionalised mediocrity and a lifetime of ignorance. (A third of the British apparently believe that Hadrian's Wall is in China, and that the Romans built Stone Henge.) The result of our neurotically anti-selective system is that children get graded meticulously, like so much fruit, into public and private schools, church and state, Muslim and Christian, comprehensive and grammar, town and county, poor and marginally less poor, and (increasingly) into black and white. When you sacrifice selection by aptitude and ability to old-fashioned concepts of class, which is what comprehensives are about, race, religion, money and social contacts enter in, and you end up more segmented than before.

On top of all this (or underlying it perhaps) is the growing disconnection between politics and the people. This would be easier to understand if our politicians were a bunch of corrupt second-raters, but actually they're not. At least not corrupt. (Sorry, that's too flip: I saw plenty of good people on all sides of the Commons, though many were damaged by the system: dumbing down operates in Parliament too). I said in my first letter that when the political function was shrivelling it was natural that politicians should shrink with it, but I didn't mean to Lilliputian stature.

Take Livingstone. Everyone treats him as if he's the duly elected Mayor of London, and the people's choice. In fact 87% of Londoners did not vote for him. The turnout in the 2,000 election was piddling, so the support of 13% was enough to give him power. On the basis of which he gets to regale us with his public-bar politics. Try to imagine the head of any other major city stating that Mao Zedung's revolution was worthwhile if only because it did away with the practise of foot-binding. Since the Chairman was responsible for the death of 70 million people, actually it did away not just with foot-binding, but with 140 million feet.

Extraordinary is think no one can find a candidate to replace him. You'll be horrified to learn that the Tories conspired to get Greg Dyke to stand. I can see the affinity. Apart from the television link, Dyke's social affectations – he was the son of middle class parents who began putting on the proly style at grammar school, and never stopped – would be another recommendation to iPod man.

Politics or parenting, schools or Scotland, wherever you look not much seems to be holding together. People live side by side yet separately, in mental isolation, with their eyes fixed warily on one another. When communities, races, classes and families become splintered and segregated to the degree they have, feelings of social solidarity erode. Society ends up like a shattered windscreen: holding together by the grace of God, even though it's all cracked to hell, so no-one has any idea where they're going.

*

The more fractured society becomes the greater our pretence of togetherness, to cover it up. That's why everyone nowadays is an anti-elitist. The old elites had the virtue of honesty, making no secret of their desire to live as far from the madding masses as they could. Now it's a Dutch auction between toffs and chavs to see how low they can go in public behaviour. The government's enthusiasm for mass events is another sign of the bread and circuses approach to social integration. The Dome was a succulent case in point. Next up in the synthetic manufacture of a national spirit, the Olympics.

Forcing new developments to include 40% affordable housing is another attempt to promote social inclusiveness by artificial means. Here's a bit of social engineering it will be fun to watch. "Balanced communities" they call it, with low-cost places for essential workers and people on housing lists, side by side with the well-off. To the extent that it aspires to enable nurses and firemen and so on to meet and mingle harmoniously with City bankers and wealthy retirees it sounds idyllic. But as you know from personal experience, you can't re-invent village life in urban communities riven by every sort of social apartheid.

A tower block I know of that's under construction is going to have 400 flats, 160 council and 240 private. The council folk will pay way below market rents. The private flats will nudge £1,000 a square foot – a million for a decent-sized, two bedroom apartment. How realistic is this? There's no lack of people who will be happy to be housed next to luxury flats, though you might wonder who in the real world will cough up a million to live next door to council tenants? A shockingly prejudiced thought, but that's how people are.

Think of it. A single great block of flats where the private lot will be on £100,000 a year (more if both work) and the others on a fifth of that figure. Imagine their different circumstances. The private types will educate their children independently, the council lot will go to the nearest, probably lousy, school. Statistically the private lot will be more likely to be married, while the council tenants will include many a single parent family, with foreseeable consequences for teenage behaviour. A model of social and racial integration? I wouldn't want to be around when the two groups meet in the lifts. One knifing in the car park and the million pound boys will be out of there, pronto, nursing massive losses.

Too cynical Catherine may say, but I don't think so. The danger of an unreal approach to society is that, like all idealism that goes sour, it will leave mayhem in its wake. Think of Sixties tower blocks. Are we saying that, provided you throw in some high-earners, this time everything will be sweetness and light? Where the income gap is not too wide, and the kids are schooled together, here and there I suppose it could work. At the more exclusive end of the scale (some of the schemes have flats selling for £2-3 million) the chances are that many owners are going to be flush and foreign. In my experience the social conscience of rich foreigners (Russians, Iranians) is somewhat less delicate than our own, and I don't see them palling up too easily with their less affluent neighbours. On the other hand if the loaded foreigners are high-class crooks (it happens), and enough of the council tenants likewise disposed, together they could engender integrated, self-sustaining communities, of a kind quite unintended.

Whichever way it goes, this is a strange society we are building.

*

All this false togetherness is one of the reasons authority is so keen on pop concerts, especially of the Bono and Geldof variety. Here is a chance for young people of all backgrounds to come together and emote about poverty while spending enough money getting stoned to keep an African child at school for a year. If our youth are genuinely conscience-stricken about Africa, how about a little personal sacrifice? Not just a one-off, feel-good concert ticket, but a continuing contribution. Think how many hungry mouths a ten percent levy on CD sales and downloads of popular music would feed. (I tried the idea once in a letter to a national newspaper, by the way, for a laugh. The result? You got it – silence.)

Our selfless youth prefer to show their support for the needy and afflicted by gathering in their tens of thousands to have a bloody good time, delighting in music whose lyrics proclaim self-indulgence of all descriptions as the ultimate virtue. And before Catherine says "your dad's getting old" let me add that it's not the sex or the booze I mind, or even the music. What sticks in the craw is the smarmy moralism.

But then these are the morals of the pop-stars they revere: the multi-millionaire models of flamboyant consumption, most of whom – and here's the nice part – hire top accountants to use every wheeze in the book to avoid paying taxes. The result is that low-income folk contribute more to the aid budget for Africa than them. All they do is go on jaunts and preach about it. The only aspect of their behaviour that is morally consistent is when they demand, against all professional advice, that Western help should not be linked to levels of corruption in the African countries in question. Never mind that Frederick Chiluba, a former President of Zambia, where people live on 50p a day, siphoned off £23 million from an aid-supported budget, mainly to buy clothes. Given the mores of the pop industry, there's a logic there. I mean a guy's gotta have his gear, right?

*

Another way to cover up the social and ethnic cracks in society is propaganda, and Livingstone, nostalgic for old-style Russia in the way others used to be for George Formby or Gracie Fields, is onto it. When I lived there everywhere you turned giant billboards depicted grinning workers linking hands in celebration of the unity of the Soviet nationalities, and I feel something similar coming on here. Posters saying "London is one" have begun appearing, and the Olympics will bring more of the same. Already we are promised new statues marking the main entrances to the city, no doubt depicting heroes and heroines of labour from all continents and races, though hedge-fund managers are unlikely to feature, even if they are Asian. The principle propaganda works on is of course that, whatever it says, the opposite is the case. That's why they need the propaganda. I do not have to remind you that, in Russia as in the Balkans, as soon as communism collapsed the posters came down they fell to murdering one another.

The way to avoid all this social fractiousness and the phoney bonhomie that goes with it is simple: be rich. Then you can flash those beneath you a benign, ingratiating smile – and have as little as possible to do with them. (It was the great Tocqueville, you remember, who said: "The French look up in anxiety. The English look down in satisfaction.") For those doing well out of New Britain PLC, barring a major terrorist incident I don't see how things can change. The problem is that for those lower down, ie the majority, I don't see how they can change either.

So we must expect the splits and cracks and social fissures to proliferate. Which leaves people your age with three choices: resign yourself to a life in a perilously fractured community, get rich – or do as you have done and get out.

*

One way to avoid disturbing reflections about the future is to stop thinking about it, and enjoy what you've got. I have no complaints about my own situation whatever, and am free to live, within reason, where and how I like. So why should I bother? After I'd gone on about the problems of our universities when I was minister an American I knew once said "George, you take too much responsibility for things." After 37 years in public service it's hard to stop, but I'm learning.

A country with demagogic leaders and an exploding population is due to suffer increasingly from the physical, psychological and cultural effects of massification, few of which will affect me. So why should I care? Most of the comfortably-off people I know confine their devotion to the public weal to caring noises over dinner. They have tacitly written off a society with which they have increasingly less in common. It would be easy to do the same.

The answer to "why should I care?" can no longer be "because there's a lot to care about." A hundred years ago you could get exercised about the lack of sanitation, or inadequate schools for the poor. Now Gordon Brown spends billions, with the result that you still risk dying in dirty hospitals or having a child stabbed at school. Not a huge incentive for the comfortable classes to get more involved, is it, unless of course they're Cameronian careerists. Now people can claim they are paying their taxes and off-load their social consciences onto the state. And if the state can't make a go of it, well tough luck on the masses.

This is a new, caring brand of social selfishness. A kind of "Sod you Jack, I'm all right" with heart. *"I do care about you, Jack my boy, really I do, your schools and your health and things. It's just that it's all getting a bit hopeless, isn't it, the way billions are spent with so little to show. Personally speaking I'm on a bit of a roll, so sod it. Not sod you personally, you understand, Jack my friend, but it."*

*

We were reflecting the other day on the spaciousness of your Ontario life, after seeing some official report about noise pollution and so on here. Even the rich aren't immune. A friend of ours, an American who's made a bit of money writing and was attracted by the lure of London, bought himself a two million plus house here and a modest country pile. For a year he and his family lived happily. Then somebody richer than him bought the two houses next door and began knocking them into one: thirty-five foot basement swimming pool, cinema room, the whole show. That was nearly two years ago, and the agony continues.

Next he discovered that a new council estate in all but name, complete with high rise flats, was being planned a few minutes from his house. Which might have been tolerable, except that at the same time he read that a flight path for the new Heathrow runway was planned to run pretty much directly over his street. Still, there was always the country house, where he could write in peace. Except that the farmer next door to him has just sold off his livestock, which didn't pay, and set up in the light manufacturing business, which does. Though only because he employs a transient labour force of thirty Rumanians and Bulgarians who are housed in caravans a hundred yards from my friend's house. Estimable workers, but who like their drink strong and their music loud.

So my millionaire is besieged: in his London house by excavators digging out the next door basement; by the promise of 1,000 new residents as near neighbours in a couple of years; by the threat of incessant noise from the skies; and by factory noises in the country. "Seems to me like you just shrunk your country" my long-suffering friend said to me the other day. "The only time I'm gonna get a moment's peace and quiet is commuting on the motorway."

Personally I'm unsettled if things get too quiet (the wife of Thomas Carlyle, I remember reading, almost went mad living in a place in Scotland where all she could hear was the sound of grazing sheep), but that is no longer a problem in Britain. I'm amazed at people's infinite capacity for decibel absorption. When we flinch at the amplification in the cinema Sarah says it's not because we're getting old, but that we belong to an intermediate generation. Younger folk don't mind so much because their hearing has been irreversibly damaged by 20, so they don't take in half of it. As for the elderly, they're deaf anyway. (It's odd how you can find yourself shouting in the ears of people half your age, as well as in those of the not-long-to-be-with-us.) So it's mainly people in their fifties or sixties, like us, too old to have had their ears coarsened by Walkmen and so forth and too young to be naturally hard-of-hearing that suffer. Never mind. If she's right soon every generation will have impaired hearing, so it's a self-rectifying problem. I must remember to tell my American friend that. It'll cheer him up.

*

Scene at a newsagents one Sunday. Behind the counter, instead of the usual smart young Pakistani, his uncle: an older, slobby-looking, loquacious fellow. Before him stands a customer who has bought *The Sunday Telegraph*. Dapper, a polite sort of person, he's keen to get away, but the slob is pointing to a headline about the Iranians building nuclear weapons.

"Why is there such big fuss? Israel has weapon and no one gives a damn. What is difference? You tell me, what difference?"

"Absolutely" The polite class of person smiles, and begins shrinking away. "It's six of one, isn't it?"

The slob will never know the difference between a democracy and a semi-crazed President responsible to a self-appointed council of mullahs, because nobody will dare tell him, certainly not the Brits. Will his young nephew? All this shrinking away. Similar thoughts a week later when I read that the US Embassy, which has been in Grosvenor Square for half a century, is moving because authority has decided it's indefensible against terrorism. The resignation is amazing. What is this place going to be in ten years time, downtown Beirut?

*

For reasons that sound embarrassingly close to yours, your brother tells me he's thinking of moving house. To date he's suffered no personal injury, but others nearby have. You know what he's like – totally frank about these things. He says he's enjoyed his rangy, post-student life but is wearying of the endless vigilance needed to live where he does and is looking for something in a more wholesome area (my word, not his).

Prodded by Sarah I went to a couple of estate agents on his behalf. The first one shrugged and said they had nothing.

"Can I leave my particulars?"

"If you wish, Sir." Another shrug.

I didn't bother. The next one – a sub-blond, sub-Chelsea and rather substantial lady pretty much waved me away on sight, but deigned to ask how much I had in mind. In today's market there's nothing more humiliating than saying you are looking for a one bedroom flat on behalf of your son or daughter. The closed eyes, the incipient smirk, the shake of the head when you mention a figure.

"Is it worthwhile…" I gesture at her desk "Registering?"

"We've nothing at the moment."

"Maybe I can leave you my…"

"No need". She hands me a card. "You can always phone."

In the property business the power structure has been inverted. It's the revenge of the estate agent. Now they behave like impoverished relations who've come into money. Suddenly, they don't want to know you. I'm not sure which is worse: the low, insinuating agent or the same person in insolent mode, who unless you have a place to sell for two plus million, or the money in cash to buy it, pretty much tells you to bugger off. There is something horribly symbolic about how these odious creatures have suddenly got the upper hand.

At one place I was honoured with a viewing, along with half a dozen others, who could scarcely fit into the exiguous, over-priced top-floor flat. They all seemed to be buy-to-let merchants, of the kind where you wouldn't want to get behind with the rent. The sight of them reminded me of the time I used to thunder away in Parliament and the press about Britain's over-priced housing, and how the solution lay in a bigger rented sector. Now I see the landlords I'm not so sure.

The flat-hunting has stopped. As your brother has no doubt told you, after wondering whether you were doing the right thing by emigrating, he's thinking of volunteering to work abroad for a stretch himself. As an IT guy and linguist he is infinitely mobile. Another reason is that in Europe (where he'll probably end up) he can buy a nice place for a sensible price that will grow instead of something ludicrously inflated that could collapse in value here. Finally, he just wants new experiences. Where will this end, I sometimes wonder? With both of you gone and us travelling more for a lot of the year, soon it'll only be your sister holding the fort in Blighty.

I suppose we're following the trend. The number of people we know who have bought something abroad and calculate the days they spend in this country hour by hour, so as to ensure they get the best tax deal, is growing apace. Next thing they'll be changing their nationality so as to qualify for non dom (not domiciled here) status, the most favourable tax deal of all, where you only pay out on UK income and not in foreign earnings. To hell with the country, it's the tax regime that matters.

*

It's so long since we saw one another I can't remember whether I told you what a great trip we had to Paris for the presidential elections. It was the first time we'd been since you decamped to Canada rather than France, and of course we kept wondering if you'd chosen the right place. The sense of a different world begins on the Eurostar train. Everything works smoothly, your fellow passengers (half of them Japanese) are ultra-polite, and you notice the absence of the yob factor you increasingly see on planes. Why would a yob go to Paris?

The place was at its glorious best in the Spring sun. It being a Sunday people were lounging on the river bank or sprawled in squares. The Place des Vosges in the Marais, where your mother parked me to read the papers while she combed the shops, was packed – the one thing Paris lacks is green space – and I found myself examining them with a sociological eye. In Britain we run a mile at the sight of people in the mass. They can be so wilfully slobby, with their more-down-dressed-than-thou outfits, their outdoor beers and radios, and their sense of collective grunge.

In the Marais a quartet played classical music while people lounged about decorously. Maybe it was me idealising the scene, but the flesh of those who had half stripped off in the sun seemed less offensive than the English equivalent, mainly because there was less of it. Obesity is on the increase in France too, though not so fast as in Britain, where an epidemic would be a catastrophe: unlike America there just isn't the space. Think of those millions squelching against one another. Even the French kids played without screaming – a product of their less indulgent upbringing.

I know it's not the suburbs, where the minorities live and which I have also seen, and I realise that about twenty percent of the youngsters in that square would be out of work. So there's a limit to what conclusions. Also Paris has become a museumified city, too perfect to be entirely human. In gaining respectability it has lost some flavour and become a deodorised city. When we lived there in the seventies it was more spontaneous, more messily attractive, more alive.

Even the politics are fairly decorous compared with ours. The only thing messy about France are its finances. We had a drink with your brother's old school friend Joseph, who is the French problem in a nut-shell. He's still got no job since he lost the one he had two years ago, but since he's being paid 80% of his salary I got the impression he wasn't trying too hard. About seventy percent of the French have it all sewn up. The rest enjoy a cornucopia of benefits, and the quality of life is way above our own. It's just that I don't see how it can last, and Sarkozy is discovering how hard it is to do anything about it: the people who go on about the need for change, which is most of the country, will be the first on the streets if their sectional interests are touched.

Maybe the British experience is relevant? The only way we got out of our rut in the seventies was by a general collapse – the three day week under Heath and the slide into trade union government that gave Thatcher her mandate. For the moment things are not that bad in France, yet the country has a sunset feeling. Sweet as life can be for a lot of people in the present I don't see the future, and neither do they. The blocked society, it has been called, for good reason.

The Brits by contrast are bubbling away on the surface but dammed up underneath, notably in terms of social mobility. Never forget that French productivity is higher then ours, largely because of education. As with Sarkozy I suspect it will take an immigrant who's made his own way up to call the place to order, and dyno-rod the blockages. The trouble is that in Britain he or she would be seduced into adopting a patrician style well before they got to the top, and develop a fondness for the status quo, certainly if they were a Tory.

Britain faces massive risks, but at least it's got a sense of dynamism.

For years France has been in elegant decline, a beautiful country illuminated by an evening glow. Maybe the Hungarian immigrant can change it, perhaps he can't. It would have been lovely to have you all just across the water, within a few hours reach, and a wonderful excuse for us to spend more time there. But I think Catherine was right to incline you towards Canada.

*

You may remember that for years I've suffered from that irritating condition, Dupuytren's contracture (the diagnostic was by a Frenchman of that name), or claw-hand in its less distinguished appellation, because the fingers contract one by one until they look like one. I say "sufferer" but there's no pain, it's just a bloody nuisance, not least because after you've had an operation for one finger it starts on another. I've had two, one on the NHS and the other private. The £1,500 was worth it: I didn't fancy going into hospital for a minor, overnight operation, catching MRSA and coming out dead, as thousands are now doing.

The first time I had it done and turned up in the Commons with an arm in a sling, in an unprecedented abandonment of his principles (he doesn't talk to Tories) Dennis Skinner asked me what was the problem – then turned my reply into a class issue. When I said it was claw-hand he refused to believe it, on the grounds that only miners suffered from that. (Actually it's hereditary, especially if you're from the West of Scotland, which a strain of our family is). Anyway another damned finger began curling last year, so I went to my NHS doctor and saw a consultant – after a wait – who said he doubted whether it was worth another operation, but to come back in sixth months to see how it was progressing. Meanwhile I read that the French had developed a miracle cure. So thanks to them and none at all to the NHS thirty years aggravation was fixed while we were in Paris in a single afternoon, for the sum of about £60, with no pain, no anaesthetic, no hospital operation, and no maddening arm in a sling.

In the MOD there is a syndrome known as NIH – not invented here – which debars them from adopting military technology developed abroad, until they're forced. The same petty chauvinism would appear to operate in the NHS. None of those doctors or specialists I saw mentioned anything about the French cure, but then if you have the best health service in the world, which officially we have, we need have no truck with lesser breeds.

Margaret Thatcher told me she was a fellow sufferer from Dupuytren's: I don't recall her thinking it funny when I said she had a French disease, and I don't suppose she could face the indignity of admitting that it is the French who have come up with a cure, still less of going there to have it fixed.

*

On the political front, still nothing to report. Both parties jabber on about facing the future, but actually both of them are straining backwards. Deep in his tormented soul Brown remains torn between old Labour moralism and modern economics, and under a modish veneer the Tories continue to revert to the patrician era. (There was a lovely picture in the paper the other day of Boris Johnson and Cameron clowning about, electioneering. Such japes, what?) I've just learnt that Cameron has a picture of Harold Macmillan in his office, which is no accident. Politically they belong to the same tribe. Everyone loved the old fraud, though actually he was something of a disaster: a master of inactivity of a kind that turns out to be less masterful than everyone liked to think.

I met him a couple of times, and on both occasions he behaved like an actor from an Edwardian play, maybe Harley Granville Barker. The first time was when I was called to the Prime Minister's table to interpret at a lunch he was giving for the Soviet minister of culture, a ghastly old dragoness called Mme Furtseva. The way he showed her round Number 10 afterwards, waving a hand languorously at this or that antique painting, as if they were family portraits, seemed calculated to imply that the old place had been in the family since God knows when.

The second time was with Lord Carrington years later, at the twenty-fifth anniversary of the Austrian State Treaty which Macmillan had signed. By then he was far gone in his actorly affectations, and enjoyed playing the old man, leaning on a stick you suspect he may not have needed and chuntering away, reminiscing. He was an amusing talker, even if his wit was of the dated variety. We were having a nightcap and Harold was swilling his whisky round his glass, doing his grandfather walrus impersonation. We got talking about the American Secretary of State, Ed Muskie, who was in town.

"Muskie, Muskie…Sounds like something from the tundra… Isn't that the fellow who cried at a press conference when somebody said his wife was a drunkard?... I can't imagine why. If someone said to be, Mr Macmillan, your wife is a drunkard, I would have replied, well you say that, but you never met her mother…"

Cameron is a bit of an actor too, though one with a limited repertoire of two expressions: the gaping political grin, and the look of wrinkle-browed sincerity. And whereas Macmillan played up to middle class nostalgia, Cameron plays down to (supposedly) classless youth. Macmillan went in for superior unconcern, Cameron's pseudo-sincerity is the opposite, but it comes to the same thing in the end. Playing at being something they're not, I sometimes think, is second nature to the Brits. That's why we have the best actors. For the same reasons (as the Indian writer Nirad C. Chaudhuri once observed) in England it is impossible to know who is intelligent and who isn't: the clever ones disguise it and the thick ones have an impermeable coating of self-confidence.

There are times when I think the entire country is acting something out, to escape reality. Everyone behaves as if we were richer than we are, by running up massive debts. We still play at empire (Blair in Iraq, Brown undertaking to cure world poverty) while minimising our own problems ("a few domestic troubles, dear boy" as Supermac would have said.) And all the time, as under Macmillan, huge problems are building up, and solutions deferred. The wisdom of doing nothing, the virtue of inaction, is an old British game, when most of the time it's because no one can think what the hell to do, or if they can, no one will dare do it.

Our national theatre benefits from an indulgent audience. I'm always struck when I travel by how few people hate us. The Americans, the

French, the Chinese, the Russians – it's enough to mention them for someone to go into a spasm. But not the Brits. They still think we stand for something, and they're right, we do, however hard it is becoming to say exactly what it is. A sort of ultimate decency I suppose. But then foreigners can be wildly out of date on the New Britain. A French-Canadian friend (no one you know), one of the most sophisticated and widely travelled people I have met, who has lived in Britain, said something recently that revealed he hadn't a clue what the New Britain is about.

We'd been at a conference together where one of the speakers, a distinguished academic, happened to be a Sir. Afterwards my friend was full of amazement at the fact that the fellow, a man on whose shoulder the Queen's sword had lightly rested, had been dressed in a denim jacket. I found myself explaining that inverted snobbery, once no more than a fad, had become the essence of contemporary Britain. The entire ruling class – by which I don't mean aristos and the like, but the largely middle-to-upper-middle class folk in charge of the media, politics, the arts and the City – take every opportunity to climb into their jeans and prate away about the Arctic Monkeys. Between them they constitute an interconnecting elite whose power and money come from playing down to the masses while keeping themselves and their children at arms length from them.

I shouldn't have been surprised by my friend's naivety. The Brits put on a good performance, so good that they themselves are easily taken in. We are creatures of convention and a new elite playing proletarian games has become the basis of our culture. Phoney to the gills it may be, but as my Canadian friend shows, it works. The problem comes when the acting becomes infinitely better than the play.

*

I can't say the nation's international status has improved since your departure, except in the eyes of private finance operators with an eye to acquiring what remains of our most prestigious firms, Boots being the latest. Of the many nationally demeaning incidents since you left the Iranian hostage incident and Prince Harry's retreat from Iraq are the most dispiriting. And that's leaving aside the cricket.

You told me the Iran kidnapping affair had made a poor impression in Canada, and I can see why. The whole thing is a nasty blow to our psychology – a miniature Suez, except that this time we were the victims of aggression who nevertheless managed to come off worst in public opinion. It wasn't too clever of us to make Gamel Abdel Nasser a hero over the Suez crisis, but to make an atavistic loon like Ahmadinejad look like a statesman takes genius. What could be less in tune with the British ethos than for the MOD to allow soldiers to sell their stories? What has happened to the British sense of dignity and proportion? How have we become such a twitchy, skittish, PR sodden, unstable race?

On Harry, everyone has missed the point, which is why the absurd undertaking to go to Iraq was ever given? His presence was always going to attract a swarm of religious maniacs and killers, to himself and his men. But then his men were never the primary consideration. From start to finish the whole business has been a fantasy, arising from the sentimental myth that the Royal family are just like everyone else. The Prince's problem over Iraq began with Shakespeare's Henry V, which amongst other things explains why Harry is called what he is.

In the play not only does the King lead his men to victory, he cares for them. That's why he goes from one to another on the eve of battle to bolster their spirits – "A little touch of Harry in the night" in the play's lovely words. And so we get Prince Harry heading for Iraq. When historical fantasy collides with modern reality the result is national humiliation. The powers that be, having made a big thing of him sticking with his men, are understandably too afraid to allow him to leave these shores. No shame should accrue to the poor lad, but every condemnation should be heaped onto the heads of his advisers for playing the game of populist ingratiation.

The main shame is borne by the British people as a whole. Hence your feelings when a Quebecois ribbed you about how King Harry today would never have made it to Agincourt. Coming after the Iran hostages it all helps to punch a hole clean through Blair's universalist pretensions. For all the high-toned rubbish written about him being no more than a simple soldier, Harry could not, in the event, go to Iraq. And for all our international activism, whether it's Blair in Iraq or Brown on aid the British cannot, when it comes down to it, sort out the world single-handed.

*

Not a good day for your mother yesterday. First she had to spend it attempting to rescue an Old Master that had been badly restored in the Sixties, in the brisk, Anglo-American fashion, so as to make it look like new. Attempting to resuscitate a ruined masterpiece is a dispiriting process. This lowering experience was not improved when she took a bus home. In Ladbroke Grove three girls aged between 16-18 tried to board. They were South Americans she thinks, but so completely anglicised they'd got themselves roaring, or rather squealing drunk. Toting bottles of vodka and plastic cups they pressed onto the platform, but the Bangladeshi driver stalwartly refused to allow them to board. (One of those occasions where a bit of Muslim principle does not come amiss.) Anyway the bus was held up for twenty minutes while the girls blocked the doors, laughing and screaming obscenities in their newly acquired Essex accents. The point of the story is that during all this little drama not a single one of the weary rush-hour passengers said a word. The great British public held hostage by a trio of sozzled teenage girls.

*

We had a great break in New York not long ago. We went because Sarah had something to look at something at Sothebys over there, and I had a few people to see, notably George Soros, on whom I planned to write something. We'd got to know him, you may remember, before he broke the Bank of England. His wife was a Whistler specialist, Sarah had restored *The Mother* for the Louvre, and George shared my interest in Russia.

Too busy enjoying New York, in the event I didn't get round to writing anything, yet sitting there in his New York office with a surreal view of the whole of Central Park, one of the things he said struck me. We were talking about the eclipse of New York by London. The main reason London was winning out as a financial centre, in his view, was that it had lowered its standards to get the business. He was especially scathing about the City agreeing to float dodgy Russian firms on the Stock Exchange, but there were other instances of increasing laxity. Eventually, he thought, we would pay the price.

Given that the City is the source of so much of our GNP, no joy there. But then George was not in a joy-dispensing mood. He was profoundly gloomy about America, which he felt had lost ground in recent years that, ground that, with the rise of China, it could never make up. On his analysis the Anglo-Saxons looked like going down together. If George turns out to be right (and I'm not sure I agree with him) and countries like China, Russia and Iran gain in influence (the Indians worry me less), all I can say is God help the world. At that point I can think of a lot of people, particularly in Europe, who'll pray for the Yanks' return, complete with poodles.

New York seems more and more charmingly old-fashioned, but they do old-fashioned well. We went to the Village Vanguard (the Thirties jazz club where Miles Davis recorded *Birth of the Cool* with Gill Evans) fearing the worst, but there was nothing phonily antique about it. You know I prefer America to Canada, and we found ourselves thinking, once more, whether it would have worked for you, but there's no point in going over that ground again. In the end its'a matter of temperament. I could live there, and so I think could Sarah. But I don't see you being at home there, and certainly not Catherine. In Canada the British echoes are more pronounced.

I was sorry our planned flit to Toronto for a second visit collapsed. Having reached 70 degrees two days before (and this was March!) the temperature dropped to sub-zero, and we couldn't get out of Newark airport. Too much ice to get off too many planes, so they just gave up. These extremes of temperature are amazing: like everything else in America, even the weather is over-engineered. And to think this is *before* God's environmental anger really kicks in.

*

When we were over with you we talked about the security position in Canada. You told me there'd been some arrests, but the main risk was of Canada being used as a base for attacks on the USA. However you rate the threat you're certainly safer there than here. In my first letter I suggested we were likely to live in the shadow of Islamic terrorism into the indefinite future. Events since then have more than borne me out. Within one year three plots have been revealed or come to court: to bring down several planes taking off from Heathrow, to murder huge numbers of people at a nightclub or shopping mall, and plans for radiation attacks. Any one of these would have been devastating, and the effect on the country's morale appalling.

Yet the mood is still one of evasion. Anything rather than confront the truth. Until Dhiren Barot, the leader of the radiation plot, was caught and sentenced, it was the fashion amongst sophisticated folk to deride the nuclear risk. Alternatively it was said that if it ever happened it would be retribution for Iraq, and therefore the fault of Tony Blair. The fact that Barot began his plans *before* we went into Iraq is rarely mentioned. Another myth that has hit the dust after these trials is the view that the guilt is ours for alienating Muslims to the point where they have no alternative but to blow up themselves and us. Most of those involved in these murderous schemes were actually young Britons who by no stretch of the imagination were marginalised or deprived.

This determination to pin the blame on ourselves reached a pathological level over the fertiliser plot. It's weird when the criticism of those who aim to massacre us is less than of those trying to defend us. This is an update of the Stockholm syndrome. In that case the victims begin by fearing for their lives and end up excusing their kidnappers and identifying with their cause. In the case of Islamic terrorism we are so apprehensive of a threat to which we rightly see no end, and so afraid of antagonising the Muslim community from whence the terrorists spring, that we turn our anger on our defenders rather than them.

Much of the public discussion has ceased to make sense, and in this irrational climate M15 cannot win. People have begun demanding a level of protection that can only exist in totalitarian societies: the Stasi and the KGB would have fixed the terrorists good, in short order. If the security services slip up – as occasionally in a democracy they are bound to – they are branded as criminally incompetent on Newsnight. The most likely reason for errors is because M15 are overwhelmed. Yet if the security services were expanded as much as they should be, their operations beefed up and their surveillance increased, watch out for Newsnight programmes claiming it is the beginning of the end of our human rights, and that picking on Muslims will alienate the community further. Then the guilt for the atrocities would be safely back where it belongs – with us.

American security experts with whom I've discussed these things say the arrests show that M15 is doing a good job. Within the limits imposed on its resources and behaviour, I suspect it is. But there's another interpretation of this sudden batch of arrests and trials: that there is a profusion of plots so great that some are bound to be discovered, and that these are only the ones we happened upon by good luck. The law of averages suggests the terrorists will get through. That is the *sotto voce* message I'm hearing from the authorities, and given the enormity of the kind of attacks that have come to light, one is all it takes.

The heart of the matter is the nature of the enemy. It's curious, is it not, how people are quite ready to say that the reputation of the Christian Churches will suffer (as it should) because of their appalling record over paedophile priests, while going out of their way to avoid suggesting that plots for mass murder by Muslim extremists cast any shadow on Islam. But then if the attacks are somehow seen as our fault in the first place, it makes a kind of crazy sense. All this nonsense shows that even failed attacks succeed in destabilising society by promoting an atmosphere of irrationality, dissent and self-recrimination.

You do not normally turn to novelists for sanity on these matters, at least not British novelists, but Martin Amis is an exception. After returning from a stay abroad and taking part in *Question Time,* whose panellists and audiences can mostly be relied on to swallow the "we are all guilty" line, he wrote:

"People of liberal sympathies, stupefied by relativism, have become the apologists for a creedal wave that is racist, mysogynist, homophobic, imperialist and genocidal. To put it another way, they are up the backside of those who want us dead."

*

Another of those surveys that tell you who are the happiest countries. We used to be well up the scale of the satisfied, but now we're slipping, it appears, and grumbling more. "Trust in society" is apparently a key factor in how happy you are, and there's certainly been a decline there. Emigration, by the way, is apparently no cure for unhappiness, according to this study, since it's indigenous people who tend to be most contented. At this point they lost me. What happens when the indigenous people become less happy because of the strains of immigration, and the immigrants are equally discontented because they're not natives and can face discrimination?

The real reason to distrust these studies however is because the countries who tend to come out top are normally the most bovinely contented. Cheery morons will put up with anything, and you could make a case that the most discontented folk are the smartest; the French – not the dumbest of people – are well down the list. So maybe the fact that the Brits are grumbling more is a sign that we're getting smarter? Meanwhile we're confident that you will integrate happily with those cheery, though not remotely bovine, Canadians.

*

Here's something that – on the face of it – should perk us all up. A Gallup poll suggests that Muslims can be more civic-minded than the rest of us, and more trusting of the judicial system, elections and the police. All good news – till you read on. The survey is confined to Greater London, which means the ghettos in the North don't feature. Secondly, you have to watch the presentation of the figures. Nine out of ten Muslims apparently believe that attacks which target civilians are morally wrong, and four out of five that integration is important. Highly encouraging, you think – till you remember that this leaves twenty percent who don't want to be fully British, or British at all. Then there's the ten percent of Muslims (ie some 250,000) who presumably think it's OK to massacre your fellow citizens in the name of your religious or political beliefs. I'm sure it must be less than that – I certainly hope so – but remember what I said in my last letter about the polls showing that 6% explicitly supported the 7/7 murderers. So not that much to cheer about after all.

The fact that the London Police Chief has now complained publicly about the absence of intelligence about terrorists from the Muslim community doesn't square with this poll either. (Most of their information comes from abroad, apparently, mainly Pakistan I assume). It's not much help saying you're keen to integrate into the community then standing aside from the biggest threat the community faces, as some Muslims are clearly doing. If you don't report potential killers of your countrymen to the authorities, what kind of a British citizen are you?

Of course it's good to know that a lot of Muslims are stalwart patriots in the making, willing to play the game by the rules of the host country. But we knew that already, from daily contacts. So all that surveys like these really show is that we are so nervous about the problem we have brought on ourselves that commentators leap on any figures, no matter how tenuous or ambiguous, to reassure us – and themselves.

*

A series of reports over the last few days is not encouraging about what it is to be young in Britain. We are the worst place to grow up as a child. We have the worst drug problem in Europe. We have far and away the largest number of lost souls – teenagers not in education or training and with nil prospects in the labour market. An increase of 40,000 more children in private education this year shows that those who can are getting out of the schools others have no choice but to attend even faster than before.

The middle classes steer a path through all this, like a woman holding up her skirts to avoid them touching the ground. But it impacts on everyone's lives through the spread of drugs, crime, the animality of public

behaviour and the vileness of much of our culture. We have no mono-
poly of these vices. They exist in Canada too, and America is of course
out there on its own, but we do seem to have developed a knack for
pushing social problems to extremes.

*

The thought came back to me during another quick flit to Paris, this time
for a marriage. Being in France always makes me think how out-of-date
our national caricatures are. Everyone goes on talking about how sane,
moderate, balanced, prudent and commonsensical we are, but the
modern Brits are not like that at all, and haven't been for some time. And
though the French can still be excitable, with a tendency to take to the
streets at the slightest provocation, they've calmed down a bit, and in everyday life can be a lot more sober than us. Certainly there's no parallel to
the Friday and Saturday night mayhem in formerly peaceful English
towns – a sign either of our changing character, or of a reversion to the
eighteenth century original. The French still drink plenty, though less than
they used to and in more civilised fashion, sitting in their cafes rather than
milling on pavements, roaring and glugging it down. In fact they're rather
balanced and commonsensical about it – the things we are supposed to
be, but aren't.

They remain as sensual as ever, but because they've never been
Puritans they don't have to make a show of how liberated they are, or act
as if they are the first people to discover how our body parts fit together.
The tide of Anglo-American commercialism is having an effect, and
some of the latest films and novels are attempting to out-do us in sex and
violence, but of course in France it's done *so* much more artistically, chéri.

We may not have revolutions, but it's Britain that has now become a
society of extremes. Look at public policies. It's lunatic to go on promising free medical treatment for all-comers. It's against every tenet of com-
monsense to have mixed ability classes, but in the delirium of our class-
consciousness, we persist. Doing away with most of our manufacturing
base even before the Chinese entered the scene is reckless economic
behaviour, but the prudent, balanced British have done that too. The

income gap and house prices are too obvious to mention. And finally it's madness to fill up every remaining nook and cranny in the country with – but I said I wouldn't mention that, so I won't.

Wherever you look moderate, step-by-step, prudent-mind Britain is way out on the fringe. Our manically fair-minded approach leaves us with crazy systems. Think of families. Instead of beginning with the self-evident proposition that two parents are better than one, though of course that doesn't mean that individuals must sacrifice their freedom and conform, or that every one parent family is dysfunctional, we start at the other end. The result is that we insist on individual rights to the exclusion of everyone else's interests, including the child's. As a result we have more singe-parent families, more teenage pregnancies, more adolescent misfits and more destitute families than anyone in Europe. And this is the country of balance and moderation.

*

After a career of public commentary on immigration lasting a good six months, I've decided never again to write or speak on the subject, something that will I suspect delight Catherine. It's too tedious and demeaning. Discussing immigration at all is deemed racist, in the way that any discussion of sex was once deemed perverted. To make things worse, such support as you got for opening the subject up came with depressing frequency from people you would run a mile to avoid.

Yet now I must have one last say, because something has happened I can't pass over. The Minister responsible, Liam Byrne, has said that large-scale immigration has profoundly unsettled the country, overwhelming public services like schools and housing, and that it is the poorest communities that have suffered most. If it failed to address public concern, he concluded, the government could lose the next election.

I couldn't have put what Mr Byrne was plucky enough to say better myself, though I did have a go in *Time To Emigrate?* To have the Minister for Immigration confirm the guts of what I wrote less than a year later is both gratifying and provoking. What is extraordinary is the lack of reaction to what he said. Where are the columns and editorials and BBC programmes saying either that the Government itself has gone racist, or (preferably) admitting that the minority of newspapers, commentators and non-political organisations like Migrationwatch were right all along to say there was a problem?

On the principle that a sinner who repenteth deserves the greatest praise, Byrne is something of a saint. He'll certainly have the majority of immigrants on his side: according to a speech by the former chairman of the race relations commission, Trevor Phillips, 54% of them think there's been enough immigration. Hardly surprising, since they and their children are amongst those who stand to suffer most from overcrowding, poor schooling, racial tensions and discrimination.

But of course Byrne was precluded from telling the whole truth. To cover the government's tracks he said that immigration has greatly enriched the country – a claim that sits strangely with his admission that it has hurt the least well-off most. To complete this outburst of honesty he should have acknowledged that it's the rich wot stand to gain – a message that would have gone down well with his Labour audience. But it would also have raised the cry "so why in God's name have you done it – and why are you going on?"

The only logic in the situation would be if the government could prove beyond doubt that a sharply increased population was economically advantageous to the entire country, the poorest included, to the point where temporary social, cultural and security problems were acceptable. But the evidence, always small, has shrunk further. Since my first letter the Governor of the Bank of England has demolished the Government's claim in a single passing remark. It was getting increasingly harder to manage the economy, he told MPs, without knowing how many people were in the country. The press reported the comment but missed the implications: if the Bank of England doesn't know the true population figures, nor can the Treasury. How then can anyone assess the profit and cost of migration, and claim that the balance is positive, if nobody knows the figures?

Enough. I'm quickly bored by the sound of my own voice, and disinclined to repeat things few people want to hear, or be forced to shout louder because they are pretending to be deaf.

*

The more I look at the economic outlook the wiser your decision to take a break from Britain begins to seem. Whether it's the bonuses in the City, the purchasing power of the pound on our shopping trips to America, or the money you sold your house for before emigrating, everything has begun to seem unreal. Economic reality has a habit of reasserting itself with a jolt, so we should be mentally prepared.

The only pleasure will be seeing Gordon Brown having to deal with a situation he himself has brought about. His favourite private joke – that there are only two kinds of Chancellor of the Exchequer, those who fail and those who get out in time – looks like coming true. Except that Gordon's got out into Number Ten. If it all goes arse over tip, being in the public sector and the media, I suppose you and Catherine would have been sheltered from the worst. But the social consequences of unemployment do not bear thinking about, and in the area where you lived you couldn't have avoided that. And this time people who are laid off won't be able to retire early, because he's blocked that avenue of escape by buggering up their pensions.

One thing is certain. If things do turn down there'll be a lot more people doing what you have done. When the country is riding high a record number of people have begun leaving. If ever the economic bubble is pricked think what will happen to the emigration figures.

*

Arthur Koestler (him again) said that the British will put up with anything, then suddenly they'll give a great sigh and the thing they've tolerated for too long is gone forever. I suppose that's what happened when they elected Thatcher, but I'm not sure it can happen again. With the prospect of seventy million people on a shrinking island – which is where we're heading – the options for action of any kind are narrowing. Fear of communal upsets means that stability will be the number one concern. The sense of paralysis is discernible in Brown's reticence since he became

PM, and in Cameron's non-programme of action.

In my first letter I said that the risks the country faced were awesome, and that there seemed an alarming sense of uncertainty in a time of plenty. What you will ask me now is whether there is any sign of those risks diminishing since the time you left? I can't say there is: in the economy, the environment, and in security the uncertainty is accelerating.

You know what it's like when you get disoriented in the Underground and ask people where the Tube you're about to board is heading? A passenger tells you it's going in the direction you hoped, yet somehow you're not really convinced, and peer out, mistrustfully, at the passing stations. At times you get a sense that the whole country is in that position. As though we were all on an over-crowded Tube hurtling towards an unknown destination, with everyone holding their breath and glancing nervously at their neighbours.

I'd better leave it there. I mustn't get into a state of mind of hoping for the worst just so I can tell you you're well out of it! I have not presented a very pretty picture of life here, but then the point of the exercise is to show that, whereas people like us have never had it so good, the younger generation seem likely to have it tougher.

I can see it's going well over there, but who knows? After the children have finished school, and assuming I'm right about us scrabbling through, you can never rule out the possibility of coming back.
Love to all, Dad.

March 2008
   London